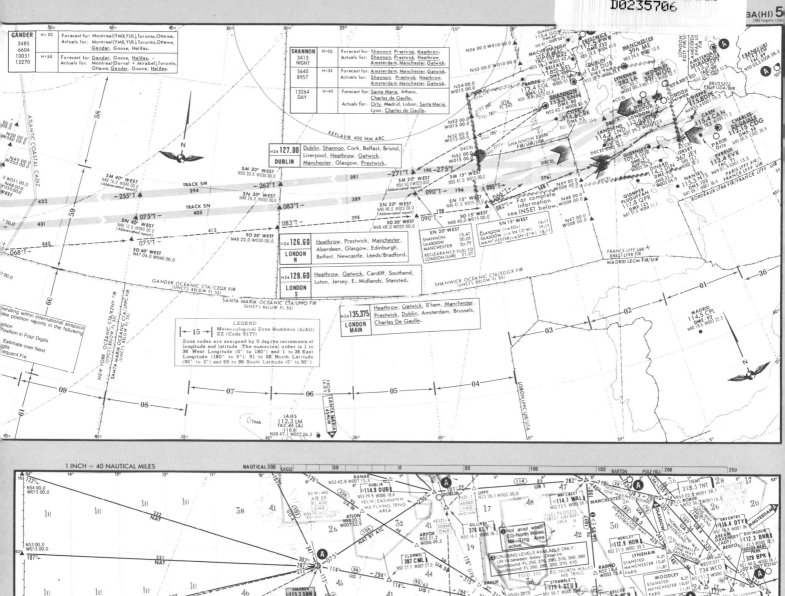

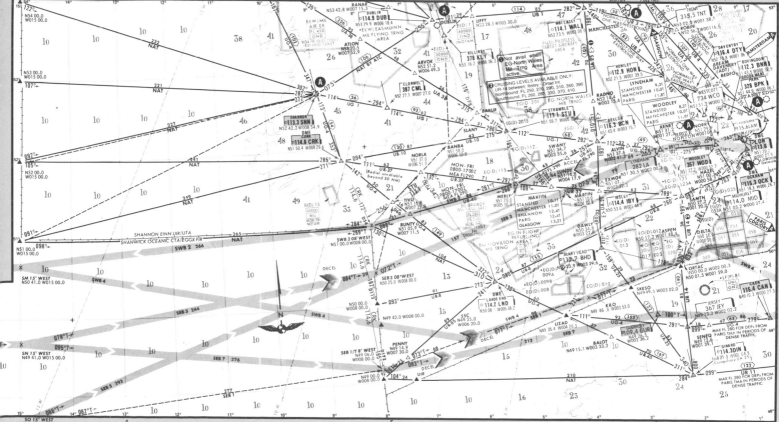

THE
CONCORDE
STORY

THE CONCORDE STORY

FIFTH EDITION

CHRISTOPHER ORLEBAR

OSPREY
PUBLISHING

Endpapers

These charts show Concorde's west and east bound Atlantic tracks, 'SM' and 'SN' respectively; 'SO' is a reserve track. The acceleration and deceleration points, labelled 'ACCEL' and 'DECEL', are the points respectively where Concorde either commences acceleration from Mach 0.95, or deceleration from Mach 2. However, the deceleration point is varied a few miles either side of the position shown depending on the conditons – aircraft altitude and forecast wind – prevalent on the day.

There are a variety of routes into the United States, however the route to New York via Linnd and Sates is the one described in the chapter, The Flight – Deceleration. Concorde must cross the boundary of the 'warning area' (W105 BDY) above 52,000 ft when that area is

'active' with military training or test flights.

The front inset shows a plan view of the runways at Heathrow with the designations as they were when Concorde entered service in 1976: 10L, 10R, 28L and 28R. The ever-reducing magnetic variation in Britain has brought their tracks closer to 090°M and, in the opposite direction, 270°M, than to the 100°M and 280°M they used to approximate to. (°M is the measure of the direction with respect to magnetic north.) Therefore, since July 1987, they have been called: 09L, 09R, 27L, and 27R.

The back inset shows the approach path to runway 4R (the right-hand of the two northeast facing runways) at Kennedy – the runway onto which the landing was made in the chapter, The Flight – Deceleration.

For a complete list of titles available from Osprey Publishing please contact:

Osprey Direct UK
PO Box 140
Wellingborough
Northants
NN8 4ZA
UK
info@ospreydirect.co.uk

Osprey Direct USA
c/o Motorbooks International
PO Box 1
Osceola
W1 54020-0001
USA
info@ospreydirectusa.com

www.ospreypublishing.com

'Oh God, who art the author of peace, and lover of concord. . .'
From the second Collect, for Peace in the Book of Common Prayer

To my wife Nicola and our children Edward and Caroline. CO

First published in 1986 by Osprey Publishing
Elms Court, Chapel Way, Botley, Oxford OX2 9LP, UK

© Osprey Publishing Limited 1986, 1990, 1994 and 2002

ISBN 1 85532 667 1

Editors: Jasper Spencer-Smith, Tony Holmes, Shaun Barrington, Ged Barker
Printed and bound in China

*This Video **Concorde - the New Era** is available to Concorde Story readers at the promotional price of £9.95 inc. p&p (£12.50 for non-UK residents, Sterling only). Send a cheque/postal order with your name and address, quoting **The Concorde Story** as a reference to: Fast Forward Productions, 22 Fleshmarket Close, Edinburgh, EH11DY*

Contents

Acknowledgements

The Concorde Story was originally published in 1986 to celebrate Concorde achieving 10 years in service. In this 5th edition, minor corrections have been made and new material added. This covers the crash of F-BTSC and the tragic loss of 113 lives, and gives details of the official accident report. It also describes the return of Concorde to service, and reflects on where the supersonic technology learnt from Concorde might lead. I would like to acknowledge the encouragement I received over the years from British Airways and the following individuals:

Peter Baker, former Concorde Test Pilot, BAC
Mike Bannister, General Manager, BA Concorde
Michael Blunt, *BA News* and Public Relations
John Britton, Chief Concorde Engineer, Airbus Industry, UK
Adam Brown, Vice-President Market Forecasts, Airbus Industrie, France
Charles Burnet, formerly of British Aerospace, Weybridge
Frank Debouck, Manager, Air France Concorde
Alain Guilldon, Beureau Enquêtes Accidents, France
David Learmount, *Flight International*
Peter Leggett, the late and former Vice-Chancellor, Surrey University and his widow Enid
Jock Lowe, former Chief Pilot, BA
Dennis Morris, BA Engineering
Donald Pevsner, President, Concorde Spirit Tours, USA
Mike Ramsden, former Editor of *Flight International*
Sandy Sell, BA Engineering
Alan Simmons, Air Accident Investigation Branch, UK
Donald Thompson for pointing out typographical errors in earlier editions
Brian Trubshaw, the late and former Chief Test Pilot, BAC
Brian Walpole (former General Manager, BA Concorde) who first asked me to write the book.

Gratitude must go to the passengers who by flying Concorde have ensured its ultimate success. Without them this extraordinary aircraft would have come to nought and there would have been no story. Furthermore, this achievement has spawned serious interest in the eventual building of a Concorde successor. Grateful thanks also to my wife Nicola, sister-in-law Angela Metcalf and daughter Caroline who assisted me with word processing, and son Edward whose analysis I valued. The greatest acknowledgement must go to the people who designed, built, maintain and crew Concorde.

Christopher Orlebar
Oxshott, April 2002

In remembrance of all those who died in the tragedy at Gonesse near Paris on 25 July 2000: the three flight crew, six cabin crew and one hundred passengers on Concorde F-BTSC and the four people on the ground.

The author with Sir Frank Whittle on the flight deck of Concorde during the filming of 'Jet Trail', a documentary about the effect of jet propulsion on civil transport. May 1984

Foreword

By Captain Mike Bannister
British Airways Chief Concorde Pilot

Heads turn as Concorde flies over. Even today, when the aircraft visits somewhere for the first time literally thousands turn out to see her. In the USA, crowds of 25,000+ block roads to airfields. Why?

It is not just because Concorde is such a beautiful aircraft but because she is also a great technical achievement. The psychologists write that she appeals to both sides of the brain – the artistic side and the technical. But she is also a commercial success adding significantly to British Airways' bottom line.

That is true today and has been for many years. But it is not what the pessimists foretold. They prophesied doom, gloom, despair and failure on many occasions. It is a tribute to the determination of so many involved with the Concorde Project that those omens never came to pass. The history of the aircraft is one of many challenges. From design to first flights, introduction into service and commercial viability through to return after the tragic Paris accident. There have been hurdles to overcome. In all these stages there have been people of vision, determination, capability and persuasion who have exceeded even their own high aspirations to ensure that the dream of passenger supersonic flight can continue.

Concorde is the only aircraft that can literally 'arrive before she's left' giving a unique opportunity to spend a full day in New York, be on the beach in Barbados before lunch or return to the UK without taking an overnight subsonic flight. She gives us mere mortals, not astronauts, the chance to travel on the edge of space, where the sky gets darker and you see the curvature of the earth. In other words to literally travel faster than the Earth rotates.

In the UK and France the Airlines, Manufacturers, Airworthiness Authorities and Accident Investigators worked tirelessly for over a year to bring about the restoration of Concorde's *Certificate of Airworthiness*. I was honoured to be part of that team and, in a period when I missed flying the aircraft that I love so much, I never doubted that the Concorde Story had many more years to run.

Captain Mike Bannister on the flight deck of Concorde

H.M. The Queen Mother's eighty-fith birthday present from British Airways was a trip in Concorde on 6 August 1985. Seen here with Captain Walpole O.B.E. (General Manager, Concorde Division of British Airways 1982-1988) (centre) and Senior Engineer Officer, Peter Phillips (right)

Preface

This book is about the conquest of flight at speeds faster than sound. It covers the synthesis of the host of disciplines which were brought together to build and operate the most superlative form of transport yet built by man – Concorde. Yet Concorde exists in the ordinary physical world. There was no divine intervention which altered the laws of nature to favour Concorde. Its success has been achieved by the devotion of countless people who have been inspired by the concept. It ranks with the architectural marvels of the world – the Pyramids, the Gothic Cathedrals and the Taj Mahal.

This book was originally written to celebrate the tenth anniversary of Concorde commercial operations, 1976-1986. Approaching the 21st anniversary it has been fully revised and updated.

What follows is a brief description of some of the technical terms and concepts that the more inquisitive reader may find useful. In some instances these are expanded in the chapters that follow.

Ernst Mach*, an Austrian physicist, observed that airflows obeyed different laws as they approached the speed of sound. In recognition of his work, the term 'Mach number' was named after him. The Mach number of a moving body is the ratio of its speed to that of the speed of sound in the fluid in which it is travelling. The fluid in which aircraft travel is, of course, the air in the atmosphere. When an aircraft's speed is the same as the speed of sound it is said to have a Mach number of one – Mach 1.

Ernst Mach was a positivist who argued strongly against the notion that matter was made up of atoms. The explanation of why the airflow obeyed different laws, as the speed of sound is approached, is much easier to explain on the assumption that atoms and molecules exist. It is therefore curious that Mach did not agree with what has now become the accepted truth.

Air is a gas which is made up of molecules moving randomly at high speed. Their speed varies with temperature. They move more quickly when it is hot than when it is cold. The speed of sound in air is the speed at which vibrations or changes of pressure are transmitted through the air. As this speed is a function of the speed the molecules move,

sound travels quicker in hot air than in cold.

At 15°C (59°F), the average temperature found at sea level, the speed of sound is about 760 mph (660 knots). Between 50,000 ft and 60,000 ft, where the temperature averages minus 57°C (−71°F), it is 660 mph (573 knots). It varies in fact with the square root of absolute temperature (absolute zero is minus 273°C (−459.4°F) thus the freezing point of water is 273° Kelvin and its boiling point 373°K).

An aircraft in flight can be travelling subsonically, i.e. below the speed of sound, or supersonically, i.e. above the speed of sound. The airflow, as Mach observed, is governed by two quite different laws depending on whether the aircraft is flying at subsonic or supersonic speeds. There is, however, a third definition of speed, and that is 'transonic'. In reality 'transonic' refers to a range of speeds typically from Mach 0.75 to Mach 1.3. It is called 'transonic' because both supersonic and subsonic (governed by their respective laws) are present simultaneously.

At first sight it is not obvious why a supersonic airflow can be present when an

*1838–1916.

The airspeed indicator on Concorde showing just over 500 knots, whilst the Machmeter indicates just less than Mach 2 corresponding to a true airspeed of 1,150 knots. The apparent discrepancy is due to the low density of the air found at 53,000 ft causing the aircraft to 'feel' only 500 knots. See the 'Flight envelope' on page 160

aircraft is flying subsonically. The reason is that an aircraft in flight separates the air. The airflow over the more bulbous parts of the aircraft (over a protruding cockpit or over the top of the wings) has to travel further than the air underneath the aircraft. Thus the air travelling the further distance over the aircraft has to travel more quickly. To be consistent with the law of energy conservation, as the 'moving' energy of the air increases, its pressure energy must reduce. Low pressure on the top surface of a wing sucks it upwards, or gives it 'lift'. When the speed of an aircraft exceeds about Mach 0.75 the faster moving air over the wings reaches Mach 1. Therefore supersonic airflow is found on an aircraft flying subsonically.

When the aircraft flies faster than Mach 1 some of the air, depending on the shape of the aircraft, is pulled along by the aircraft, so that part flows subsonically over the surface. Usually by the time the aircraft has reached about Mach 1.3 all the airflow over it is supersonic. Flight at transonic speeds was to prove more difficult than flight at supersonic speeds.

As an aircraft flies it experiences resistance from the air. This is known as 'drag'. The amount of lift compared to drag that an aircraft experiences at a given speed is a measure of its aerodynamic efficiency. This is known as the lift to drag ratio, commonly written as L/D. Drag is caused by the shape of the aircraft (form drag), by the surface of the aircraft (skin friction drag) and by the work the wings have to do to give lift (induced drag). The first two increase with speed, while induced drag decreases with speed.

At speeds below about 300 knots (1 knot = 1.15 mph), the airflow over an aircraft behaves like an incompressible fluid (like water). Above 300 knots the molecules of air, having had less 'warning' of the impending disturbance, become compressed. The 'warning' travels at the speed of sound. As the aircraft travels closer to Mach 1 the molecules have progressively less time in which to redistribute themselves before the passage of the aircraft. Now they build up and make, at Mach 1, a distinct 'compression wave' or 'shock wave'. This wave, analogous to a bow wave of a boat, increases the drag. Hence the notion that there was some kind of barrier at Mach 1, although projectiles like bullets had exceeded the speed of sound since the early 1700s. At the rear of an aircraft flying above Mach 1 is another compression wave where the air reverts to its original condition, having steadily reduced to a lower pressure during the passage of the aircraft. These two shock waves can usually be heard on the ground as a double boom.

At first sight it is difficult to visualise that

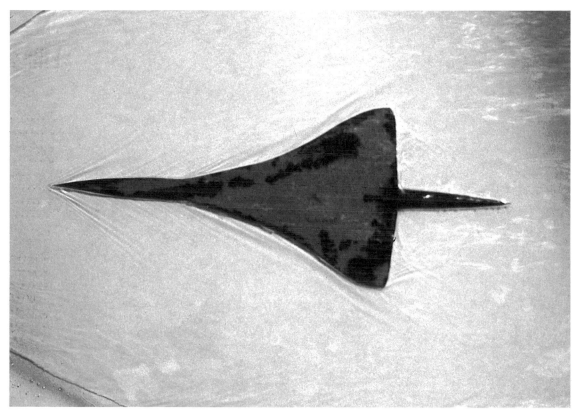

The shock waves formed in the air around a supersonic aircraft are analogous to the waves formed by a moving boat. Here water is flowing over a thin silhouette of Concorde to demonstrate the analogy. Although these waves are formed in just two dimensions, the shock waves on an aircraft are in three dimensions, forming a cone at the nose

the air ahead of an object moving at subsonic speed starts to redistribute itself before the arrival of the object. Observation of light airborne objects, like snowflakes or thistle seeds, becoming wafted over the windscreen of a moving car demonstrates the effect. Heavier objects like grit and raindrops do not deflect. Should the car accelerate towards Mach 1, the deflection of even the light objects would not happen. Their first 'knowledge' of the car would be the car itself.

Once the sound barrier had been 'broken' another barrier appeared – the heat barrier. The faster an aircraft flies the more it is heated by the air which surrounds it. This is not an effect which is suddenly manifest, as it is present at all speeds, but does not become significant until the aircraft is travelling supersonically. It is caused by the compression of the air as it is accelerated during the passage of the aircraft. When any gas is compressed its temperature rises, as is readily observed when pumping up a

Wind tunnel models of Concorde were used to check its viability throughout the speed range. Here flight at slow speeds, requiring high angles of attack, is about to be investigated

bicycle tyre. The end of the pump becomes very hot due to the compression of the air within it. On an aircraft this effect is known as kinetic heating.

The temperature rise in degrees centigrade can be calculated approximately by squaring the true airspeed in mph of the aircraft and dividing this by 100. At Mach 2, about 1,320 mph, the rise is 174°C (345°F); at Mach 3 it is 392°C (737°F). These quantities are for the point experiencing the greatest temperature rise, usually the tip of the

aircraft's nose, where the air is accelerated to the speed of the aircraft. To this figure must be added the static air temperature. Above 37,000 ft this averages minus 57°C (−71°F), varying from place to place over the globe. At Mach 2 the final top temperature is thus 117°C (243°F) and at Mach 3 it is 335°C (635°F). Kinetic heating has an immense bearing on the choice of cruising speed for a supersonic transport aircraft (SST) and the materials from which it will be built. Aluminium alloys can easily cope with temperatures up to about 130°C (266°F); higher than that, more expensive titanium alloys must be used.

To monitor the temperature experienced by the nose of fast moving aircraft there is a gauge in the cockpit. It simply reads degrees centigrade. There are other instruments like the altimeter and compass which say, with a fair degree of accuracy, how high the aircraft is and in which direction it is pointing. There is one instrument, however, which to the untutored eye appears as if it is constantly telling a frightful lie (unless it is observed at sea level) and that is the airspeed indicator.

At sea level the speed shown on the airspeed indicator corresponds quite closely to the True Airspeed (TAS). But as the aircraft climbs into the thinner air the indicator registers an airspeed which is less than true. At Mach 2 and 55,000 ft the true airspeed would be 1,150 knots, but because of the low density of the air, the indicated airspeed is only 500 knots.

Aircraft are flown with special reference to indicated airspeed since this is a measure of what the aircraft feels. Knowledge of what the aircraft 'feels' tells the pilots how the aircraft can perform; how close it is, for instance, to losing the ability to give lift (stalling). Or, in the case of Concorde, how much extra thrust will be required to overcome the high induced drag when flying at landing speeds.

Indicated airspeed also shows the pilot how great an angle of attack the aircraft is experiencing. The angle of attack is the angle between the aircraft and the flow of air. As the speed falls so this angle increases, thus lift is maintained. If constant altitude is to be maintained during deceleration, the aircraft must be pitched up to compensate for the increased angle of attack. When descending to land, Concorde has quite a high pitch attitude (11°). This is because of the high angle of attack (14°) associated with low indicated airspeed.

The Background

The Gloster E28/39 Britain's first jet propelled aircraft, which first flew 14 May 1941. Its Whittle-designed, Power Jets engine gave a modest 850 lb of thrust. The engine planned for the US SST was to have produced close on 70,000 lb of thrust. The big fan engines of the mid-1990s are capable of delivering well over 100,000 lb of thrust

'Pull steadily, watch the altimeter, don't flap and don't expect anything much to happen until below 15,000 to 20,000 ft . . .' This advice was contained in a document written by George Bulman, Chief Test Pilot of Hawker Aircraft in 1943. It was intended for pilots who found themselves in aircraft diving at speeds close to that of sound.

A number of Allied fighter aircraft had experienced strange effects when diving at such speeds during the Second World War. Not the least of these effects had been the dangerous tendency for the controls to do the reverse of what was expected of them and for the whole aircraft to buffet and shake, sometimes to the point of structural failure. To preserve frontline fighter pilots and to investigate flight at speeds close to Mach 1 – thus forestalling any German advance in the new science – a series of high speed dives was planned.

The aircraft chosen for these investigations was the Photo Reconnaissance Spitfire (PR Mark XI) fitted with the Merlin 70 engine. Such a Spitfire was capable of climbing to 40,000 ft – high even by the standard of the subsonic jets of the mid-1990s. To achieve the highest speeds the power dive had to be started from as high as possible. For that and the reason of its relatively thin wings, the Spitfire PR Mark XI was considered a suitable aircraft for research into flight at transonic speed.

Some time in 1943, Squadron Leader Martindale, a test pilot for Rolls-Royce in civil life, found himself in a 45 degree dive from 40,000 ft. After 36 seconds from the start of the dive, descending through 29,000 ft, the Spitfire attained Mach 0.9. From about Mach 0.75 upwards some of the airflow became compressed and therefore subject to different aerodynamic laws. The Spitfire experienced increased drag, loss of lift and a tendency to pitch further nose down. Uncorrected the nose-down pitch would increase the dive angle. To prevent this the pilot would pull the stick back to apply 'up elevator'. At transonic speeds such action exposed the aircraft to another risk. Due to lack of stiffness in the tailplane and the great force of a compressed airstream on the up-going elevator, the leading edge of the tailplane could bend upwards leaving the elevator trailing in the slipstream. This resulted in the controls achieving the reverse effect of what was expected, namely pitching the aircraft further nose down. This effect is quite separate from the nose dropping due to the redistribution of the lift.

Entering the warmer atmosphere the Spitfire found itself in an environment where the speed of sound was greater. Although still travelling at roughly the same true airspeed, its speed with respect to the speed of sound (Mach number) was lower. The danger now was that the laws governing the airflow at the slower speeds would suddenly be restored. The 'up-elevator', which had maintained the dive angle could now, at the smaller Mach numbers, reassert itself with unnerving suddenness, pulling the aircraft out of the dive at such a rate that the wings might fold upwards, or flutter like a flag. There were no ejection seats in those days.

These investigations into flight at speeds close to Mach 1 would have been given immense publicity in peace-time. In the event they were cloaked in war-time secrecy and by the time the story was told, it appeared rather pedestrian compared to the rocket- and jet-propelled attempts on the sound barrier going on in the late 1940s. It is of lasting tribute to the Spitfire that it behaved better at such speeds than some of the later aircraft of supposedly more advanced aerodynamic design.

The Rolls-Royce Merlin 70 engine, which powered the PR XI, had been developed and fitted to the Spitfire Mark IX in response to a formidable new fighter fielded by the Germans in 1941: the Focke-Wulf 190. The increased performance of the Merlin 61 was largely due to the effectiveness of its supercharger. This added 70 mph to the top speed and 10,000 ft to the Spitfire's maximum altitude. In consequence it out-performed the Focke-Wulf 190.

A supercharger is a device that compress-es the air before it undergoes further compression in the cylinders of a piston engine. The supercharger on the Merlin 61 engine had been refined to near perfection by a brilliant young engineer at Rolls-Royce in Derby – Stanley Hooker.

Stanley Hooker (later Sir Stanley Hooker) had been recruited in 1938 by the works manager of Rolls-Royce Ernest W. Hives (later Lord Hives of Duffield) with the somewhat enigmatic words: 'You are not much of an engineer, are you?'! Hooker's work on superchargers was soon to have great relevance in the development of the jet engine, since the centrifugal compressors of the early jet engines were similar in principle to, although much larger than, the supercharger of the Merlin. The jet engine turned out to be the most suitable power plant for continuous supersonic flight. Eleven years after his work on the Merlin supercharger, Stanley Hooker began the transformation of the Bristol Olympus engine, destined, in its most superlative version, to power Concorde.

The 'barrier' to greater speed from the Spitfire during its transonic dive was due to two effects. One was the large increase of drag it experienced as the compression waves built up at Mach 0.9; the other was the loss of thrust experienced by the propeller. The combined effect of aircraft forward speed and the turning speed of the propeller ensured that the outer portions of the propeller blades were travelling at supersonic speeds. At such speeds the propeller becomes very inefficient. Thus the Spitfire lost thrust just as its drag increased. A rocket-propelled, rather than a gravity-assisted, Spitfire might have been able to maintain Mach 0.9 for longer.

Rocket propulsion has the advantage over other kinds of propulsion in that the thrust it generates is not dependent on the forward speed of the aircraft. Nor is its thrust dependent on altitude, if anything it increases as the pressure of air around it decreases. Although rocket-propelled air-craft are spared the need of having any kind of air intakes, they suffer the greater burden of having to carry extra fuel weight in the form of liquid oxygen (or some chemical suitable for combustion with the fuel). They therefore do not give propulsion suitable for sustained flight.

Happily by 1943 there had appeared an engine which looked capable of giving sustained thrust both at subsonic and supersonic speeds. This was the jet engine. This new engine gave thrust not through a propeller, but by virtue of its high speed jet efflux. The fact that its intake might be in a supersonic airflow would be, if anything, a bonus, since the incoming air could be slowed down and therefore 'supercharged'

The Rolls-Royce Merlin engine of a Spitfire, showing the circular supercharger casing to the rear. Stanley Hooker's work on the supercharger transformed the performance of this engine

prior to entering the compressor on the engine, making the engine yet more efficient.

The inventor of the jet engine principle, Sir Frank Whittle, said that he was regarded at the time as a crazy optimist. One of his early proposals (in 1935), envisaged an engine giving 111 lb of thrust to a 2000 lb aircraft travelling at 500 mph at an altitude of 69,000 ft. It is anyone's guess what people would have said had he predicted that a 350,000 lb aircraft (including the fuel) would be capable of travelling at 1,320 mph at 55,000 ft with each of its four engines giving, at that altitude, 10,000 lb of thrust.

Jet-propelled flight became a reality in Britain in 1941 with the first flight of the Gloster E28/39. A Whittle-designed engine, the Power Jets W2/700, was chosen, in 1943, as the power plant for Britain's first supersonic project: the Miles M52 (E24/43). It was hoped optimistically that the M52 would exceed 1,000 mph (about Mach 1.5) in level flight. There was a great deal of controversy over the choice of wing section for the aircraft. Thin wings, suitable for supersonic flight, seemed to be the obvious choice, but their lack of efficiency at subsonic speeds meant that the aircraft would not be able to climb to such a high altitude as one fitted with conventional

wings. The higher the altitude, the higher the Mach number that could be attained in the ensuing dive. Once comfortably supersonic it was hoped that the aircraft could level off maintaining speed – engine thrust having increased to cope with the higher drag associated with supersonic flight.

The W2/700 was one of the last engines built by the Power Jets Company. Under the leadership of Frank Whittle, a small and dedicated team working in appallingly primitive surroundings near Rugby in England (Sir Stanley Hooker referred to the unit as Whittle's rabbit hutch) had researched, designed and built a viable jet engine. After an unsatisfactory period of liaison with the Rover company, Rolls-Royce became involved with Power Jets and, under the leadership of Stanley Hooker, set about developing and producing the jet engine in quantity.

The lineage of the modern jet engine owes far more to the early British engines than to the jet engines developed in Germany. On observing the immense length of runway required by the Me 262 (the German jet-powered fighter) on take-off, an onlooker remarked to Frank Whittle, who was also present, that it was no wonder that Hitler wanted to extend the Third Reich.

Soon it became evident that more research was needed to give sufficient thrust to the M52. The reason that the Ministry of Supply gave for the cancellation of the project in 1946, however, was that they were concerned for the safety of its pilot. In 1948, a pilotless, rocket-propelled, scaled down version of the M52 did achieve about Mach 1.4, which proved that its planform with straight wings could cope with supersonic flight. However, at the end of the Second World War, British design was influenced by swept wings which gave better performance at both supersonic and high subsonic speeds.

Before the outbreak of the Second World War a German scientist, Professor Adolf Büsemann, had published findings that suggested that swept wings would perform better than straight wings in supersonic flight. One significant reason for this is that the shock waves generated at the nose of an aircraft miss the wing tips if these are swept back. Thus there is not the added complication of an interference between wings and shock waves. Astonishingly these findings, freely available to all, went unnoticed.

Equally remarkable was the failure of the Allies to understand why the wings were swept on the rocket-propelled German fighter (the Messerschmitt Me 163 – Komet). The Komet was a tailless swept-winged interceptor, which was very fast, achieving Mach 0.8 (about 550 mph) for short periods. The Allies believed that its speed could be ascribed to its being rocket-propelled. The reason for the swept wings was thought to be so that adequate control could be retained in pitch (the control of the longitudinal angle of the fuselage about itself). Though both beliefs were partly correct, what was not understood was that swept wings allowed the aircraft to fly at speeds closer to Mach 1, since the increase in drag was delayed until these higher speeds were reached.

From the description of the Spitfire tests, it will be remembered that some of the air becomes supersonic over an aircraft even though that aircraft is travelling subsonically. It is the portion of the supersonic airflow which causes the drag rise.

Thick wings experience this transonic drag rise at lower Mach numbers than thin wings. Wings must support the weight of the aircraft and have within them some space to contain fuel. High speed aircraft need both strength and as much space for fuel as possible. The conflict can be resolved

The Me 163B Komet, Germany's rocket-propelled interceptor, the design of which was based on research by Dr. Alexander Lippisch, 'father' of tailless and delta winged aircraft. Rocket propulsion was available for 8 to 10 minutes, giving speeds in excess of 550 mph. Its swept wings allowed flight at high subsonic Mach numbers before the transonic drag rise took effect. The planform of the D.H. 108 was somewhat similar to this aircraft

by sweeping the wings either forward or back. Although the ratio of the thickness of the wing to the distance from leading to trailing edge remains constant, the sweep-back makes this ratio 'appear' smaller to the airflow. Now the air is less disturbed by the passage of the aircraft, so the aircraft can fly faster before the compression waves start to apply their drag increase. The benefit of this discovery, made by Professor Albert Betz (a German aerodynamicist), has been applied to jet-propelled airliners, virtually all of which have swept back wings.

To research flight with a swept-winged aircraft, the de Havilland company modified a Vampire, a single engined, straight-winged fighter, with its tail and fin surfaces connected via twin booms to the wings. The booms and the tail surface were removed, swept back wings fitted, and a swept fin was placed over the rear end of the fuselage. It resembled the Komet in many outward respects. The DH108 was partly intended as a research aircraft for what became the Comet airliner. At that time the philosophy among several British aircraft manufac-turers had been that it was desirable to perfect a 'flying wing' to reduce the aerodynamic drag and the extra weight caused by tailplane surfaces. Sadly, after the loss of several such aircraft, to lack of control in pitch, this philosophy had to be abandoned.

'Flying wings', as tailless aircraft were

dubbed, would have had to carry their payload within the wing. For people to stand inside the wing it would have had to have been at least 7 ft thick. The wing span would have been huge to cope with such a thickness. Furthermore without a tailplane there was no way of aerodynamically balancing wing flaps. Without flaps either the landing speed would have had to have been very fast or the wing too big for efficient cruise. It would thus have been an uneconomic proposition – the de Havilland Comet had a tail!

Two other British aircraft design philo-sophies had their origins in the immediate post-war era. One was to produce a wing capable of sustaining laminar flow. Hitherto the flow of air over a wing had always been impeded by that little turbulent layer of air close to the wing known as the boundary layer. Laminar flow control promised a very marked reduction in aerodynamic drag.

The other philosophy was the notion that the aerodynamic drag associated with the engines and intakes could be reduced by placing the engine air intakes at the wing roots feeding air to engines that were 'buried', as on the Comet 4, rather than podded, as on the Boeing 707.

The laminar flow concept failed largely because it seemed impossible to retain a completely clean wing. Even a squashed insect, acquired during take-off, upset the laminar flow. Removal of the boundary layer

The D.H. 108, Britain's first transonic swept winged aircraft. Control in roll and pitch on aircraft without tailplanes has to be achieved through the surfaces on the trailing edge of the wing. John Derry exceeded the speed of sound in this aircraft (VW 120)–the first British aircraft to do so

The de Havilland
Comet 1, Britain's
great leap forward in
the post-war aviation
era. Stresses at the
right angular corners
of the windows were
higher than
predicted; hence the
metal fatigue that led
to fatal crashes. But
for the accidents de
Havilland might have
retained their world
lead in jet airliner
construction

through minute holes drilled in the surface of the wing was another solution, though rather impractical, at least in those days. However, laminar flow control was put forward again in the mid-1980s as a means of reducing drag on an Advanced Supersonic Transport (AST).

The presence of a boundary layer can be readily observed on a car windscreen during rain. Even when driving at 70 mph the smaller drops remain stationary. The larger ones which protrude out of the boundary layer are moved by the airstream but not that quickly. It is some millimetres away from the screen that the speed of the airstream assumes its expected value.

Although the concept of buried engines worked, it was not such a satisfactory answer to the drag and weight problem as the solution developed by the Americans. For their 707, Boeing placed their engines in pods slung beneath and slightly ahead of the wing, on pylons. The engine intakes benefited from a clean airflow not disturbed by the unpredictable behaviour at the junction of wing and fuselage. Furthermore the distribution of the engine weight to the wings meant that this part of the total weight did not have to be borne through the wing root. Thus this part was lighter too.

The de Havilland Comet 4. The windows are now oval-shaped following experience with the Comet 1. The engines are buried at the wing roots - a philosophy preferred in Britain to the underslung pods chosen by Boeing and other US manufacturers. The pods outboard on the wings are fuel tanks

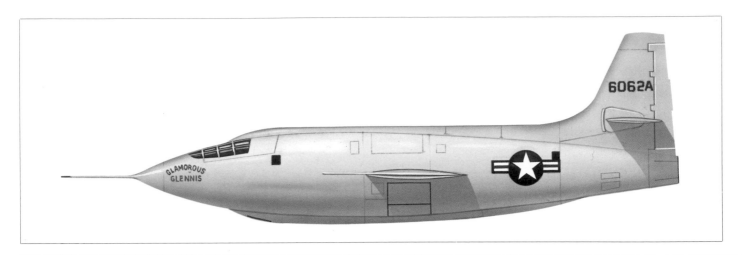

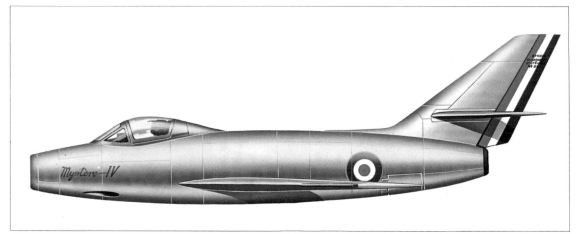

Opposite *The Bell X1 in which Chuck Yeager became the first pilot to exceed the speed of sound, in October 1947. It had straight but thin wings and a tailplane situated out of the slipstream from the wing*

Left *Dassault Mystere IV. This swept-wing French fighter-bomber was in production by 1955, and it provided useful data about flight at transonic speeds*

This advantage does not favour aircraft with rear fuselage mounted engines.

In 1948, John Derry, Chief Test Pilot of de Havilland, became, more by accident than by design, the first pilot in Britain to exceed Mach 1, in a DH108 during a test flight investigating transonic flight. Whilst attempting to recover from a dive at Mach 0.97, his aeroplane exceeded the vertical and achieved Mach 1.02. He was lucky to survive. Geoffrey de Haviland son of the founder of the firm had been killed in a DH108 almost exactly two years earlier probably having experienced similar very severe oscillations in pitch.

By the early 1950s data had been acquired which would make the next steps in supersonic flight slightly easier. The first aim then was to build a jet fighter capable of intercepting the mammoth Russian nuclear bombers which were under development, and were capable of cruising between 30,000 and 40,000 ft at around Mach 0.8.

The fighter had to have an excellent rate of climb and at least double the bomber's speed for a successful interception long before the bomber could reach its target. The second aim was to build a supersonic bomber which, because of its speed, would itself be very difficult to intercept.

Long range supersonic flight, however, was going to be much more difficult to achieve than the short duration dash required of an interceptor. But should a bomber become a reality then a transport derivative could follow, such was the pattern generally established during the 50 years of aircraft development. But as far as the development of an SST was concerned, the introduction of missiles even capable of intercepting supersonic bombers at high altitude was to upset this evolutionary pattern. The SST would have to be developed almost in its own right.

Left *Boeing 'Dash 80' prototype of the 707, showing the American philosophy of placing the engines in pods mounted beneath and ahead of the wings. The wings were swept back more than those of the Comet, allowing flight at a higher Mach number before the rise in transonic drag*

The Formative Phase

The Fairey Delta 2. Fairey believed that the delta wing with no tailplane was the optimum solution for a supersonic aircraft. Peter Twiss achieved a new world air speed record of 1,132 mph in the FD2 in March 1956. An FD2 (BAC 221) was modified with wings to the 'Ogee' planform to research separated airflow

Prompted by the preponderance of designs for supersonic interceptor aircraft that appeared in the early 1950s people began to wonder whether a civil supersonic transport (SST) could one day be a possibility. With London to New York flight times being of the order of 18 hours and more, especially against headwinds and with refuelling stops, the idea of doing the same journey in a fifth of the time must have seemed preposterous.

Nevertheless Sir Arnold Hall, director of the Royal Aircraft Establishment (RAE) Farnborough in the early 1950s, asked Morien Morgan, already involved with the Advanced Fighter Project Group, to chair a small committee to look into the possibility of building a civil supersonic transport. The reported findings, in 1954, suggested that it

might just be possible to fly 15 passengers from London to New York at Mach 2 in an aircraft with an all up weight of 300,000 lb (136,000 kg). For comparison Concorde carries 100 passengers (up to 128 with reduced space between seat rows) over that range with an all up weight (maximum take-off weight including the passengers and the fuel) of 408,000 lb (185,000 kg). The envisaged 15-seater SST was based on the design of the Avro 730 supersonic bomber project that was cancelled in 1957. It had thin unswept wings with engines mounted on the wing tips. But for an SST to be economically viable, a better aerodynamic shape would have to be devised.

Such a shape did appear with dramatic impact, in the form of the British Fairey Delta 2. On 10 March 1956 Peter Twiss

(Chief Test Pilot of Fairey Aviation) exceeded the previous world airspeed record, held by the American Colonel Haynes in an F100 Super Sabre, by the handsome margin of 310 mph. A reheated Rolls-Royce Avon RA5 turbojet propelled the FD2 at the astonishing speed of 1,132 mph (Mach 1.7).

In November 1956 the Supersonic Transport Aircraft Committee (STAC) was formed, chaired by Morien Morgan, one of the greatest proponents for civil supersonic flight. Hearing evidence from 17 interested bodies, comprising the aircraft industry, airlines and ministries, its conclusions were reported in 1959. The result was Concorde which ten years later made its maiden flight.

Contributors to its success were the FD2 and the P1, both offsprings of Morien Morgan's Advanced Fighter Project Group which had been formed in 1948. The success of these two aircraft banished the notion of some kind of intractable barrier at Mach 1, the speed of sound. It is interesting to look at the different design philosophies.

Both designers produced a different planform: the P1 with swept wings and a tailplane, while the FD2 a delta wing without a tail. Tailless designs had encountered many problems, as exemplified by Geoffrey de Havilland's experience in the DH108, hence English Electric wanted to ensure stability and control through use of a

tail surface, especially for flight in the tricky transonic range. Fairey believed, however, that a 60 degree delta with powerful trailing edge control surfaces would provide a stable aircraft throughout this range. After all, experience had pointed to the fact that tail surfaces were a major source of aerodynamic buffet at transonic speeds – why run this risk by having a tail at all?

As it turned out both designs were supremely successful. In different ways both contributed to Concorde's eventual success: the FD2, because it was converted into the modified delta shape that was to be applied to Concorde; the P1, because a great deal was learned about the variable exhaust nozzle on the Rolls-Royce Avon engine, a necessary device for the efficient use of a variable thrust reheat system. It is the variable exhaust nozzle system on the Olympus engine, as fitted to Concorde, which ekes out every last remaining ounce of thrust and fuel economy from the jet efflux both with and without reheat.

'Reheat', or 'after-burner' as it is known in the United States, is a device which can be fitted to the rear of the main jet engine, within the exhaust duct, to give an extra 'push' to the aircraft. It consists of a ring of nozzles which spray fuel to be burned in the engine exhaust gases, which still have sufficient oxygen to support combustion, prior to

P1 Lightning. The tail surface can be clearly seen. The English Electric designers considered that inclusion of a tail would give the stability and control required for supersonic flight provided it was positioned away from the wake of the wing. The exhaust nozzles of the two Avon engines are mounted one above the other. The nozzles could vary the area of the exit orifice— wide open with full reheat in use, and diminishing with intermediate amounts of reheat. Perfection of variable jet nozzles was essential before a commercial SST could become a reality

The buckets or secondary nozzles on Concorde. The left-hand picture shows the nozzle in its divergent position as it would be in supersonic flight. The right-hand picture shows the nozzle as it would be for take-off, the gap allowing ambient air to break up the boundary to the jet efflux making it less noisy. For their position to give reverse thrust, see page 104

Opposite, top Sir Barnes Wallis with a model of Swallow. Although the cockpit and undercarriage have been extended for this photograph the wings are in the fully swept position for supersonic flight – a combination that would not have been found in practice. Surrounding Sir Barnes are examples of his earlier engineering efforts including bombs, airships, the Wellington bomber

Inset A polymorphous photograph of Swallow showing the extent of the variable geometry. Note that the engine pairs on the wingtips were to have been hinged. There was no fin

*See appendix (page 157).

its leaving through the exhaust nozzle. As the velocity of the jet gases are so much greater with reheat on, the exhaust nozzle must vary in area of accommodate two situations. On the FD2 the reheat was either on or off, thus the exhaust nozzle only had the two positions - wide open or open. On the P1 the reheat was variable so the exhaust nozzle had to be variable as well. On the Olympus 593, as fitted to Concorde, not only is there a variable nozzle to accommodate the reheat, but there is a secondary nozzle which, amongst other things, forms a divergent duct for efficiency during the supersonic cruise. Furthermore the primary nozzle area varies continually, even without reheat, thus keeping the Olympus engine constantly in tune*.

The Supersonic Transport Aircraft Committee (STAC) met regularly from November 1956 until March 1959. Among its recommendations was one which strongly favoured building a long-range SST to carry 150 passengers from London to New York non-stop with a cruising speed of not less than Mach 1.8. There was also a recommendation for the construction of a shorter range SST to cruise at Mach 1.2. The committee regarded cruising speeds approaching Mach 3 as feasible, but technically difficult due to the heating effect discussed in the Preface. At Mach 3 the highest temperature experienced by the fuselage is around 335°C (635°F) thus not only is it much more difficult to keep the occupants cool, but the skin has to be made from the more expensive alloys of titanium and perhaps even from stainless steel. The cheaper and

well tested aluminium alloy, although highly satisfactory at temperatures up to 130°C (265°F), does not cope with temperatures of over 300°C (572°F) at all. A Mach 3 version was regarded by the STAC as a possible second generation SST.

Between London and New York a cruising speed of Mach 3, compared to Mach 2, would reduce the total journey time by about 40 minutes, about 20 per cent. The real gain of a Mach 2 airliner was that it could more than double the speed of the current subsonic airliners, which were designed to cruise at just above Mach 0.8. Any economic gains associated with the yet quicker journey times made possible at a speed of Mach 3 would be more than wiped out by the fact that a Mach 3 SST would cost disproportionately more to build. Development costs were put at £75–£95m for the Mach 1.8 SST and £50–£80m for the slower shorter range versions, at 1959 values. It was considered that they would cost about 50 per cent more to operate than a similarly-sized subsonic aircraft.

Following the recommendations of the STAC, feasibility studies were commissioned by the Ministry of Defence, then headed by Duncan Sandys. Bristol produced studies of an SST with a conventional fuselage and slender delta wings, but Hawker Siddeley provided a study for an integral layout – a slender delta with a longitudinal swelling in which would be housed the passengers – virtually a slender delta flying wing.

Duncan Sandys' somewhat infamous defence White Paper in 1957 had put a temporary halt to the development of manned military aircraft in Britain (including the Avro 730 supersonic bomber) in favour of missiles. So a rather stunned aircraft industry must have welcomed the opportunity to research and possibly build an SST. By 1959, when Duncan Sandys had commissioned the feasibility studies for an SST, plans for the new British Supersonic Tactical Strike Reconnaissance Aircraft – the TSR2 – had been unveiled. However, in 1966 Britain's Labour government cancelled – among other aircraft – the TSR2. To quote Sir Stanley Hooker on British military aviation policy: 'We were in, we were out, then we were in again and finally out. It was more like a boat race than a policy.'

Among other designs which were also put forward at about this time was the Swallow designed by Sir Barnes Wallis, an aircraft in which variable sweep had been taken to the extreme. The engines, mounted outboard on the wings, were pivoted and could be used for stability and control in place of aerodynamic surfaces. Furthermore their movement with the wing sweep contributed to the balance of the aircraft. Aerodynamic balance is maintained on Concorde by moving the fuel to change the centre of gravity.

An 'arrow' planform is attractive because it is very efficient aerodynamically at supersonic speeds. To keep the drag down on Swallow, the pilots would have had a retractable cockpit. Studies for advanced supersonic transports make use of the 'arrow' planform; but without recourse to variable geometry, the 'arrow' cannot be so extreme as that of Swallow. In the unswept

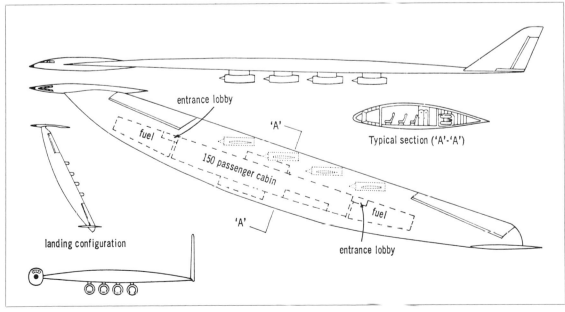

entrance lobby

fuel

'A'

Typical section ('A'-'A')

150 passenger cabin

fuel

'A'

landing configuration

entrance lobby

The slewed-wing proposal from Handley Page. Runways would have had to have taken on different proportions if this 1961 idea had taken root!

arrangement, the engines on Swallow were very far from the centre-line. This would have given the pilots quite a control problem following an engine failure. In spite of Wallis' original thinking, it might have been difficult to make the arrangement work without the modern electronic technology now available. Boeing's main study for an SST (the Boeing 2707-200) proposed using variable geometry, but with the engines fixed beneath the tailplane.

Another quite revolutionary and somewhat odd looking proposal was for the Handley Page slewed wing. Although lift to drag ratios (L/D) are good in theory with such an arrangement, the control problem looked extremely complicated. However, it too would have benefitted from the digital computers of the 1980s. A slewed wing aircraft with fixed fuselage is under development at NASA in the USA. Nevertheless this still appears a rather unlikely solution to the problem of how to design an SST.

A third proposal envisaged a slender delta with a large number of lifting engines to give it a vertical take-off capability. No less than fifty such engines were thought to be necessary on a transatlantic SST! The rate of fuel burn of the lifting engines was expected to be very high – and the result of them all failing to start simultaneously prior to landing would have left the aircraft in a somewhat dangerous state.

These three proposals (and the Boeing 2707-200) failed to exploit the discovery that extra lift could be obtained by allowing the airflow to separate over the upper surface of a slender delta wing. To give lift, under normal circumstances, the flow of air over a wing must not separate from the wing. The airflow travels slightly further over the top surface than under the bottom surface and so has to move more quickly over the top than the bottom. As it accelerates its pressure drops. In this way the wing is 'sucked' upwards, rendering lift to it and to whatever the wing is attached. Should this airflow become turbulent, thus breaking away from its ordered flow, the lift will suddenly reduce; the wing is then said to 'stall'. At the tip of a wing in normal flight is a small vortex – a kind of horizontal whirlpool of air caused by the higher pressure air underneath spilling over into the lower pressure air on top, an effect which can be highlighted by the use of smoke in a wind tunnel (it is somewhat akin to the whirlpool seen over the plug of an emptying bath). Such a vortex, on a larger scale, can be harnessed to give extra lift to a slender delta wing in slow speed flight.

A big contribution in the study of flow separation was made by E.C. Maskell of RAE. He and the late Dr. Dietrich Küchemann, head of Aerodynamics at RAE (who had been a scientist in Germany during the Second World War later 'inherited' by Britain,) laid the foundation of this new technique.

Furthermore, the slender delta wing behaved very satisfactorily during transonic and supersonic flight. This was the breakthrough – the discovery of a planform which theoretically could remain unaltered throughout a vast speed range. There would be no need to fit flaps and slats, which add so much to the weight and complexity of conventional airliners. A practical test was needed to prove both that the theory was correct and that no dangerous side effects would prevent it being applied to an SST.

Consequently the feasibility programme that was commissioned following the final report from STAC, included a contract to Handley Page to build an aircraft to test what the flying paper darts, beloved by schoolboys, had suggested: that vortex lift could give sufficiently stable lift to allow a slender delta flying at low speed to be controllable.

The resulting aircraft was the experimental Handley Page 115. It was powered by a single Viper jet engine. Although its 76 degree swept wings gave the illusion that it was built for great speed it was designed purely to explore flight at low speeds – it did not even have a retractable undercarriage.

The handling of the HP 115 was better than anyone had dared to hope. It gave excellent lift at slow speed. Even landing in a cross-wind, a situation which might have caused difficulty, was trouble-free.

Success with the Handley Page 115 proved that the resulting SST would not have to be lumbered with flaps and slats to enable its wing to give sufficient lift at take-off and landing speeds. If it had one small vice it was that as the speed became slower the drag caused by the wings giving lift became greater. Although this obviates the need for air-brakes, the extra drag has to be overcome by increasing the thrust. Provided there is plenty of thrust available, all is well; but the danger lay in the pilot not spotting the speed loss and thus not applying the extra thrust required by the lower speed. Without proper monitoring of the speed it could fall off to the point, not of the wings being unable to give lift and so stalling, but

to the point where there was not enough thrust to overcome the extra drag associated with the low speed. To overcome this problem it was recognised that such an aircraft would have to be fitted with an automatic throttle. Indeed on Concorde there is just such a device and it works extremely well too. However, Concorde is surprisingly easy to fly in the very rare event of the auto-throttle not being available.

Although the slender delta promised to have a better lift to drag ratio (L/D) at supersonic speeds than other planforms the

Before the main landing gear can be retracted it has to be shortened so that it can fit into the undercarriage bays. The 'chines' - aerodynamic surfaces on either side of the nose - are there to reduce side slip. A vortex forms on the upstream surface which generates a force which pulls the aircraft straight. Without these the fin would have been taller to avoid being blanketed during flight at high angles of attack

Shock waves around a wind tunnel model of Concorde. The shock waves are three dimensional forming a cone at the nose. Compare these with the two dimensional ones generated around the Concorde silhouette model with a flow of water shown on page 9

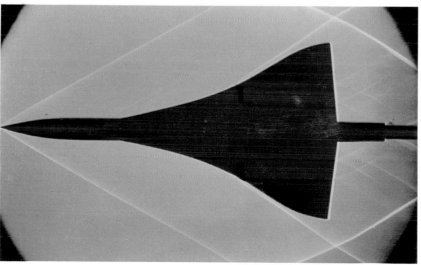

The HP 115 in flight near Farnborough. The slender delta wing was fitted with detachable leading edges, allowing various aerodynamic shapes to be tested. This aircraft proved that a separated airflow could give lift at slow speeds. First flown in August 1961, its success paved the way for Concorde by showing that complex high lift devices for slow speed flight would not be necessary for slender deltas

unpalatable fact remains that there is a drag rise as Mach 1 is exceeded. In fact the L/D drops, on Concorde, from about 12 at Mach 0.95 to 7.5 at Mach 2. How then was the future SST going to have enough range to cross the Atlantic?

Happily jet-engine efficiency can be designed to improve with speed, more than compensating for the loss of aerodynamic efficiency. The projected SST was expected therefore to travel further (or at least as far) on a gallon of fuel at its supersonic cruising speed as it could at its subsonic cruising speed, expected to be in excess of Mach 0.9. This fortunate state of affairs is brought about because the efficiency of the turbojet engine is very much enhanced if the air is precompressed prior to engine entry. At speeds in excess of Mach 1.4 sufficient precompression can be arranged to occur inside the intake system where the air is slowed – hence compressed – to about half

According to some commentators the cost of developing Concorde was increased by one third due to its being a collaborative project. There were two production lines – one at Bristol (Filton) in England, and the other at Toulouse in France. Duplication of jigs and tools were two elements in this process, whilst transporting pieces made in France to Britain and vice-versa was another. Here the 'Guppy' is being loaded with a British built tail-fin and tail-cone for transport to Toulouse. Airbus Industrie (consortium of four countries) were the benefactors of the collaborative experience gained from the Concorde project

Opposite The number 4 engine intake on a Concorde. The two moveable 'ramps' can be clearly seen inside the top of the box. The extent of the movement on the forward one (labelled 'DO NOT USE . . .') can be clearly seen on the vertical dividing wall between this intake and its neighbour (to the right of this picture) in the form of 'rubbing' marks. Correct positioning of the ramps to focus the shock wave on the intake's lower lip was fundamental to engine efficiency in supersonic flight. During subsonic flight the ramps are raised, as shown here See appendix (page 157)

the speed of sound before it reaches the engine. Nobody doubted that the intake system would need some kind of variable 'throat' so that it could cope efficiently with various speeds and especially those in excess of Mach 1.5. Since engine efficiency improves with speed up to Mach 3, there was a great incentive to go as fast as the kinetic heating of the structure would allow – Mach 2.2 appeared the most attractive speed if a well-tried and tested aluminium alloy were used.

However, Mach 2.04, which reduced the maximum temperature from 156°C to 127°C (313°F to 261°F), was ultimately chosen since the lower temperature gave less of a problem with the oil and fuel.

By the late 1950s, it was realised, tantalisingly, that aerodynamic and thermodynamic development had progressed far enough to allow an SST to become a reality. The question now became: would disappointments with the performance of British civil aviation spur Government and Industry into turning the theory of a paper dart into a practical SST?

British civil aviation in the years after the Second World War had hoped to equal or better anything the Americans could produce. It was true that two major projects had been abandoned – the Princess Flying Boat and the Bristol Brabazon. But on the credit side the pure jet de Havilland Comet 1 and the turbo-prop Vickers Viscount were about to appear. At Bristol another potential world beater, the turbo-prop Britannia was also taking shape.

The Britannia, it was hoped, would replace most long-range piston-propelled airliners. The engine chosen to power the Britannia was the Proteus. Originally designed to fit within the wing of the Brabazon, it had an air intake arrangement which caused the air to turn through 180 degrees before entering the engine. At 20,000 ft in the moist air found over the tropics ice formed at the 180 degree elbow causing the engine to flameout (stop) on an early Britannia. Fears of a similar, if not worse problem over the Atlantic brought matters to a head. However, the moisture content over the Atlantic at 20,000 ft is not nearly as great as it is over the tropics. According to Sir Stanley Hooker a relatively easy modification would have sufficed. Nevertheless for worldwide operations a total cure had to be found. In the end a system of igniter plugs solved the problem and BOAC accepted the Britannia – some two years late – and just in time to be overtaken by the jets on the North Atlantic, notably the Boeing 707. Instead of 180 only 80 Britannias were sold, and a jet-powered version of the Britannia was beyond the

The Bristol Britannia. The big British hope of the 1950s. Icing problems on the Bristol Proteus engines delayed its entry into service. Too soon it was overtaken by the long-range jet airliners.

resources of Bristol. The Britannia did serve with the Royal Air Force in the transport role, and many of the ex BOAC aircraft saw service with holiday charter and freight airlines throughout the world.

The designers of the medium-range jet-powered Comet 4 had, by 1958, overcome the devastating problem experienced with its direct forerunner the Comet 1. The corners of the windows had not been made strong enough to withstand metal fatigue with the result that three Comet 1s had experienced explosive decompression in flight. This salutary lesson caused the designers of Concorde to proceed with caution in every field and not least in the area of aircraft structure. The Comet 4 inaugurated the first transatlantic jet passenger service in October 1958 – two weeks before the Boeing 707.

It had been galling for Sir George Edwards, Chairman of Vickers, that BOAC had been allowed, by the British Government, to purchase the Boeing 707 from America in 1956. In the previous year, BOAC

and the RAF had turned down the British equivalent to the 707 – the Vickers VC7 (V-1000 in its military form). Based on the Vickers Valiant bomber, it had engines buried in the inboard section of the wing with intakes at the wing roots. The VC7 was scrapped, to be replaced by the Vickers VC10.

The Vickers VC10, with its clean wing and four rear-mounted engines, was originally conceived as an airliner capable of operating from high altitude airfields on hot days over the old 'empire' routes. Later its range was increased to compete with the Boeing 707. Although it was beloved by passengers as soon as it appeared in 1962, it was too late to sell in large numbers - the Boeing 707 had got in first. It typified the frightful divergence in the relationship between the British Government, the nationalised carriers (BOAC and BEA) and the aircraft industry. The Government, according to Sir Basil Smallpeice (Managing Director of BOAC from 1956-1963), had expected BOAC to support the British Aircraft Industry by buying British aircraft it did not want and then having to bear some of the financial burden incurred during the final stages of the development of the new aircraft. At the same time BOAC was expected to pay the Government a fixed rate of interest on the capital borrowed. It was galling to BOAC that a large quantity of that capital, in 1957, had had to be spent on acquiring ten DC7Cs to fill the gap caused by the late delivery of the Britannia 312. Thus BOAC regarded the VC10 with a great deal of caution, fearing that the Government would force them to have a large number of VC10s they simply did not want. In the end some kind of compromise was reached, but not without acrimony.

Forewarned is forearmed. Sir Basil Small-peice and Sir Matthew Slattery of BOAC made it very clear to the British Government in 1960 that although they would be delighted to assist with any future SST, this would be at no financial risk to the airline and no orders would be placed unless the SST made economic sense. In the end the Government agreed to underwrite that risk.

It is true that there had been one British success – the short-haul Vickers Viscount, with sales exceeding 400. However, by the late 1950s and early 1960s, in the words of Sir Stanley Hooker, 'We've lost in the civil market to the Americans. Now these Boeing 707s and DC8s cannot possibly last for more than about ten years. Therefore in order to collar our fair share we must look towards building a supersonic airliner with a European partner.'

A Concorde model painted in BOAC livery. By the time it made its first commercial flight, BOAC (Overseas) had merged with BEA (European) to become British Airways. The VC10s in the background at Heathrow represent the last large all British airliner, and barely 50 were built.

Agreement with France

By 1961, Britain had convinced herself that it was both highly desirable and technically possible to build an Atlantic range (3,700 statute miles) SST. There was one piece of the jigsaw missing, however; could a suitable partner be found to share the large cost of such a project? The right choice of partner, it was hoped, would lead not only to a successful SST but to co-operation in a host of other fields. A European partner, for instance, might pave the way for Britain's entry into the Common Market. At that time Russia and America were pouring millions into the exploration of space, without, apart from technical advance, any prospect of financial return. An SST promised technical advance and a financial return, the latter largely on the grounds that speed had always attracted customers.

Partnership with an American company was considered. But the Americans were more interested in Mach 3 designs. Such speeds had already been ruled out by the British designers on account of the kinetic heating problem.

The only European country with the

ability to undertake such a project in the early 1960s was France. The nation had to rebuild its once proud aircraft industry from the ashes of the Second World War. She was, in 1960, one of the few nations – with

Russia, the United States, Sweden, Britain and Canada – to have designed, built and tested supersonic aircraft. Nevertheless the French Aircraft Industry would benefit enormously from Britain's technical know-how which had been enhanced rather than destroyed by the Second World War. As it turned out, Britain was to benefit from France's determination to see the project through.

Starting with the straight-winged Trident, first flown in 1953, France had built a series of supersonic research aircraft. It was the Trident which on one occasion caused some concern in the echelons of the British Radar Warning System. Charles Burnet (BAe Weybridge) who witnessed the incident said: 'One evening in the late 1950s a worried controller phoned Boscombe Down to find out if there were any test aircraft airborne from there at that time. Apparently a target had been detected flying down the Channel from the *east* at over 1,000 mph – it turned out to be the French Trident!' This aircraft was powered by two wing tip-mounted turbojets and a rocket unit in the fuselage.

After this came the delta-winged Gerfault which was capable, in 1954, of exceeding Mach 1 by use of a turbojet alone – without reheat or rocket assistance. But most spectacular of the French research aircraft was the Nord Griffon. It had a propulsion unit which consisted of a turbojet within a huge outer casing. This outer casing formed a ramjet. The turbojet engine was used for slow speed flight and for starting the ramjet. The Griffon achieved Mach 1.85 in 1957 (about 1,240 mph).

Ramjets work on the principle that due to the high forward speed, usually above Mach 1.5, there is sufficient natural compression of the air to supplant the rotating compressor of a turbojet. No compressor means no need for a turbine to drive the compressor hence no moving parts. Air entering the intake becomes compressed, is then heated by the burning fuel giving thrust to the engine as it accelerates out of the propelling nozzle. A ramjet does not give efficient propulsion until speeds of around Mach 4 are reached.

Many missiles are propelled by ramjets, but only once they have achieved a suitable speed, usually gained from a rocket engine. Concorde travels too slowly to benefit from ramjet propulsion.

On the civil side the French had some success with the subsonic twin-engined Sud-Est Caravelle airliner. Its nose section was in fact the same as the British de Havilland Comet's. There was a lot of collaboration. Incidentally Concorde was to inherit, via this lineage, the triple hydraulic system labelled blue, green and, as a backup, yellow, which was originally fitted to the Comet.

Concurrent with the Nord Griffon were the swept-winged Mystères and the delta-winged Mirage fighters. The next logical step for Sud Aviation, as it had become by 1961, was to investigate the possibility of

Concorde 02 – the French-constructed pre-production aircraft F-WTSA displaying both makers' names against an Alpine backdrop. By the time this picture was taken Sud Aviation had become Aerospatiale. Each country was to operate the aircraft that it had constructed. Note the extended tail cone compared to the prototypes and British pre-production Concorde 01. Every minor improvement was vital in order to achieve the design range and payload of at least Paris to Washington. The greater the fineness ratio (length to maximum diameter) the better the lift to drag ratio (about 7¹/₂ on Concorde at Mach 2, although 10 or 11 is desirable in a successor). Keeping fineness ratio high on a design with a shorter fuselage compromises internal volume

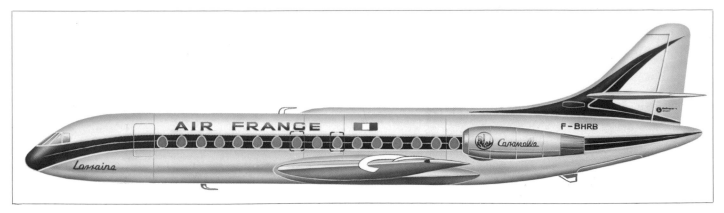

The Sud Aviation Caravelle. This successful French airliner had two rear-mounted engines. The nose owed its lines to the de Havilland Comet, as can be clearly seen

building an SST. Sud Aviation had been formed from Sud-Est, run by George Hereil, the original proposer of the Caravelle, and Sud Ouest.

Accordingly, at the Paris Air Show of June 1961 there appeared a model of a slender delta SST called the Super Caravelle. Although never built, it was designed to carry a payload of 70 passengers over 2,000 miles.

The Super Caravelle was thus not to have transatlantic range. In fact there was to be some wrangling between the British and French over this question of range. The British, in spite of a mild flirtation with an 'M-winged' medium range Mach 1.2 aircraft, had never considered it worthwhile to build anything with less range than London (or Paris) to New York. The Super Caravelle bore a remarkable resemblance to the BAC 223, the latest proposal from Archibald Russell, technical director of Bristol Aircraft which, by late 1961, had become part of the British Aircraft Corporation (BAC). Included in the merger were Bristol Aeroplane Co Ltd, English Electric Aviation Ltd, builders of the P1 Lightning, Hunting Aircraft Ltd and Vickers-Armstrong (Aircraft) Ltd, builders of the VC10 .

The BAC 223 study had followed a proposal for a larger version – the Bristol Type 198 which had been considered too ambitious to gain Ministry approval.

The Type 198 design had been originally submitted as one of the feasibility studies which had followed the recommendations of the STAC. With transatlantic range at a cruise speed of Mach 2.2, it was to have had six Olympus engines in a bank on top of the wing under the fin. The projected all up weight was to be 385,000 lb, with a passenger load of 132. Concorde turned out to be only four per cent heavier with a similar load carrying ability and four Olympus engines of increased thrust instead of the original six.

The BAC 223 on the other hand, although still with transatlantic range, had a proposed weight of 270,000 lb and was to be powered by four under-wing mounted Olympus engines. This question of size as well as range was already causing much controversy. A great deal of unnecessary expense was incurred building tools and jigs for designs that were not produced.

Duncan Sandys, perceiving the political and economic advantages of collaboration between France and Britain, had encouraged Sir George Edwards, Chairman of the new BAC, to explore the possibilities of co-operation with his French opposite number, Georges Hereil of Sud Aviation. At first, there did not appear to be much of a basis for co-operation due to the differing range philosophies. So discussions centred around collaboration on a common engine, on systems, electrics and hydraulics.

To achieve better coordination, the French Minister of Transport and Britain's Minister of Aviation met in September 1961. This resulted in a firm directive to the participating firms to resolve their differences. But collaboration proved more difficult for the airframe manufacturers, whose ideas on range were becoming more entrenched, than for the engine manufacturers. There was only one engine that could sensibly be used for both the medium and long haul SST: the Bristol-Siddeley Olympus.

Bristol Aero Engines had persevered privately with the Olympus in spite of Government policy which had decreed, in 1957, that there would be just the one large engine programme, centred on the Rolls-Royce Conway engine. Had it not been for the wisdom and foresight of Sir Reginald Verdon-Smith, Chairman of the Bristol Aeroplane Company, there would have been no engine immediately available and suitable for an SST.

There followed more meetings between

the respective ministers to encourage collaboration. There was little result at first, other than the making of a few conciliatory gestures – the building of the tail section of the Super VC10 was subcontracted out to a Sud Aviation subsidiary.

Then in 1962 de Gaulle came to power in France. General André Puget replaced Georges Hereil, while in Britain Julian Amery became the Minister of Aviation. These changes propelled the two countries into an agreement with one another. De Gaulle saw this as a way of improving the French Aircraft Industry while Puget, unlike Hereil, was on the same wavelength as George Edwards; Amery was to seal this concord with an unbreakable treaty.

Just before the signing of the treaty the Americans became perturbed by the progess being made in the field of SSTs in Europe. Accordingly Eugene Black, ex-Chairman of the World Bank and a

The Mirage III. The French pursued the delta planform after the British success with the FD2. The Mirage has been a great success for the French aircraft industry

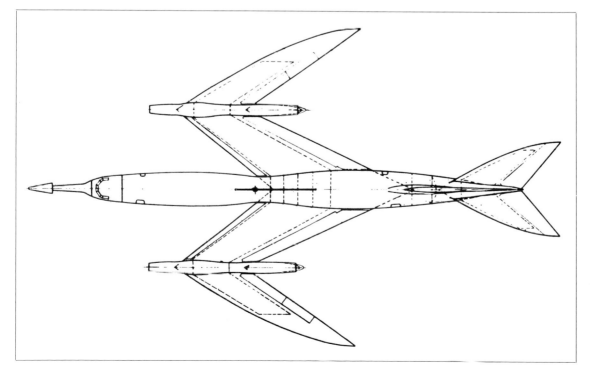

The medium range M-winged Mach 1.2 proposal from Armstrong Whitworth. The cone at the nose would have kept the nose shock wave clear of the wings. Area ruling, apparent where the fuselage is waisted, was intended to keep the drag down. Concorde was not quite long enough to have required area ruling

The Rolls-Royce/SNECMA Olympus 593–610 engine, powerplant for Concorde. Between 50,000 and 60,000 ft at Mach 2 it is the world's most efficient aero engine, with more than 40 per cent thermal efficiency. With re-heat on take-off it delivers over 38,000 lb of thrust, during the supersonic cruise around 10,000 lb

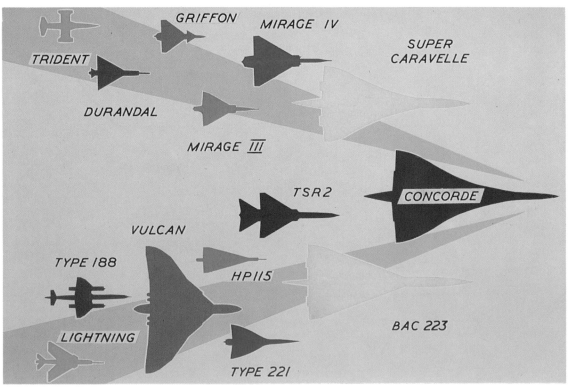

Concorde's family tree. The Super Caravelle and BAC 223 were only design studies. The Type 221 was a modification of the FD2

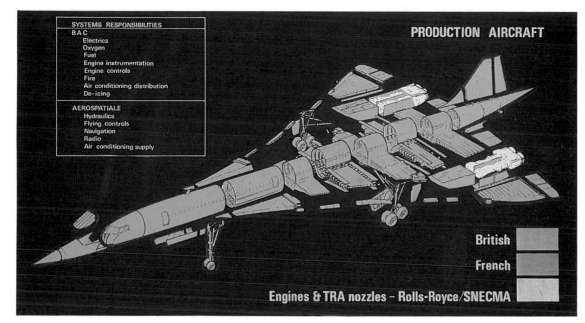

PRODUCTION AIRCRAFT

British

French

Engines & TRA nozzles – Rolls-Royce/SNECMA

The distribution of responsibilities for the manufacture of Concorde. Broadly the breakdown between France and Britain was 60:40 for the airframe and 40:60 for the engine

prominent and influential individual in the US corridors of power, attempted to dissuade Julian Amery from continuing with his plans. According to Geoffrey Knight (one time director of BAC) in his book *Concorde the Inside Story* this merely had the effect of encouraging Amery to go ahead. The Americans were afraid that Britain's gamble was going to pay off. It turned out that Eugene Black was about to become Chairman of a high-powered committee set up to study the possibility of the United States building an SST.

On 29 November 1962 an agreement between the governments of France and Britain was signed and registered at the Hague. The agreement comprised seven articles. It included clauses about each country having equal responsibility for the project, bearing equal shares of the cost, and sharing equally the proceeds of sales. Two aircraft – a long-range and a medium-range one – were envisaged. Every effort was to be made to carry out this programme with equal attention to both the medium and long-range versions. There were to be two integrated organisations taken from British and French firms – BAC and Sud Aviation for the airframe, Bristol Siddeley and SNECMA for the engine – which were to make detailed proposals for carrying out the programme. There was no break clause. The agreement was signed by Julian Amery and Peter Thomas (Parliamentary Under-Secretary of State, Foreign Office) for the United Kingdom and G de Courcel, French Ambassador in Britain, for France.

It was the first time in history that such a collaborative organisation had been set up.

The bureaucratic machinery that was to control the project ensured three things. First that every decision was minutely and critically examined by both partners. Secondly, as a result of the first, a superior aircraft was to evolve. Thirdly, the process would take longer and cost more than if it had been organised individually or with one country having design leadership.

The first flight of the prototype was expected during the second half of 1966, while the first production aircraft was due at the end of 1968, with a Certificate of Airworthiness (C of A) being granted at the end of 1969. In the event, the first prototype flew in March 1969, and the C of A was granted in late 1975.

The development costs of the project in 1962 were put at between £150m and £170m. The division of responsibility was to be 60:40 between France and Britain on the airframe and 40:60 on the engine. For various reasons connected with inflation, devaluation of the pound, the reworking of the design in 1964 for just the long haul version and the longer time it took to complete, the project eventually cost, as we shall see, rather more!

Britain was not yet a member of the Common Market. As one commentator put it 'Concorde was conceived before the two contracting partners were joined in wedlock.' In spite of the agreement, membership of the EEC by Britain was put off a further nine years. So even this act of European unity, in the face of American aviation technology, was not enough; de Gaulle was still suspicious of Britain's special relationship with the United States.

Taking Shape

An SST has to operate in an extraordinarily hostile environment. At Mach 2 it experiences a freezing airflow but of such force that the fuselage is heated to the boiling point of water, shock waves tear at every angle on its airframe, and all this occurs at an altitude where the atmospheric pressure is a tenth of its value at sea level. Only military aircraft flown by pilots, equipped with sophisticated oxygen supplies and wearing pressure suits, had ventured to these extremes and then usually only for minutes at a time. The SST was designed to carry ordinary airline passengers in complete comfort and safety for hours at a stretch. Could the fusion of British and French philosophies possibly produce such a craft?

Judging from the expected timescale of the project there was confidence that success would come quickly. The physics of obtaining lift throughout the speed range was understood. The loss in aerodynamic efficiency at speeds above Mach 1 would be more than compensated by the improvement in the efficiency of the intake and engine combination achievable at Mach 2. A certain amount of ingenuity would be called for in some areas – notably in the engine air intake, air conditioning and fuel systems. Novel techniques, like the redistribution of the fuel in flight to maintain the balance of the aircraft, would have to be developed.

The aircraft also would need to behave in a way that pilots had been trained to expect. A slender delta-winged aircraft with no horizontal tail surfaces behaves differently from a swept-winged aircraft with a tail. It is less naturally stable at speed – a conventional aircraft is designed so that a speed increase over the tail surface causes an extra downforce on the tail. This pitches the aircraft into a climb which, without a thrust increase, restores the speed. Also its ratio of pitch to roll is different from a conventional aircraft because of its length and small wingspan. Rather than rely on excessive training time to teach pilots new techniques it would be safer to fit the aircraft with computers to give it the feel of a conventional aircraft.

The design was revolutionary. In spite of the very best endeavours of the designers there was no way of predicting the

The full scale wooden mock-up of Concorde at Filton, England. This was used to evaluate emergency evacuation systems as well as being an example of the appearance of the finished aircraft. In 1976, when the first BA crews were being trained, this hangar also housed a plywood Concorde flight deck complete with droop nose – a British design responsibility. Fully equipped with instruments and electrics it was originally used for evolving an ergonomic layout. Largely responsible for the transformation of the prototype flight deck into one suitable for ordinary airline use was BOAC's Flight Development Manager Captain Jimmy Andrews. At first and unprecedented at that time, the project involved the airlines interested in acquiring Concorde and various pilots' unions. This airline participation diminished when their options to purchase evaporated. Ultimately only the teams from Air France and BA remained.

The first Concorde ordered by BOAC was given the registration G-BOAC. By the time it was delivered in 1976, the airline had become BA. BAC Weybridge built the forward fuselages

An Avro Vulcan with five Olympus engines. The centre one – the Olympus 593 – is shown here undergoing icing trials. Water droplets, simulating flight in cloud, were released ahead of the intake from the device beneath the nose. An unchecked build up of ice within the intake and over the first compression stages of the engine would radically affect performance. Heat applied either electrically or from hot air on vulnerable surfaces overcomes the problem

interaction of all the systems before the first flight of the prototypes. There might be some totally unforeseen side effect which could take years to iron out, like some quirk in the airflow affecting just one engine, necessitating a control condition peculiar to that engine. Indeed such a problem did arise, but mercifully a simple solution was found.

Having designed a practical aircraft, it would be worthless unless it were safe.

Making the structure safe, yet light, would stretch the powers of the designers. Having built the structure it would have to be tested to limits beyond those that could be explored in flight. To achieve that full scale versions of the airframe would have to be dedicated to ground-testing. All the stresses and strains of high altitude flight would be applied to them, including the repeated heating and cooling of the airframe, experienced on each supersonic flight.

Very high altitude flight is advantageous to an SST since it can fly at a far lower indicated airspeed for a given true airspeed (see page 11). At 60,000 ft travelling at Mach 2, or 1,150 knots true airspeed, Concorde only 'feels' 435 knots of airspeed. Fighter aircraft have to be built with sufficient strength to withstand turbulent air at indicated airspeeds in excess of 700 knots. Such a speed, apart from being quite unnecessary for an SST, would call for a stronger and therefore heavier structure. With the very small margin available of payload weight to total weight, the SST could not be allowed to have the luxury of a high indicated airspeed limit. The indicated airspeed limit on Concorde varies with altitude, reaching a maximum of 530 knots

A full sized rig was made to check the working of Concorde's fuel system. Apart from supplying the engines, the fuel is used to move the centre of gravity rearwards during acceleration and forwards prior to landing as well as being a medium for cooling the air in the air conditioning system and cooling the engine oil

at 43,000 ft. A typical limit for a subsonic passenger jet is 350 knots.

Off-setting the advantage of flying high is the disadvantage that the fuselage has to be made strong enough to withstand high differential pressures. To give a cabin altitude of 6,000 ft when the aircraft is at 60,000 ft requires a differential pressure approaching 11 lb per square inch (psi). Hitherto the limit for subsonic jets had been about 8 lb psi which gave them a cabin altitude of over 7,000 ft at an aircraft altitude of 37,000 ft.

Large aircraft require a multitude of systems: electrics, hydraulics, navigation, undercarriage and flying controls to name but a few. Systems fundamental to the safety of the aircraft must have back up systems. Some systems on Concorde were to have additional back up systems. For instance, Concorde is fitted with four methods of lowering the undercarriage: two of them from different hydraulic sources; one by letting it down by its own weight; and a fourth by use of compressed air.

Before passengers could be carried every conceivable combination of failures and consequent recourse to back up systems

The four undercarriage legs on Concorde are seen here at half travel. The length of the main gear legs is governed by having to keep the rear of the engines clear of the ground at the high aircraft pitch angles associated with take-off and landing. The tail gear is there as a precaution against this eventuality. The camber on the wing (roughly the amount that the leading and trailing edges are bent downwards), can be seen from this picture. It helps to minimise the rearward movement of the centre of lift with increasing Mach number, thus the requirement to move the centre of gravity so far rearward is also minimised

The Concorde production line at Toulouse, France, the other line was at Filton, England. It is doubtful that any future collaborative project on the scale of Concorde would have duplicate production lines. Development continued even after the 'production' aircraft were being built. Thanks to a US 'Change of Requirement', twenty-two titanium straps (two between frames 9-20 - roughly between the front door and the leading edge of the wing) had to be incorporated. These are fixed internally within the top of the forward part of the fuselage from floor level on one side to the other. The straps were 3 inches wide but only 12 thousandths of an inch thick. This modification was retrofitted, at no little expense, to the earlier Concordes but included in the later versions. Every aircraft has to be equipped with a means of passenger escape and, for over water flights, life rafts. On Concorde the four forward exits are equipped with inflatable 'Slide/rafts' - a slide that can be converted into a raft. In this picture the extent to which the overwing exit has to open in order to accommodate the slide/raft box fixed to its lower half, here resting on the wing, can be seen

had to be explored. Might the warning of a failure of one system cause the pilots to take inappropriate action? Just prior to Concorde entering service it was discovered that the loss of some of the hydraulic pressure to the flying controls during the early stages of the take-off run resulted in an instruction to the pilots to abandon the take-off. This required the application of the wheel brakes, themselves requiring hydraulic pressure supplied from the source whose failure caused the take-off to be abandoned. Although hydraulic pressure to the brakes could be restored in seconds, that would be too late for an aircraft travelling at 270 ft per second: the aircraft would overrun. So an instantaneous and automatic change-over from one hydraulic supply to another had to be the solution.

Safety at the level of system failures was one thing, but would the SST be able to survive a potentially more catastrophic incident? Would it be controllable during conditions following the simultaneous failure of two engines on one side? The answer had to be 'yes'. But when the British and French prepared to join forces in 1961, experience of such incidents had not been good.

The world's first big supersonic jet was the four-engined, delta-winged American Convair B58 Hustler. It was not capable of surviving a single engine failure at Mach 2, let alone two on the same side. Even flight at other speeds was risky – a B58 crashed during a display at the 1961 Paris Airshow. Deaths of B58 crew were common occurrences in spite of their being housed in escape capsules. It would be small comfort for a Concorde passenger to think that the pilot and his crew were similarly protected while he was not!

No country had yet been called upon to award a Certificate of Airworthiness for the transport of the fare-paying public in an SST. New rules had to be introduced. Every detail of the new aircraft would suffer the expert scrutiny of the civil aviation authorities of Britain, France and, as a prospective purchaser, the United States.

There are conflicting requirements on any aircraft. On an SST such conflict is extreme: too strong and it would be too heavy; too efficient at one speed, it might be unflyable at another; highly efficient engines at Mach 2 might be noisy on take-off. Compromise and ingenuity would find solutions, but the margins were narrow. The payload to maximum take-off weight on the long range

Concorde 01 – the first pre production aircraft inside the 'Brabazon' hangar at Filton, Britain. Note the shorter tail cone found on this and the two prototype Concordes, and the original secondary nozzle system visible here on number three engine. On production aircraft this was replaced by variable 'buckets'

The Concorde production line at Filton, England. Concorde 202 (G-BBDG) can be seen in the background. These hangars had originally been built for the production of the Bristol Brabazon

airliners of the 1960s was 10 per cent; the Boeing 747s of the 1970s give 20 per cent. The SST would be lucky to achieve 5 per cent over a 3,500 nm range. A small error in performance would remove the ability to carry any payload between London and New York.

The small predicted payload to weight ratio did not daunt the supporters of the SST. The difference would be restored by the greater number of Atlantic crossings achievable by one aircraft. The price of fuel was expected to remain constant, even fall a little! The sonic boom, however, did cause concern.

An aircraft travelling at speeds above Mach 1.15, depending on atmospheric conditions, causes a double boom to be audible on the surface. Should this preclude supersonic flight over populated land, the medium-range SST espoused by the French would be a non-seller, as there are too few viable medium range routes which fly over the sea (see sonic boom propagation photograph, page 58).

In 1966 the designers hoped that two very similar SSTs would be built. The medium-range version would have space for more passengers and less fuel whilst the long-range version would reverse the mix. They discovered, however, that each design compromised the other. Coupled with thoughts about the sonic boom, this finally killed off the medium-range SST.

Nevertheless the two prototype Con-

cordes 001 and 002, whose building had commenced in April 1965, could not be described as long-range SSTs. The same applied to the two pre-production Concordes – 01 and 02. The final production version of Concorde (serial numbers from 201 to 216) was not only a long range SST but also came very close to Archibald Russell's original specification – the Bristol Type 198. Designing, tooling and building of three different versions of Concorde added very greatly to the cost and the time spent on the project. On top of this problem, the whole project had duplicate headquarters, at Filton and Toulouse, mainly for political reasons. With hindsight it is absolutely remarkable that such a fine aircraft as Concorde could have had such a complicated beginning.

No less troublesome to the project were the various changes of government on the British side. No sooner as one government takes over, its predecessor's activities come up for scrutiny. The Labour Government which took over from the Conservatives in 1964 was a case in point. It was only the agreement between France and Britain jointly to build an SST – an agreement that had been registered at The Hague – which prevented cancellation of the project.

Pressure had also been mounting from America for Britain to abandon various aviation projects – among them the TSR2 supersonic military aircraft. Why should the United States lend money to Britain only to

G-AXDN (Concorde 01) landing at Farnborough. Here the aircraft is at an angle to the oncoming airflow (angle of attack) of some 14°, so with the attitude (angle of the longitudinal axis of the aircraft to the horizontal) at 11°, the descent angle is 14° −11° which is 3°. This is the normal descent slope (known as the 'glideslope') to the runway. However, at this attitude the pilots would not have been able to see the runway over a nose pointed and streamlined for supersonic flight, hence the nose and visor are lowered, as shown here. Over the leading edges of the wings there is a wisp of condensation caused by the sudden decrease in air pressure (and therefore temperature) in the vortices over the wings. The use of this separated airflow to give lift over the wings is described on page 24, and further illustrated in the picture of Concorde's first landing on page 48. The markings under the port wing were to measure the extent of the build up of ice. Concorde 01 is now displayed at Duxford, near Cambridge

André Turcat in Concorde 01 F-WTSS, which became, under his command on 2 March 1969 from Toulouse, the first Concorde to become airborne. Compare the prototype with the 'production' version of the flight deck on page 82. The four 'fire handles' are here positioned on the central portion of the 'glare shield'; later versions have automatic control switches, the fire handles being moved to the overhead panel within reach of the Flight Engineer

fund aircraft projects which would compete with the American aviation industry? According to Julian Amery, the British minister who had concluded the agreement with France, the Americans had insisted that Concorde should be stopped. George Brown, the Minister of Economic Affairs of the new 1964 Labour Government denied that this was so. Following publication of Geoffrey Knight's book *Concorde the Inside Story* in 1976, Lord George Brown accused Mr Knight (in a letter to *The Times*, 7 May 1976) of getting 'almost every strand of his story wrong', although he admitted that he had not read the book. Nevertheless Geoffrey Knight later confirmed that there had indeed been US pressure against Concorde.

At industry level the story was different. From Boeing (the company chosen to build the US SST) came support for the European project. At first sight it might seem odd that a rival should support a rival, but this support was mutual. Each company felt that

if its rival was allowed to continue, then its own chances were bettered. This was borne out by the plethora of difficulties that faced Concorde as soon as the United States SST project was cancelled in 1971. Sadly much of that difficulty came from ill-informed political manoeuverers. Happily that lobby has become far better informed.

On 2 March 1969, the day before I joined BOAC, these difficulties lay in the future. On that day, André Turcat (director of Flight Test Aerospatiale) was to attempt to take Concorde 001 into the air for the first time from Toulouse. As an observer of the television coverage I can well remember the occasion. Bad weather had delayed the flight but at last Concorde 001 was lining up for take off. About 30 seconds worth of take-off run would prove whether the preceding seven years had been spent in vain; they were not, she flew. It was an amazing moment.

Only the low speed and low altitude range of the flight envelope (combination of speed

and altitude at which an aircraft is allowed to fly) were to be explored on this day. Did the indications of speed and altitude correspond to those of the chase aircraft? The undercarriage was not even raised. Take-off and flight proved to be possible, but could the slender delta be made to land?

Some 35 minutes later Concorde 001 was on final approach at Toulouse, and all looked well. On touchdown, two clouds of dust and smoke were whisked from the wheels into the vortices over each wing. Maskell and Küchmann had been right: a separated airflow had given lift even to an aircraft as big as Concorde. Though fully aware that far better pictures would be immediately available I nevertheless photographed the event from the television screen to have, as it were, a personal record of Concorde's first landing (see page 48).

Some minutes later surrounded by cameras and microphones André Turcat announced in French and English. 'The big bird flies'. Far greater men than one future

Concorde pilot could now turn their attentions to future demands, secure in the knowledge that the first hurdle had been safely surmounted.

Just over one month later the British-assembled prototype Concorde 002 took-off from Filton with Brian Trubshaw (Chief Test Pilot of BAC) at the controls. John Cochrane was the co-pilot and Brian Watts the Flight Engineer. As the flight deck is over 35 ft above the runway on main wheel touch-down, of key assistance in landing is the radio altimeter. Concorde has two radio altimeters, on this occasion both failed, so the landing at Fairford, Concorde's British test flight base (on account of its long runway), had to be done by eye.

Just under six years of testing and building were to elapse before Concorde's first commercial flight. During that time crises of all sorts presented themselves: environmental, political, technical and economic. Concorde's surviving of them all, ranks as a modern wonder of the world.

On the flight deck of Concorde 002 Brian Trubshaw (Chief Test Pilot BAC) and John Cochrane (BAC Test Pilot) – the pilots of the first test flight of 002, 9 April 1969. Note the large empty box at the centre of the instrument panel – space for a 'moving map display' which was later removed. In 1974 John Cochrane was responsible for landing 002 safely after an over-quick extension of the left main gear broke its main side stay. The gear was strengthened after this incident

First flight of 001 at Toulouse, 2 March 1969
Below G-BSST, 5,500 hours of flight testing, about four times as many as for a similarly sized subsonic aircraft, were necessary before Concorde could enter scheduled service.

Opposite page Concorde 002 arriving at Fairford at the end of her maiden flight, 9 April 1969. Fairford, rather than Filton, was established as the British test base on the insistence of Brian Trubshaw.

Right Concorde's first landing at Toulouse, 2 March 1969. This shot, from a black and white television screen, clearly shows the vortices etched by the smoke from the tyres on touchdown

The Other Supersonic Transports

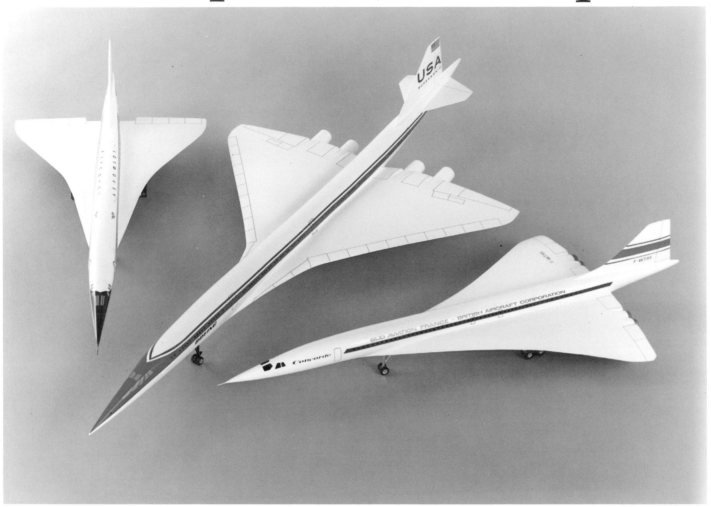

Of the three SSTs only Concorde became successful. The swing wing B2707–200 having proved too ambitious a project, Boeing resorted, in 1969, to the 2707–300 version (shown here as a model at centre). By 1971 the US government withdrew support even for this programme. On the left is a model of the first version of the TU 144 and on the right a model of a prototype Concorde showing the original visor – fitted only to the two prototypes

The flight deck of the Boeing 747 is situated above the first class passenger cabin. The decision to put it there was so that it would be easy to convert the airliner into a freighter. This could be done by fitting a cargo door in the nose and removing the seats. Boeing believed, during the design phase of the 747 in the mid 1960s, that supersonic transports would render their jumbos obsolete as passenger carriers, but not as freighters. They had good reason for their belief: the Concorde project had started in November 1962 and in June 1963 President Kennedy had announced that the US would develop an SST.

That announcement came after much lobbying of the President by the FAA (Federal Aviation Authority) administrator, Najeeb Halaby. He warned of dire consequences if the US were unable to build a challenger to Concorde, adding that the

President could conceivably find himself flying in a foreign aircraft. In the same way that Russian success had spurred on the US space programme, Concorde, especially after Pan Am announced its intention to buy six, catalysed the US reaction to SSTs. They would build one too.

To compensate for a late start the US SST had to be much larger and faster than Concorde. To this end a competition was planned, administered by the FAA, to look for the best airframe and the best engine. On 31 December 1966 it was decided that a Boeing design with swing wings (designated B2707-200) and powered by four General Electric engines was the aircraft to carry the US into the supersonic passenger age. The runner up in the competition had been the non-variable geometry Lockheed L-2000 – a proposal of similar shape to Concorde. Had the Lockheed version been

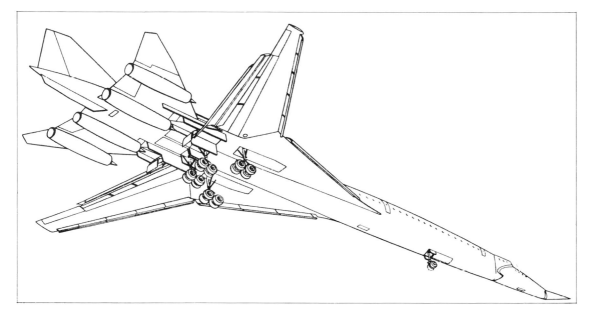

The Boeing 2707-200
of 1966. Note the
presence of flaps and
slats further
complicating the
engineering problems
already associated
with the swing wings

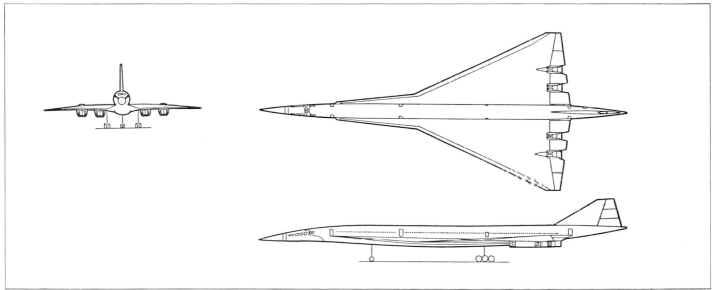

chosen, history might well have been very different. In April 1967 President Johnson gave the go-ahead for the next phase, a four year $1,600m prototype programme. Unlike previous US civil projects this one was to be financed on a 90:10 Government to industry ratio, changing to 75:25 for cost over-runs.

Half as long again as Concorde, the B2707-200 at 318 ft would have been the longest aircraft ever built. The design was intended to carry over 300 passengers at Mach 2.7 (about 1,800 mph) over 3,900 statute miles at altitudes up to 70,000 ft. Not only would its swing wings (fitted with conventional flaps and slats) give it a good take-off and landing performance, but they would give a higher aerodynamic efficiency at subsonic cruising speeds compared to a fixed delta design. Its maximum weight was to have been 675,000 lb (306,000 kg) almost one and three quarter times that of

Concorde. Each of the GE4 turbojet engines would have been capable of producing nearly 70,000 lb of thrust – not quite double that of Concorde. Due to the kinetic heating experienced at Mach 2.7, a titanium alloy would be required, such high temperatures (as hot as 260°C/500°F) being too great for aluminium alloys (see page 11).

By any definition it was an ambitious project and very quickly ran into difficulties. The hinge mechanism for the swing wings presented the greatest problem. For maximum effectiveness swing wings must have their pivots as close to the centreline of the aircraft as possible, since the greatest benefit of increased wing span can be so achieved. However, this interfered with the undercarriage and the positions of the engines. For it to be worth having swing wings their associated machinery must not be too heavy. By 1969 it appeared that their

History might have been very different had Lockheed's much simpler proposal for an SST, the L2000, been chosen instead of Boeing's highly complex swing-wing version. Since 1960 Lockheed had gained immense supersonic experience from the SR-71 'Blackbird' (Mach 3+) project. So they might have had a prototype L2000 built before the mood against a US SST had gained momentum

The (US) General Electric GE4 turbojet engine of the late 1960s exceeded 63,000 lbs thrust on test. Four of the world's then most powerful jets would have propelled the B2707. Silencing such an engine would have been difficult. The GE90 turbofan (up to 115,000 lbs thrust) is a contender for the projected Very Large Airliner (600 tons +) of the 21st century, and with its lower jet exhaust velocity would be naturally quieter – hence the Rolls-Royce/SNECMA proposal for the Mid Tandem Fan arrangement for a Concorde successor

The Boeing 2707-200. By the time this version of Boeing's variable swept winged SST had appeared, grave doubts as to its viability were being voiced. Here a 'Canard' has appeared to overcome shortcomings in pitch control

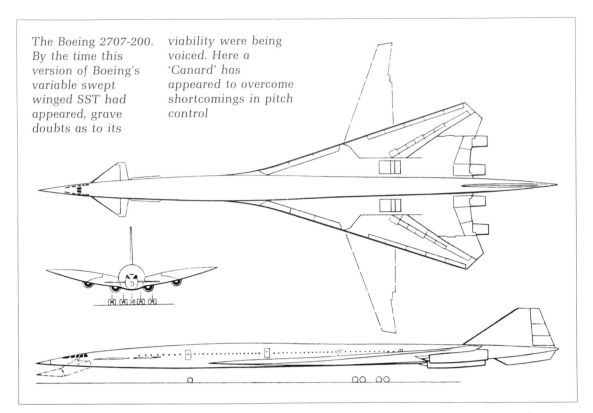

Above *The double-jointed droop nose on this model of the Boeing 2707-200 displayed at the Boeing Museum of Flight during Concorde's visit to Seattle in November, 1984*

Opposite top *A good view of the underside of the later version of the TU 144. Compare the arrangement of the undercarriage, the intake boxes and the presence of a canard with the earlier version of TU 144*

weight might be such that no payload could be carried.

So Boeing, unable to continue with the swing-wing project, submitted another design for FAA approval. The B2707-300 was somewhat similar to Concorde but it had a more marked double-delta wing and a tailplane. The same engines and as many of the original systems as possible were to be used. This time about 250 passengers were to be accommodated and the expected range was to be about 4,200 statute miles. But with a Mach 2.7 cruising speed, a titanium alloy, as yet not finally developed, would have been necessary. In comparison to Concorde's very simple arrangement of six elevon surfaces, the B2707-300 had a tailplane as well as control surfaces on the trailing edge of the wing. As with Concorde, the design of the B2707-300 became more difficult as it progressed. By 1970 political and environmental opinion was hardening against SSTs. Their future looked uncertain.

The environmentalists found allies among the US politicians critical of government expenditure on civil programmes. Had the same politicians withdrawn financial support from environmental programmes, then there would have been no joining of forces. As it was, both parties wanted the US SST to be cancelled. Notable among the politicians was Senator William Proxmire. Among the environmentalists were groups that delighted in such names as 'The Committee for Green Foothills' and 'Friends of the Wilderness'.

On 24 May 1971 they won their victory. The Senate and the House of Representatives both voted against further funds being made available for the US SST. For a sum of money about equal to that spent by Britain on Concorde, the US aerospace industry had nothing to show but tons of paperwork. Boeing's workforce at Seattle was drastically cut. Bleak though it was for Boeing, the Concorde protagonists knew

that their task was now harder. Without an American contender the full force of the environmentalists, flushed with victory, would be focused on them. Even the presence of the Soviet SST (the TU 144) would not count much in Concorde's favour. The technological mood in America, galvanised into such an intensive exploration of space by early Russian success had been assuaged by the moon landings. The TU 144 now appeared a relatively minor threat to prestige. The new creed among some in the US seemed to be: 'If you cannot beat them, then question the morality of their projects.'

In Russia nobody appeared to question the anachronism of an egalitarian state producing an aircraft suitable only for commissars. The TU 144 was not a copy of Concorde although superficially it looked very similar. It was supposed to be able to carry 121 passengers at Mach 2.35 (1,550 mph) over a distance of 4,000 statute miles — a performance which, on paper, was slightly

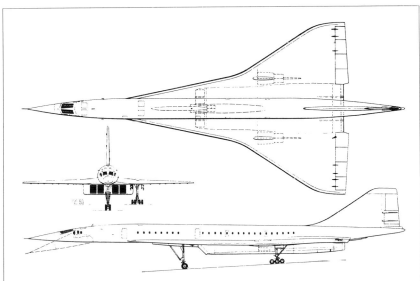

The first version of the TU 144 had the four separate engine intakes ducts contained within a single box. Note the absence of a canard. Although superficially similar to Concorde's wing in two dimensions, the TU 144's wing lacks the complex three dimensioned shaping found on Concorde

'The woods decay, the woods decay and fall, The vapours weep their burthen to the ground, Man comes and tills the field and lies beneath, And after many a summer dies the swan' from Tithonus *by Tennyson.*

Decaying Soviet technology in a Moscow wood, the Tupolev Tu-144 as seen by Mark Wagner (photographer for Flight International) *September 1993.*

In March 1996, after ten years of storage, a modified TU144L with new Kuznetsov NK-321 turbofans, was rolled out at Zhukovsky air base for six months of joint Russian-US (NASA) flight research

There still remains information on Novosibirsk in the computer of the Concorde simulator at Filton. Had the TU 144 been a success, a trans-Russian route might have been possible. Note the runway lights visible through the windscreen when this picture was taken with the simulator 'pilotless' and 'frozen' on final approach

superior to that of Concorde. 'Concordski', as the TU 144 was dubbed, had a less complicated wing than her European rival. Instead of the ogival form with the curved leading edge joining the two angles of sweep-back, as on Concorde, the TU 144 was more distinctly a 'double delta'. The wing also exhibited less camber droop and twist than Concorde's. The four long engine intakes for the NK 144 turbofan engines were arranged in one box underneath the centreline but with dividing walls between them. The main gear was away from this box, retracting into a bay which protruded into blisters above and below the wing surface. There were no underfloor holds; baggage and freight were to be carried in panniers stowed between the two cabins and in a compartment to the rear over the engines.

The TU 144 however chalked up several 'firsts'. On 3 December 1968 she made her maiden flight, two months ahead of Concorde. In June 1969 Mach 1 was exceeded and in May 1969 Mach 2 was achieved. The respective dates for Concorde 001 (F-WTSS) were October 1969 and November 1970. However, there were problems with the Russian design as Sir George Edwards, Chairman of BAC, had pointed out to the Russians in 1967. The engines were in the wrong place, too close inboard; presumably they had been so positioned to make the aircraft easier to control in the event of engine failure. The engines were 'turbofans' and this would impair efficiency during supersonic cruise. The wing was not sufficiently sophisticated which would impair effectiveness and efficiency throughout the speed range.

At its appearance in the 1973 Paris Airshow, the TU 144 looked to have been radically redesigned. The pairs of engine intakes were now in two separate boxes, placing the engines further outboard, while the main undercarriage legs now retracted into a compartment within the engine intakes. A retractable 'canard' or foreplane appeared, placed above, and just to the rear of the flight deck. Extended, the canard would improve low speed flying characteristics by giving a lifting force to the front of the aircraft. This would now be countered by the elevons to the rear of the wing controlling the aircraft in pitch (and roll) going a few degrees down, thus giving 'flap' effect to the wing. Retracted, the canard would not interfere with the supersonic airflow. The Boeing 2707-200 (swing-wing)

design eventually included a canard too; but it was non-retractable and was there to assist control in pitch. To be fair, Concorde also appeared in progressively superior forms, but never with such a radical change as that exhibited by the TU 144.

Tragically the new version of the TU 144 crashed at the 1973 Paris Airshow. It appeared to be attempting to recover from a dive, but no really satisfactory explanation has been put forward for the disaster. On 26 December 1975 the TU 144, which apparently had not been modified greatly following the tragedy, entered service

between Moscow and Alma-Ata, capital of Kazakstan. It carried mail and freight over this 1,800 statute mile sector and flew at about Mach 2.05, between 52,500 and 59,000 ft for much of the distance.

By 1985, if not years before, the TU 144 was out of service. There were unconfirmed reports of another accident, but such events, unless they involve foreigners, were usually cloaked in soviet secrecy. There is no evidence to believe that the TU 144 ever achieved its design range and payload. On the contrary, it almost certainly had to use the afterburners (reheat) during Cruise, and

so it is unlikely that it had sufficient engine efficiency to fly transatlantic ranges.

This failure had one effect on Concorde. There had been plans for a trans-Soviet service by Concorde to Japan stopping at Moscow and Novosibirsk. With no TU 144 to take up reciprocal rights, the Soviet authorities were unlikely to approve a scheduled Concorde route over Russia. A last memorial to this plan remains. In the computer for the Concorde flight simulator at Filton there exists information about Novosibirsk, available should BA crews ever have needed training for this airfield.

A Stormy Beginning

Concorde 01 with shockwaves visible in the supersonic exhaust flame. Upstream of the 'petal' type secondary variable nozzle on 001 were 'blow-in' doors for engine silencing. For reverse thrust separate buckets angled the exhaust flow forward through louvres positioned top and bottom of the jet pipe. The later version of secondary nozzle combined the three functions: silencer, divergent duct and thrust reverser. The British Concorde was test flown from Fairford. However, the New York noise abatement procedures were evolved in Casablanca (Morocco, Latitude 34N). There, proximity to the equator was also useful. With the higher tropopause over the equator than over the poles (circa 55,000 ft cf 30,000 ft), the temperature drops as low as –80°C (cf –45°C). Concorde, suddenly encountering cold air during a demonstration to The Shah of Iran, shot into a barely controllable climb. Curing this alarming characteristic nearly delayed Concorde's entry into service

Early in the 20th century, self-propelled road-going vehicles in England had to be preceded by a man with a red flag. The rule did not reflect the politics of the day but was made because of the vehicles' speed. Whether those who criticized Concorde were motivated by this type of conservatism will never be known; nevertheless there was vociferous opposition against SST's in general and Concorde in particular. The criticism came from all quarters: journalists (on both sides of the Atlantic), an English bishop, politicians (mainly from America), and many other individuals. Their arguments were based on economic and environmental grounds and were often completed with the question: 'What's the use of people travelling so fast in any case?'

When the American SST was cancelled in 1971, a US Senator declared that if the project was worth financing then Wall Street, not the Government, should do it. By 1976 Concorde had absorbed in development costs alone about £500m from Britain and the same amount from France – rather less it was said, than that spent on the abandoned US SST. Concorde certainly had rather an expensive aura to it. Nevertheless it would be churlish for any American politician to maintain that the successful US civil transports, like the series of Boeing and Douglas passenger jets, had not benefited financially from the military contracts that paved the way for their development. But with no military counterpart, the US SST as well as Concorde had to be developed and paid for almost from scratch.

Concorde's development bill had suffered in three ways: firstly from inflation; secondly from the costs associated with having two equal partners (according to one source this accounted for as much as 30 per cent of the bill); and thirdly from having produced three substantially different versions of the aircraft – the two prototypes, the two pre-production aircraft and finally the production series. It was easy to see the critics point of view: that vast amounts of money had been spent so that the 'idle' rich could save a few hours travelling time. But Concorde was never designed for the idle. On the contrary it was designed for busy people who add to the wealth of their businesses and the economies of the free world. Given that each generation benefits from the preceding one, would every Concorde critic, had he been in a position to do so, have protested at the development of the car in the days when it was exclusively used by a minute proportion of the population.

Even as late as 1976 critics were pressing

for Concorde to be abandoned on economic grounds. But by then the development phase was virtually over, so cancellation would have ensured that all the money spent and experience acquired would have been largely in vain. Those who suggested that Concorde's development money should really have been allocated to other more 'worthy' causes were being over optimistic. It is unlikely that the small amount that would have been made available by cancellation in 1963 (about £40m) would, as a matter of policy, have been channelled elsewhere.

A more serious criticism is that Concorde prevented investment in other aviation projects. Would the projected BAC 3-11 (a wide bodied, twin engined, medium range airliner) have survived in the early 1970s? Or would Britain have remained a full member of the European Airbus consortium? As for the BAC 3-11, the answer is probably yes bearing in mind that governments often withdraw their support from aviation projects; but without the agreement to build Concorde, the Airbus Consortium would not have come into being when it did, so the second question is hypothetical.

Alongside their economic arguments, critics added environmental ones. One criticism was that the ozone layer might be dispersed and the ultra-violet light shield removed thus causing skin cancer to become endemic. Others mentioned physical damage caused by sonic booms, passengers suffering excess doses of radiation from solar flares, pollution of the atmosphere with poisonous emission and finally Con-

corde being too noisy on or near the ground.

Concorde's manufacturers patiently answered all these questions. On the first point, ozone is present in the stratosphere, which is the layer of atmosphere above the tropopause. Between the tropopause (average altitude 37,000 ft) and the surface of the earth, is the troposphere, which is that part of the atmosphere where weather occurs. (See Appendices, page 160.) Concorde's engines emit nitric oxide which reacts with ozone to form nitrogen dioxide. Without 'cleansing' from the troposphere, the stratosphere would lose ozone and gain nitrogen dioxide. It was feared that without absorption by the ozone the extra ultra-violet light from the sun could cause a higher incidence of skin cancer. However, an American investigation, called the Climatic Impact Assessment Program (CIAP), refuted the current theory that the 30 SST's then scheduled to enter service would have any detectable effect on the stratosphere. Furthermore natural variations in the quantity of ozone would make the assessment of the impact of even 125 Concordes flying four hours per day above 50,000 ft impossible to discern.

On the sonic-boom problem, the British desire to build only a long range SST was based on the belief that sonic booms would usually be intolerable over populated land, but would be allowable on long-range routes which were over oceans, desert or tundra. On some others a small detour adding maybe 100 to 200 miles (5 to 10 minutes flying time) could allow continuous supersonic operation through avoidance of

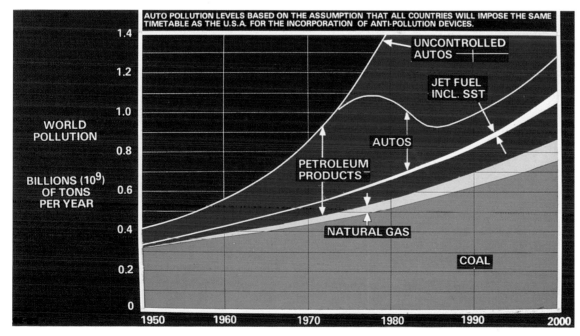

A pollution chart published in 1976 showing the very small amounts of pollution attributable to jet engines, let alone SSTs

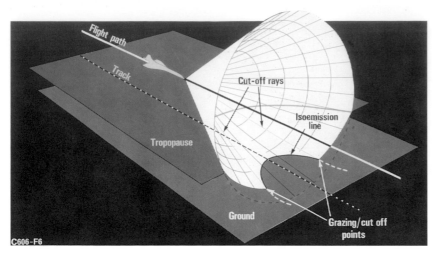

The direction of the 'ray' path of the shock wave is at right angles to the line of the wave. As the shock waves descend into the warmer air near the earth's surface their path bends concave to the sky. Thus shock waves generated by aircraft at low supersonic Mach numbers are not heard on the surface, having been refracted upwards, in a way analogous to a mirage

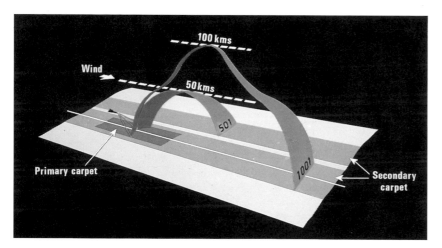

A portion of the upgoing wave can be refracted back to the surface forming a secondary boom. The guns of the western front in France, during the First World War, were heard faintly in certain places in England, on still evenings, further from them, than in others, closer to them, due to this effect. During the winter when the upper westerly winds are stronger, eastbound Concordes decelerate through Mach 1 further from a 'boom sensitive' coast to minimise this effect

Under some conditions the shock wave can bounce, as shown here. The amount of energy returning to earth from these effects is tiny. Loose windows can sometimes be rattled by them, as by a gust of wind. The reflected and refracted boom is usually inaudible unless the ambient noise is virtually zero

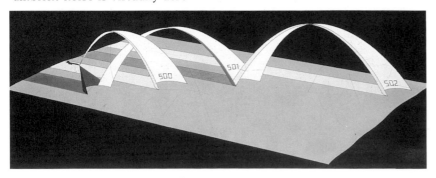

'boom sensitive' land. Where there was no way round, the higher subsonic cruising speed of an SST would give it a small edge, about 100 mph, over the majority of subsonic aircraft. Most Concorde routes do include a small proportion of flight at Mach 0.95.

On the question of solar flares, Concorde is fitted with a radiation meter. The usual dosage rate of cosmic radiation over the latitudes between London and New York at 55,000 ft is around 1 millirem per hour (about twice that found at 35,000 ft). Solar flares could cause the dosage rate to exceed 50 millirem per hour. In every case so far, the presence of radiation from a solar flare has been forecast since the flare can be seen about a day before the associated radiation reaches the earth. If radiation were encountered Concorde would descend to an altitude where, shielded by more atmosphere above, the radiation rate is lower. A survey used in 1976 showed that such evasive action would have had to have taken place five times during the previous 39 years. No radiation warnings from space were received on Concorde during the first 10 years of commercial operation. Although the dosage rate on a subsonic aircraft is half as much, the occupants experience the effect for twice as long, thus receiving a similar quantity to that received by a Concorde passenger. Furthermore subsonic flights over the Poles, where the radiation is higher, possibly exposes the aircraft's passengers to more radiation.

Placing this all in context, an individual's dose of radiation from all sources, including cosmic rays, X-rays, television sets and atmospheric nuclear tests accumulates to about 100–150 millirem per year, and one transatlantic crossing in a subsonic or supersonic transport adds 3 millirem to that total. There are greater dangers to be found from crossing the road than from this. Suggestions that Concorde should only be staffed by stewardesses beyond child bearing age, just turned out to be stories designed to attract popular press headlines.

As far as the pollution of the atmosphere is concerned only hydrogen-fuelled engines are completely 'clean' – that is if the water vapour they emit is ignored. Fossil-fuelled engines also emit water vapour. Often the critics could not make up their minds whether the presence of extra water vapour would 'cut off the sun's rays from the ground and bring on a new ice age', or 'give rise to a "hot house" effect and overheat the

earth'. In practice the earth's weather systems are infinitely more responsible for the distribution of water vapour than aircraft can ever be. As for other pollutants, cars are nearly ten times worse per seat mile than Concorde, and there are many cars.

Of the most serious concern to the critics was the noise that they believed Concorde would cause at airports. For efficiency at supersonic speeds SSTs then had to be fitted with engines which have a high velocity jet efflux. The shearing effect of this efflux with the static air to the rear of an aircraft causes the major part of the noise. Consistent with retaining an efficient engine, Concorde's manufacturers had gone to enormous lengths to reduce engine noise. They had concentrated on two areas. One was to break down the sharp boundary between the moving and static air and the other was to try and increase the quantity of air flowing through the engine so that it would give the same thrust with a lower exhaust velocity.

The first line of attack saw the development of a device called 'spades'. These were designed to break up the efflux by protruding rectangular metal plates into the jet pipe to splay out the jet efflux during take-off, to

be retracted when engine silencing was not required. The 'spades' appeared quite promising in miniature, but failed to be sufficiently effective on the full-scale engine, and were abandoned. Another device called 'buckets' was more successful. Consisting of a pair of doors rather like eyelids, they are set to the rear of the jet pipe of each engine, being visible from the outside of the aircraft. During flight at low speed they mix the static and engine exhaust air thus breaking up the noisy boundary. On landing they are used as thrust reversers by closing off the jet pipe and deflecting the efflux forward; in supersonic flight they form a divergent exit nozzle (see photograph on page 22).

The second line of attack on the noise front involved computer control of the relative speeds of two engine shafts allowing the engine to 'change gear'. This happens after Concorde takes-off and allows a greater mass of air into the engine, thus causing the velocity of the jet efflux to be reduced without the loss of thrust. Such a process can only be applied after Concorde has sufficient forward speed for the intakes to swallow enough air; insufficient air could lead to a surge (backfire).

Whatever the manufacturers achieved in

Concorde 002 on take-off. The 'production' Olympus engine has a modified combustion chamber which eliminates these smoky emissions. Also changed were the auxiliary inlet doors from the 'scoop' (shown here), to the 'blow-in' type. The variable 'ramps' are visible in the intake entrances. The failure and throwing forward of one of these from number 4 intake and its ingestion by the number 3 engine during a test flight at Mach 2 on 001, caused a double engine failure. The subsequent safe return to base proved the soundness of Concorde's basic design

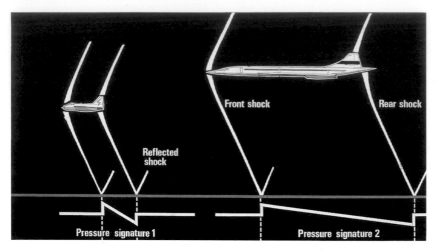

The pressure signatures from supersonic aircraft of different lengths. Note this diagram does not show the refraction of the shock waves due to increasing temperature and changing winds as they approach the earth's surface

Front shock

Rear shock

Reflected shock

Pressure signature 1

Pressure signature 2

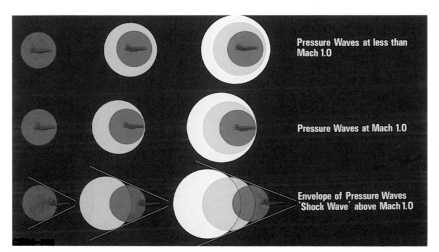

Pressure Waves at less than Mach 1.0

Pressure Waves at Mach 1.0

Envelope of Pressure Waves 'Shock Wave' above Mach 1.0

the way of noise reduction, the crews having reduced to minimum thrust consistent with climbing, to comply with noise abatement procedures had to eke out every last ounce of the aircraft's performance. However, such procedures had not been finally and accurately formulated for use during the route proving flights flown by Concorde during the summer of 1975. Concorde was thus rather noisier than she should have been, with the result that the American anti-Concorde lobby found some rather willing allies in Britain.

The worst aspect of the anti-Concorde campaign was the way in which the critics were quite happy to see Concorde written off before being allowed into New York without a fair noise trial. There was much discussion in the media about this but eventually, when services began, the combination of the relatively light take-off weights (less fuel is required on a New York to London sector than vice versa) and the meticulous application of the noise abatement procedures kept Concorde's noise well within limits. The protestors melted away. Since then Concorde has made many firm friends with the people in New York.

Nevertheless a second generation SST will have to be quieter than Concorde. Several fully laden Concorde departures per day can be tolerated by most people but one every ten minutes from the more land locked airfields could be problematic.

The noise monitoring posts at Kennedy. The two most desirable runways for Concorde on take-off are 31L and 22R. By turning away from the noise sensitive areas after take-off, most of the noise impact of Concorde at Kennedy was avoided. Runways 4L, 4R and 13L are never used by Concorde at transatlantic take-off weights

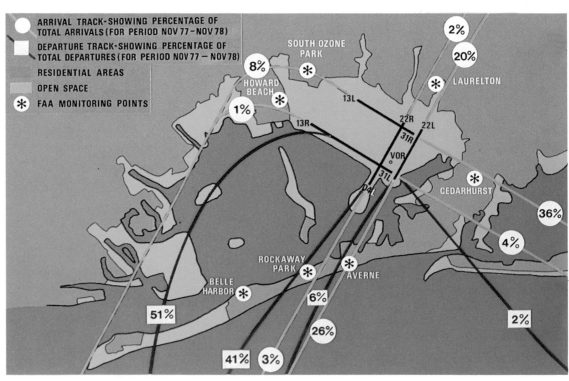

ARRIVAL TRACK - SHOWING PERCENTAGE OF TOTAL ARRIVALS (FOR PERIOD NOV 77 – NOV 78)

DEPARTURE TRACK - SHOWING PERCENTAGE OF TOTAL DEPARTURES (FOR PERIOD NOV 77 – NOV 78)

RESIDENTIAL AREAS

OPEN SPACE

* FAA MONITORING POINTS

SOUTH OZONE PARK

2%

20%

8%

LAURELTON

HOWARD BEACH

13L

1%

13R

22R 22L

31R

VOR

CEDARHURST

36%

31L

4%

ROCKAWAY PARK

AVERNE

BELLE HARBOR

6%

2%

51%

26%

41% 3%

Opposite
The build up of the shock waves. As the aircraft approaches the speed of sound, the molecules of air progressively have less 'warning' of the approach of the aircraft. Above Mach 1 a shock wave forms, tangential to the spheres of disturbance. Some Concorde critics appeared to think that Concorde formed a shock wave at any speed. Under normal conditions, due to its refraction in the warmer atmosphere beneath the aircraft, the shock wave from Concorde only reaches the ground when Concorde exceeds Mach 1.15. The shock wave first reaches the ground about 50 miles after the 'acceleration point'

In January 1976 the final battle for entry to New York still lay in the future. British Airways and Air France were patiently putting the finishing touches to a plan for a joint take-off into the supersonic era; the British with a Concorde from Heathrow and the French with a Concorde from Charles de Gaulle.

On 21 January 1976 I stood with my wife, camera at the ready at the take-off end of runway 28 left at London's Heathrow airport. Around us were crowds of people, some were wearing heavy looking 'service' earphones connected to electronic devices wired up to microphones on poles. Concorde would not start her commercial supersonic service unrecorded! We listened to a local radio broadcast. At 11.40 precisely the commentator announced that Concorde had begun to roll. Next came the distinctive sound of the four reheated Olympus engines. Then Concorde GBOAA came in view, climbing out over the approach lights

*Airlife, 1984

This publicity photograph, inset, was taken on Concorde G-BBDG (202) as can be seen from the instrumentation on the engineers' panel which was different from that ultimately fitted to the production Concordes

The most extensive test programme ever undertaken for a commercial airliner (5500 hours of which 2000 were supersonic) included cold weather trials – Concorde 02 at Fairbanks, Alaska (Latitude 65N)

Opposite page In contrast to her difficulties in 1976 and 1977 Concorde has become a welcome visitor to many US destinations. In November 1984 Concorde G-BOAB visited Boeing Field at Seattle, Washington State. Mount Rainier can be seen in the background. For the visit the Boeing Museum of Flight displayed a model of the cancelled US SST project, the B2707-200; they also organised a supersonic flight by Concorde out over the Pacific and back for one hundred passengers to raise funds for the museum

of the reciprocal runway, with the undercarriage retracting. Commercial supersonic services had begun.

As the British Concorde, under the command of Captain Norman Todd, with Captain Brian Calvert as second-in-command and Senior Engineer Officer John Lidiard, reached her subsonic cruising altitude over the English Channel, the crew heard that the Air France Concorde F-BVFA had had an equally successful departure. The odds, people had said, were heavily against achieving a simultaneous take-off, but as so often in the past Concorde had proved the pessimists wrong.

Concorde F-BVFA flew to Rio de Janeiro via Dakar; G-BOAA flew to Bahrain. Included amongst the guests on G-BOAA were Sir George Edwards (Chairman of BAC) and Sir Stanley Hooker. On arrival at Bahrain they were invited to a banquet at the New Palace by the Amir of Bahrain. Sir Stanley Hooker, in his book *Not Much of an Engineer*,* said: 'Eventually we entered the fabulous dining room, ritually washed our hands and took our places around the gigantic U-shaped table. I was next to the Minister of Foreign Trade, who spoke perfect English. We each had a waiter in full court uniform, each pair of guests being supervised by a steward . . . I was about to turn to the Minister and say "How far sighted and generous of your government to allow us to bring the Concorde here on its first scheduled flight" when he said to me "what a great honour you have done our country by bringing your magnificent Concorde here on its inaugural flight!" Considering the violent hullabaloo that was going on in New York, and that nobody else would allow us in, it was difficult to find the right answer!'

Left to right *Senior Engineer Officer John Lidiard, Captain Norman Todd and Captain Brian Calvert – the crew of the inaugural service to Bahrain on 21 January 1976 on Concorde G-BOAA.*

The Turn of the Tide

During the early days of supersonic services to Bahrain in 1976, Concorde was hardly ever out of the headlines. 'US warned against ban on Concorde'; 'Court challenge on Concorde go-ahead'; 'Red light delays Concorde'; 'Boeing tries for rival to Concorde.' Under this headline from *The Times* (3 April 1976) Mr Lloyd Goodmanson, Boeing's design director said '. . . much of the official opposition to giving British Airways and Air France landing rights for Concorde was based on pure jealousy of their commercial lead rather than environmental considerations.'

Concorde had many vociferous friends and enemies. But for Concorde to succeed she needed landing rights in the United States, and at New York in particular.

Two production lines for Concorde had been set up at vast expense, one in Toulouse, France, and the other at Filton, in Britain.

Apart from the availability and skills of a work force, production lines require the necessary jigs and tools, but above all factory space. In 1974 the Governments of Britain and France had approved the building of 16 production Concordes. This was in spite of Pan American and TWA having decided in 1973 not to take up their options on buying Concorde. It was hoped that now Concorde had started services, these airlines might change their minds.

Iran Air and China Airlines had also shown an interest in Concorde, but they, in line with the rest of the world's airlines, were keeping very quiet on the subject. Production lines cannot remain open indefinitely while aircraft cannot go on being produced without prospective customers, and Concorde production facilities would have to make way for other work. By 1976 it was deemed that it was up to Air France and

Meeting at Dulles tower. Scheduled Concorde services to Washington's Dulles airport began on 24 May 1976

Opposite page A slender delta pivots around the slender CN tower. Concorde is a frequent visitor to the Toronto Airshow in Canada

British Airways to make a success of the new supersonic era. However, without permission to fly to the USA, this appeared almost impossible.

On 4 February 1976, after protracted wrangling, the US Secretary of Transportation, William T. Coleman, finally gave approval for British Airways and Air France to commence services for a 16 month trial period; one Concorde each per day to Washington and two each per day to New York. On 24 May 1976 Concorde services began to Dulles airport at Washington, owned by the Federal (US Government) authorities. In the words of Brian Calvert, Commander of that first flight: 'Planning started for what, it was decided, would be another spectacular – this time a joint arrival. We agreed that on this occasion the British Airways flight would land first – simultaneous landings were a little too much to expect.' The two Concordes performed perfectly, as they had done almost exactly four months earlier at the start of their commercial careers.

Landing Concorde at Dulles International airport Washington, was one thing, but permission to do so at Kennedy airport, New York, owned by the Port of New York Authority, was another. Coleman had implied that Federal pressure might be brought to bear on the Authority, but it became increasingly apparent that there would have to be a legal battle before Concorde could gain rights into New York.

Those rights were finally granted, and amidst threats of the greatest car-borne anti-SST demonstration, Concorde 201 (F-WTSB) arrived in New York on 19 October 1977. In command was Aerospatiale's Chief Test Pilot, Jean Franchi and on the flight deck with him were Captain Brian Walpole (BA Flight Technical

Manager) and Captain Pierre Dudal of Air France. The following day with Captain Walpole in command, Concorde took off from runway 31L (the left hand of the two north-westerly facing runways at New York). For the first time Concorde made the famous left hand climbing turn, started at 100 ft above the runway. That turn, which was regarded as cheating the noise meters by some critics, had been the subject of much practice, both at other airfields and in the Concorde simulators. The turn, the maintenance of the correct speeds, the cutting back of the thrust, the re-application, the cutting back and finally the re-application of thrust had been calculated precisely to correspond with Concorde's proximity to noise sensitive areas. The take-off was a success, the noise minimal. In one sense the protestors had won a great victory: Concorde had been made to be acceptably quiet and other airliners had better follow Concorde's example. On 22 November 1977 British Airways and Air France commenced supersonic services to New York.

Had there been no delay in starting the New York service, there might have been further orders for Concorde. But however 'well dressed' Concorde had appeared, no purchasers were forthcoming while she had 'nowhere to go.'

In December 1977 British Airways, in conjunction with Singapore Airlines (SIA), extended the London to Bahrain Concorde service to Singapore. During performance and hot weather trials in September 1974 the first 'production' Concorde (G-BBDG), with Brian Trubshaw and Peter Baker (Assistant Chief test pilot BAC) at the controls, had flown supersonically over India. Supersonic overflying permission was now withdrawn so the Concorde route to Singapore had to go to the south of Sri Lanka adding some 200 nautical miles (10 minutes flying time). By December 1977 minor modifications and improved operating procedures had increased Concorde's range, so, what would have been unattainable in early 1976, was by then quite possible. However, after three return flights the Malaysian government withdrew flying rights over the Straits of Malacca. After more negotiations with the Malaysians the route reopened in January 1979 and was operated until November 1980. Concorde was flown to Singapore by BA crews with the cabin alternatively being staffed by BA and Singapore Airlines cabin crews.

World recession brought about a drop in

Concorde's load figures between London and Singapore. This, coupled with the financial arrangements between British Airways and Singapore Airlines, put a greater share of the burden of loss onto British Airways, finally causing the route to be abandoned. A particular Concorde had been earmarked for use on this route (G-BOAD), being painted in Singapore livery on the left hand side, and in BA colours on the right. This was the first and, by 1990, the only Concorde to have appeared in colours of an airline other than those of Air France or British Airways. Sadly, as the route closed down, the BA flight deck crews returned home from their postings in Singapore. With an excess of crews, some would leave and others be redeployed in the airline. Morale which was usually very high, took a temporary dip. G-BOAD was restored to BA livery.

Earlier that same year the agreement between Air France, British Airways and Braniff which enabled Concorde to continue through to Dallas, Texas, from Washington (changing to an all American crew just for this sector), was wound up. The route lasted from January 1979 until June 1980. Braniff was, by 1996, the only American airline to have operated Concorde, albeit subsonically. They had hoped to gain experience with the aircraft for eventual supersonic services to South American destinations. In the meantime Concorde's high profile would have helped their marketing effort. But world recession and the deregulation of American internal airline routes had stretched Braniff's resources, so their Concorde operation experienced unacceptably low loads. On the Washington to Dallas sector the Concordes bore their home airlines' livery, the only noticeable external change being the dropping of the 'G' in the registration. The British Concorde had been changed from the usual British registration of (G-BOAA) to a 'G' followed by an 'N' two single digit numbers and then the two final letters of the original registration letters (G-N94AA).

To give Concorde a boost during the time when services were declining, several Concorde crew members chartered the aircraft, giving people flights on Concorde at a fraction of the cost of a transatlantic fare. The first one to do so was a Concorde stewardess, Jeannette Hartley, who organised charters, at no little financial risk to herself. In 1981 my wife and I chartered Concorde to celebrate Britain winning the Schneider Trophy contest. The last contest was won in 1931 by an RAF team captained by Squadron Leader A. H. Orlebar*. In 1981 Concorde flew on two occasions, at 340 mph, almost exactly 1000 mph less than her cruising speed, around the final course which was situated between the Isle of Wight and Portsmouth (England). The speed of 340 mph was chosen since it had

Overleaf *G-BOAD showing Singapore Airlines colours on the port (left) side, taking off from Heathrow for the nine hour journey to Singapore*

*A cousin of the Author.

NEW YORK POST, THURSDAY, MAY 12, 1977

"Damn the court, DON'T LET IT LAND!!"

*Opposite
Concorde G-BOAA
with the Anglo
American registration
G-N94AA during the
period when Braniff
operated Concordes
between Washington
Dulles and Dallas
Fort Worth. Note the
curves on the leading
edge of the wing,
necessary for the
smooth transition
from lift generated by
vortices, roughly
below 250 knots, to
lift from a
'conventional'
attached airflow,
generated at the
higher speeds*

*Concorde was
chartered on 12 and
13 September, 1981,
by the author to
mark this event.
Each of the
passengers received
a certificate as
shown below. The
captain on those
occasions was John
Eames, the author
was First Officer and
Senior Engineer
Officer David
Macdonald, the
Flight Engineer*

been the average speed of Flt. Lt. John Boothman's winning Supermarine S6B in 1931. Two Schneider trophy pilots flew on Concorde to celebrate the 50th Anniversary of the final victory: Air Commodore D'Arcy Greig (1929 team) and Group Captain Leonard Snaith (1931 team).

Other Concorde crew members followed suit.

On Concorde's financial side, a review in February 1979 of the ability of British Airways to make a profit with Concorde had concluded that it could not do so by ordinary commercial standards. Accordingly the Labour Government decided to write off the £160m of Public Dividend Capital (PDC) associated with BA's acquisition of its five Concordes. In November 1979 an Industry and Trade Select Committee, chaired by Sir Donald Kaberry MP, was convened. This was to investigate Concorde. Quoting from the report of their investigations (published in 1981): '...this [the writing off of £160m PDC] meant that the whole fleet, including the initial inventory of spares, was entered in the British Airways balance sheet as a fully depreciated asset – that is to say a gift from the taxpayer. For their part British Airways had to pay to the Government 80 per cent of future Concorde operating surpluses (the so called 80:20 agreement), though these were to be calculated after the offset of any operating deficits incurred after the review and also the amortised cost of any post-review expenditure.'

The BA partnership deal with Singapore Airlines (SIA) on the Singapore route negotiated by Gordon Davidson (Concorde Marketing Director, BA 1975–1979), appeared promising for BA, but it had dashed

Government hopes of SIA purchasing at least one of the remaining unsold Concordes – two in Britain and three in France. Later the best return for the Government appeared to come from placing the two unsold

SCHNEIDER TROPHY
50th Anniversary Flight by
British airways **Concorde**

1931   1981

British

Presented to

_____

who flew in Concorde to mark the event
on 13th September 1981

Christopher J. Weber

70

British Concordes with British airlines. When Gordon Davidson moved to British Caledonian, rumours started of BCal operating a supersonic service to Lagos, but this came to nothing. For a period BA operated one of the two surplus Concordes when one of its Concordes was undergoing modifications. Ultimately BA acquired the two remaining Concordes, making seven in all.

According to the Report, the UK had

spent about £900 million on Concorde by the end of 1980. Furthermore the Government was still having to finance the support given by the manufacturers to the project, expected to total £123 million for the five years beginning 1980/81.

During the commercial life of an aircraft, its manufacturers not only undertake to supply spare parts, but just as importantly to supply a 'support' service in the form of carrying out development work and monitoring performance, suggesting or insisting, where necessary, on improvements or modifications. Overseeing this process are the aviation authorities in whose countries the aircraft are built and registered – the CAA (Civil Aviation Authority) in Britain. These aviation authorities have the full backing of their country's law behind them. Such support is usually financed out of the profits from the sales of spare parts and ancillaries to airlines operators.

In the case of Concorde, monitoring of the aircraft's performance was, in the early days of operation, a very expensive business. Not least of those expenses were the two test specimens – full-sized Concorde fuselages dedicated to being tested on the ground. Quite early in the programme the stress test specimen in France had been purposely tested to destruction, but the one at Farnborough, was still by 1980 costing several millions per year to run. This Concorde had been dedicated to being 'flight cycled', which included the heating and cooling process experienced on every supersonic sector. Profits through sales of spare parts would not raise anything like enough to pay for the Farnborough rig, nor enough to pay for the necessary, but diminishing, development work associated with Concorde. Accordingly, the four manufacturers – Aerospatiale, British Aerospace (successors to BAC), Rolls-Royce and SNECMA – were funded for their responsibilities to Concorde by their respective governments.

In October 1978 the jigs used to manufacture Concorde were removed from the Brabazon Hangars at Filton for storage at Wroughton, near Swindon in Wiltshire, against the possibility that there might be a demand for more Concordes. However, the French had, by December 1977, not only removed but disposed of their jigs; with their capability gone further production of Concordes would have been an extra expense. On 31 December 1980 it was announced that the production phase of Concorde had ended, but it was not until

The Stress Fatigue Specimen at CEAT (Centre d'Essais Aeronautique de Toulouse), one of the two complete Concorde airframes dedicated to structural tests. This specimen was not subjected to heating and cooling to simulate a supersonic flight cycle, as was the one at Farnborough

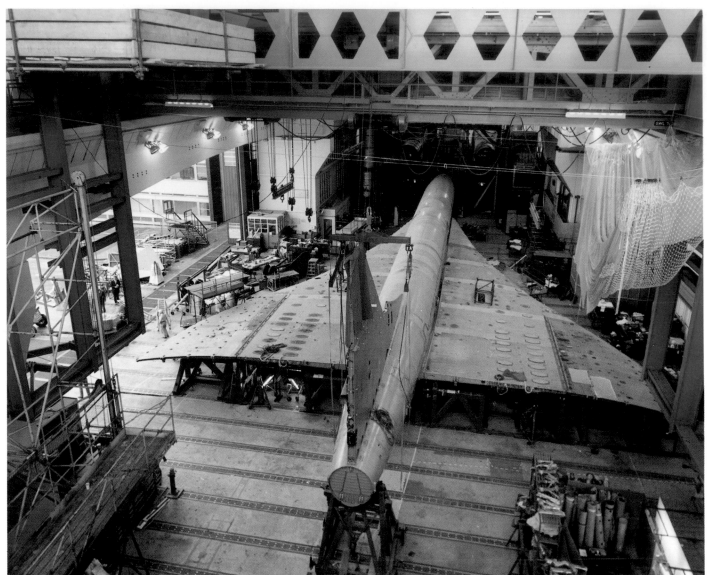

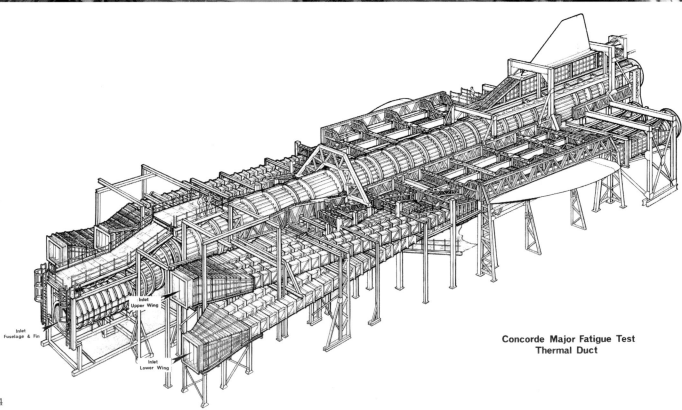

Inlet
Fuselage & Fin

Inlet
Upper Wing

Inlet
Lower Wing

**Concorde Major Fatigue Test
Thermal Duct**

October 1981 that disposal to scrap merchants of the stored British jigs began. About this time Federal Express investigated the use of Concorde as a supersonic parcel carrier, but this also came to nothing.

The Select Committee, charged to look into Concorde affairs, had to face some rather unpalatable truths. No more Concordes would be sold, the funding of the manufacturers would bring no return to the Governments, and the two airlines concerned did not seem able to operate Concorde profitably. It had been asked to make recommendations specifically on the question of costs due to be met out of the public purse. Was there, it tried to answer, a case for continued expenditure, which although unjustifiable in financial terms, might confer other benefits on the UK, such as prestige or the basis for starting a second generation SST? Then, more sinisterly, from Concorde's point of view, the Committee was to investigate how the cost of immediate cancellation would compare with the cost of continuing and how a proposal to cancel would affect relations between the UK and France.

The Committee heard evidence from representatives of British Airways, the British manufacturers of Concorde (British Aerospace and Rolls-Royce), the Minister of Trade and Industry (Norman Tebbit, an ex BOAC pilot), and the Deputy and Assistant Secretaries of the Department of Industry. Representing Concorde's paymasters, the Select Committee had every right to question the commercial decisions made by the companies responsible for servicing and operating Concorde.

It appeared that the writing was on the wall for Concorde, the more so since the return of a Conservative Government in May 1979. There is no doubt that they wished Concorde to continue if at all possible, but not at any price.

The change of government in Britain also saw a change of policy towards the nationalised industries. In Febuary 1981, Ross Stainton retired as Chairman of the British Airways Board, and Sir John King took over. He had been charged by the Government to prepare the company for privatisation. Having suffered disappointing financial results, attributable to the world recession, the moment had arrived to study every aspect of the airline with the view to cutting costs and increasing revenue. Nevertheless, the new leadership was more keen than the old on retaining Concorde.

All too frequently large organisations become conscious that their staff can lose a sense of identity and pride in their work. Following the period of recession, the restoration of morale in British Airways was regarded as a most important part in its march back to profitability. To this end, 'profit centres' were set up within the airline. One such centre was the Concorde Division. In May 1982, Captain Brian Walpole, who had been Flight Manager Technical was

Opposite, top *The Concorde Fatigue Specimen at the Royal Aircraft Establishment (RAE), Farnborough. Although fully visible, here the airframe was festooned with ducts connected to a hot air supply in order to simulate the heating and cooling experienced by a Concorde on a supersonic flight. Each 'flight' was minutely monitored by computers. With sufficient experience to allow Concordes to fly well into the 21st century, this specimen was dismantled in 1985*

Opposite, below *The Concorde Fatigue Specimen engulfed by its thermal duct. The thinness of the wing tips and top of the fin meant that they would not suffer significant thermal fatigue, hence they were not under test. The fuel tanks were filled, the cabin pressurised and jacks were used to 'load' the airframe as on a real flight*

The BA 195 being prepared for service at Heathrow on a winter's evening. Later, from the west, the sun will rise on this Concorde for the second time in the day. For a while during the early 1980s the livery excluded the word 'Airways'

First Concorde to Pittsburgh! British Airways - 11 May 1985

Concorde is frequently chartered to destinations all over America. On this occasion, two weeks after the unveiling of the new livery, Concorde was used to publicise the opening of the Jumbo service between London and Pittsburgh via Washington

Opposite top *Washington Dulles, September 1985, passengers disembarking from G-BOAA via the 'Mobile Lounge'. Once loaded the lounge is lowered prior to being driven to the terminal building. After a 50 minute turn round the aircraft will be en route to Miami.*

Centre Concorde *G-BOAA inaugural service to Miami from London via Washington, 27 March 1984. The 1 hour 20 minute sector from Washington to Miami is flown at subsonic speeds over land then at supersonic speeds over the sea south of Wilmington, North Carolina*

asked by Gerry Draper (BA Commercial Director) to become General Manager of this new division. As his assistant he brought with him another Concorde pilot, Senior First Officer W. D. (Jock) Lowe. Broadly they divided their responsibilities into two, Walpole looking into ways of increasing revenue and Lowe at ways of reducing costs. The appointment of practising pilots to these positions represented a welcome change from tradition. However, it must be stated that their predecessors in Commercial Division had worked very hard for Concorde's success in conditions which had not been easy. At that time Concorde passenger loads were falling from their peak in 1979 while costs consistently exceeded revenue.

Within months of their new appointment Concorde was faced by a new crisis. In August 1982 Ian Sproat (MP) wrote to Sir John King stating the Government's intention to cease funding the British manufacturers support costs for Concorde and asking British Airways if it wished to take on this responsibility. If BA were to decline, in the words of Keith Wilkins (Head of Planning, BA): 'The supersonic project would terminate.' Termination in Britain at this stage would probably have meant termination in France as well. The date set for this was 31 March 1983.

President Mitterand, unlike his predecessor, did countenance a review of Concorde's financial performance when he came to power in 1980 and Concorde was on the agenda of the Anglo-French summit of 1981. However, at no time in Concorde's history had Britain and France both shared the same opinion regarding cancellation, hence its survival. In Britain at this time, the

Government perceived that by 1983 or 1984 the 80:20 agreement might even be producing a return from which the support costs could be financed, especially since the cancellation of the Singapore route. But Government involvement of this kind was not within the philosophy of the Conservative party in power. Probably for this reason, rather than from wishing to stop Concorde, did Ian Sproat write to Sir John King stating the Government's intention of ceasing to fund the British manufacturers.

*See page 73.

An Air France Concorde being prepared for service at Kennedy in October, 1985. By 1984 Air France Concorde operations became profitable on the Paris New York route. Runway 22R is one of those preferred for a Concorde take-off on the basis of restricting noise (see page 60). There are no similar restrictions for Concordes landing at Kennedy

The BA reply indicated that they were very willing to examine the possibility of taking over the support costs, but they would have to be given time to examine the implications. The Government agreed to another year being made available before the axe would finally fall on public money funding the British manufacturers. In the meantime a Department of Trade and Industry Review Group headed by Mr Bruce MacTavish of the Civil Service, would negotiate with BA for the handing over of the Government's responsibility to BA. The BA negotiating team were led by Mr Keith Wilkins (Head of Planning), with Captain Walpole (General Manager Concorde Division), Jock Lowe (Planning Manager Concorde), Sandy Sell (Engineering), and Peter Brass (Accounting).

The team's first job was to find out whether Concorde could make a sufficient operating surplus to fund the British manufacturers' support costs. Their second, and no less important, task was to analyse the manufacturers' activities with a view to reducing costs without impairing service, especially in areas of flight safety. This would rule out any development work not called for jointly by manufacturers and BA. The team were modestly optimistic that Concorde revenue which, had, in the period 1979/80 to 1982/83 been dropping, would improve as the recession passed. Over optimism was not only unwarranted, but might have upset the negotiations. Equally too much pessimism might have brought the negotiations to an untimely end. It took eighteen months to find a satisfactory formula.

The main points at issue were the terms surrounding the acquisition by BA of Concorde spare parts owned by the Government (and useless to anyone other than a Concorde operator), the winding up of the 80:20 agreement soon expected to give government a small dividend, and the replacement of the Government by BA in the contracts with the British manufacturers (British Aerospace and Rolls-Royce). On this particular issue it was fundamental that BA could withdraw unilaterally from the Concorde project at its own discretion without having to finance the British manufacturers if Air France continued Concorde operations. BA made it clear to the Government that they would not pay for the continuation of the operation of the test rig at Farnborough. This had been a major element in the support costs and by 1984 the

full-scale Concorde structure had experienced sufficient 'flight cycles' for the Concordes to continue, at their present rate of use, well into the next century*. In the end BA took responsibility for the dismantling of the rig.

The funding of Concorde's French manufacturers would not necessarily be altered by the proposed changes in Britain – that was a French matter. Hitherto the French manufacturers had received payment from the French Government. In the early 1980s the French Government had promised Air France that it would bear a higher proportion of its Concorde operating loss. In return it reserved the right to dictate where Air France operated Concorde. With the result that the Rio de Janeiro, Caracas and Mexico through Washington routes were abandoned leaving Air France a single daily return Concorde service between Paris and New York. In 1984 Air France operations became profitable.

In April 1983, as discussions between BA and the Government continued, a 30 minute documentary programme about Concorde appeared in the QED series on BBC1. I was technical consultant to the producer, Brian Johnson, and was present as First Officer to Brian Walpole on the London to New York

service which was filmed. (The Flight Engineer on that sector was Senior Engineer Officer Bill Johnstone.) Brian Walpole, during an interview on the programme, made it very clear that Concorde in future would have to stand on its own two feet: 'I believe it can, and, given a reasonable response from Government, Concorde will continue.' Although the tide had started to turn in favour of Concorde before the transmission of that programme, it was from that moment that Concorde ceased to be regarded as a loss maker. Gone were the tiresome yet familiar gibes about its poor prospects.

Slowly and inexorably the negotiations eroded the major outstanding differences between the Government and BA. In the end a sum had to be agreed which BA would pay to the Government for all the Concorde spares, Concorde G-BBDG (202) which was grounded at Filton minus engines and much equipment, the Farnborough Concorde test structure, as well as buying its way out of the 80:20 agreement. In March 1984, eighteen months of detailed analysis were brought to a swift conclusion. In a meeting lasting not more than a quarter of an hour, reminiscent of bargaining in an eastern bazaar, Gordon Dunlop (Finance Director of BA) and the Government representatives agreed on a figure: £16.5m. Concorde was saved.

Great credit is due to the people whose determination found a way of preserving this unique aircraft in service. In particular, Bruce MacTavish as negotiator for the Government and Keith Wilkins astute leader of the BA team deserve great praise. Brian Walpole's and Jock Lowe's infectious enthusiasm and dedication to Concorde were great motivators throughout. During all the negotiations Concorde continued in service thanks to everyone connected with the operation maintaining faith that somehow Concorde would have a successful future.

A Conservative Government spawned Concorde and ensured its right to life through an unbreakable treaty with France in 1962. Twenty-one years (and a few months) later, another Conservative Government severed almost all its financial connections with Concorde; the supersonic airliner had come of age. With expanding charter services and improving figures on the scheduled routes (London to New York and London to Washington and Miami), the commercial future of Concorde in British Airways looked bright.

Top
Maintenance at Heathrow, and here Concorde is festooned with gantries designed for ease of access

Above
The 9½ ft diameter cabin without seats. The outside rails on which the seats are fixed are mounted so that they are not stretched due to the elongation of the fuselage which is at 100°C during cruise, compared to the 22°C of the cabin

Right
The walkway around the nose, here at 12½° down, is contoured to fit precisely. The gap in the nose is open for access to the weather radar scanner. Note the windscreen wipers revealed with the visor down

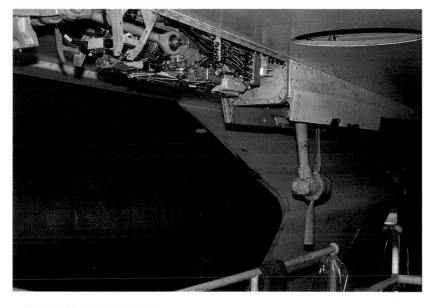

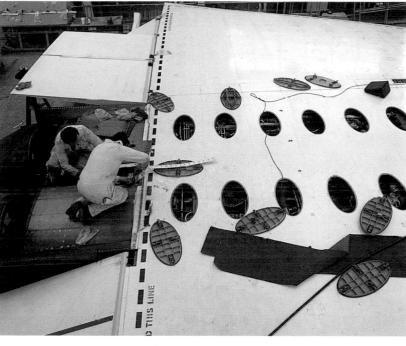

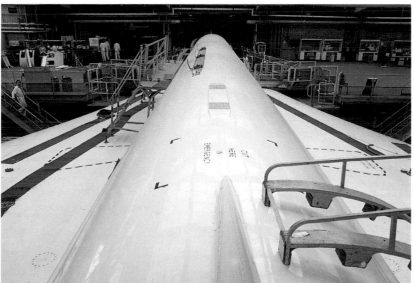

Above left
One of the hydraulic jacks responsible for moving the elevons. Normally it is signalled electrically; although there is an 'emergency' mechanical signalling system, there is no 'manual reversion'. Should hydraulic pressure from the engine pumps fail, a slip-stream driven hydraulic air turbine can be deployed to supply pressure, seen here ahead of the jack

Middle left
Concorde inspires great dedication and enthusiasm among all those whose privilege it is to contribute to the supersonic operation, not least from the maintenance engineers, the unsung heroes of the Concorde Story

Above
One of the eight fan-cooled 'carbon' brake units on Concorde. The development of carbon fibre instead of steel represented a great weight saving. Thanks to Concorde such brakes have become common place on subsonic airliners

Below left
A view forward from the tail fin during maintenance

The Flight – Acceleration

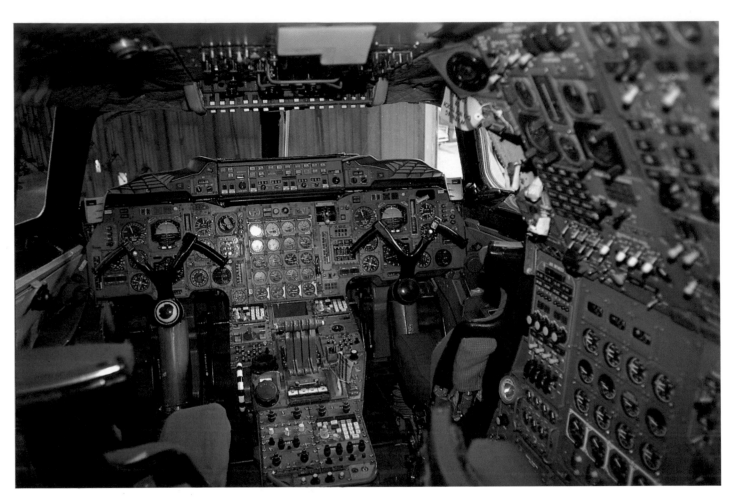

The flight deck. The two control columns with their familiar 'ramshorns' shape can be seen. To the right is the Flight Engineer's panel. The nose and visor were down when this picture was taken during a period of servicing in the hangar. Unpowered, the instruments display red failure flags

'Ladies and gentlemen. This is the First Officer, Christopher Orlebar,' comes the voice on the cabin address system. 'We are climbing through 20,000 ft and are just accelerating through the cruising speed of a Jumbo jet: Mach 0.85, 550 miles per hour. We are flying over the track of Brunel's Great Western Railway – another great engineering project – towards Bristol, and in particular Filton, from where this Concorde first flew in 1979.

'The time in New York, if you would like to reset your watches is five minutes to six. We expect to arrive in New York at a quarter past nine. Having left London at ten thirty, you do not need to be an Einsteinean physicist to work out that that will make us one and a quarter hours younger by the time we arrive at Kennedy airport. Although we travel backwards in time it is not sufficiently far to call our destination by any of its original names – Idlewild, or New Amsterdam.

'In six minutes from now we shall be switching on the after-burners. You will feel two small nudges as they come on in pairs. They give extra thrust to the engines to overcome the increased air resistance found during supersonic flight. We accelerate and climb, and by 43,500 ft we shall have achieved Mach 1.7, at which point the after-burners will be switched off. In case there are no thermodynamicists among you I will explain why. By Mach 1.7 the engines will have become very much more efficient due to the increase in airflow through the intakes, which precompresses and slows down the air before it enters the engines. There is then sufficient thrust to overcome the increased air resistance caused by those shock waves which appeared just below Mach 1. We continue to climb and accelerate, reaching Mach 2 just above 50,000 ft. Thereafter we climb gently as we use the fuel and so become lighter, maintaining Mach 2, or thereabouts, until we reach today's ceiling of about 58,000 ft – in any case not above 60,000 ft which is as high as we are allowed to fly.'

Another voice now, this time in the headsets of the crew, from the Air Traffic Controller at West Drayton: 'Speedbird Concorde one nine three*, London. You are cleared to climb at the acceleration point. Cross eight degrees west at or above flight level four three zero (43,000 ft).'

'Roger. Cleared to climb at the accele-

system, which allows landings in visibilities down to 200 metres (656 ft) with a 'decision height' (whether to land or to go up again) of 15 ft (4.5 metres). Whatever the weather at the destination, the aircraft must be able to divert to an alternate airfield whose weather would allow an ordinary manual landing. The weather at the en-route alternate airfields is also checked. These might be needed in the event of engine failure when Concorde would be forced to decelerate to

*In 1987 the flight number of BA 193 was changed to BA 001.

Senior Flight Engineer Tony Brown (left), Captain John Massie (centre), and the author at the flight briefing in the Queen's Building at Heathrow. In 1994 British Airways moved its Flight Crew Briefing Centre from the Queen's Building in the central area to The Compass Centre on the north side of the airport

ration point. Cross eight degrees west flight level four three zero or above. Speedbird Concorde one nine three,' comes the reply to London Air Traffic Control. Soon Concorde will be travelling at almost two and a half times the speed of a Jumbo jet.

Two hours previously the three flight deck crew of BA 193* assembled in the Queen's building at London's Heathrow Airport.

'One hundred [passengers] booked. You have Alpha Foxtrot on stand Juliet 2.' Armed with this information and a list of the six cabin crew members, the three crew, consisting of Captain, First Officer and Flight Engineer, go to be briefed. They study the weather, the fuel flight plan and other relevant information concerning airfields, navigation aids and route information.

The weather forecast at the destination and alternate airfields is of fundamental significance. Is fog likely? Concorde is fitted with a Category Three automatic landing

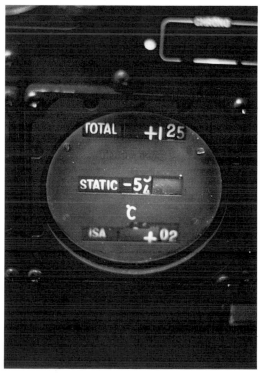

Air temperature gauge on Concorde at Mach 2. The outside air temperature is shown in the 'static' box. The tip of the nose in the 'Total' box and the deviation from the International Standard Atmosphere in the 'ISA' box

subsonic speeds where the range is not so great.

The forecast winds between 50,000 ft and 60,000 ft are studied. They are usually less strong than the winds found up to 40,000 ft. Very rarely do they exceed 100 knots. On average they blow from the west at 30 knots. Cruising at 1,150 knots true airspeed, a 100 knot headwind has less effect on Concorde than on a Jumbo which cruises at 480 knots. Over a 2,000 nautical mile (nm) distance a 100 knot headwind gives Concorde a ground speed of 1,050 knots increasing the flight time by 10 minutes, but a Jumbo with a ground speed of 380 knots would take 65 minutes longer over the same distance. The tracks followed by subsonic aircraft over the Atlantic are varied from day to day to take account of the winds. The supersonic tracks, however, are fixed by the minimum distance consistent with over-water flight where the sonic boom is acceptable.

The temperature to be found at altitude is also of importance. The average over the Atlantic constantly varies, but is of the order of minus 55°C (−67°F) at Concorde's cruising level. A few degrees warmer and the fuel requirement is greater and vice versa. For efficiency the engines prefer cold air. There is a greater mass of oxygen in a given volume of air at a given pressure, in cold air than in hot air.

The fuel required to carry 10 tonnes of payload (100 passengers and their luggage) and 15 tonnes of spare fuel over the 3,150 nm between London and New York is typically 77 tonnes (depending on winds and temperatures). Nevertheless the fuel flight plan is meticulously checked. For taxiing at London 1.4 tonnes are added bringing the total to 93.4 tonnes – some 2 tonnes short of full tanks. The expected take-off weight with these figures is 180 tonnes. The expected flight time on this journey is 3 hours and 23 minutes.

Equipped with the paperwork the crew are driven to the aircraft on stand Juliet 2. At this stage the gleaming paintwork showing off the new British Airways Concorde livery (unveiled 25 April 1985) is somewhat hidden by hordes of service vehicles, fuel bowsers, luggage and catering trucks and transport vans. The passengers congregating in the special Concorde lounge glimpse the unique supersonic nose serene above the white-overalled activity beneath.

It is almost impossible for the passenger, viewing all this activity, to imagine just how many lifetimes of thought and effort

preceded this moment of sublime anticipation: flying the world's only successful supersonic airliner. Yet as these words were written, powered flight by men in heavier than air machines has happened within the life of many living people and commercial supersonic flight was 10 years old.

The 'safety' checks having been completed in the cockpit, the pilots remain on board while the Flight Engineer checks the exterior of the aircraft. He will inspect, amongst other things, landing gear, tyres, engine intakes and the elevons (the flying control surfaces) to the rear of the wing, which look, without hydraulic pressure, rather like flaps in the 'down' position. As he does so he steps over power cables,

refuelling hoses and the high-pressure air hoses for use during engine starting. Finally he rejoins the pilots going through their 'scan' checks. Lights, instruments and audio warnings are all scrutinised. 'Pull up, pull up!' says an insistent microchip from the loudspeakers. It is the terrain avoidance system under test. Another voice, taped and transmitted from the tower, announces: 'This is Heathrow information Romeo, zero eight one five weather, wind two nine zero degrees, one five knots . . .' The data is copied down, relevant for calculating whether conditions are suitable to allow 180 tonnes of Concorde to take-off from runway 28 left (the southerly of the two west facing runways at Heathrow).

Although more crowded with instruments than other airliners, the cockpit in Concorde is equipped with the familiar ones: altimeters, airspeed indicators, artificial horizons and engine temperature and pressure instruments. However, the Mach-meters are calibrated up to Mach 2.4, and on closer inspection switches and gauges of systems unique to Concorde become apparent – engine air intake controls, primary and secondary engine nozzle indicators and a centre of gravity meter – but despite diligent searching, there are no flap and slat levers. To the untutored eye it is as foreign and daunting as a cathedral organ is to the tone deaf. But to the crew it is like home; a place that both gives and demands nurture.

'Good morning gentlemen.' It is the Cabin Services director introducing himself to the flight deck crew. The cabin, with the new 'space-age grey' upholstery, has been meticulously checked by the six cabin crew, as has the food and drink to be consumed during the flight. However well the aircraft is operated technically, it is the cabin crew who must supply the ambiance and good feeling that will make the passengers say: 'We had such a good flight . . .' Dedicated to Concorde they meet the challenge. They are lucky since they can see the fruits of their dedication – satisfied passengers. But the cabin crew are trained in other equally vital tasks affecting the well-being of the passengers; they must be experts with all the emergency and survival equipment that is carried on board.

No less dedicated, but behind the scenes, are the thousands of individuals who have made the flight possible. The shifts of engineers, the refuellers, the catering staff, the Chairman, the ramp controller, the Chief

'Number four uplifted four quarts,'

'No performance A.D.D.'s, but there is a history on number two H.F. radio, it is very slow to tune.'

'Speedbird Concorde one nine three, cleared to New York Brecon one foxtrot, squawk two one zero three, track Sierra Mike.'*

'Cleared to start, one two one nine for push'.

The clearance is read back by the crew to the tower.

'Fifty three and half for take-off with a burn-off of 900 kilograms' comes another statement. It is akin to the tuning up of an orchestra.

The Captain or First Officer may fly the aircraft. Today it is the First Officer's turn, so the Captain acts as co-pilot to the First Officer although he retains overall command. Thus the captain reads the 'before start check list'. Henceforward all actions are co-ordinated between the three crew as a team, and each one, where possible, monitors the other's actions.

'Altimeters' says the Captain.

'QNH one zero one five set, eighty, six eighty, normal and 20 ft on the radio altimeter' comes the reply. Later: 'INS one, two and three'. Concorde is navigated by three inertial navigation systems (INS). Once programmed with the latitude and longitude of the starting point of the aircraft, they will continually read out the aircraft's position. Programmed with a route (a series of turning or 'way-points') the auto-pilot will steer the aircraft along that route. All three computers are checked.

'ASI bugs and pitch indices' says the Captain. 'Vee one, one six zero; rotate, one nine five . . .' These are the relevant take-off speeds. The first one, 160 knots, is the decision speed. Up to this speed the aircraft may safely stop within the runway distance; beyond, the take-off may be continued safely even with one of the four engines out of action. On this journey the aircraft will be 'rotated' (that is pitched up) to 13 degrees at 195 knots (225 mph) to become airborne at 217 knots (250 mph).

The loadsheet is checked. Ninety of the one hundred passengers have turned up and are on board; there are ten 'no-shows'. The zero fuel weight and the zero fuel centre of gravity have been programmed into the relevant computer. They are finally checked. Fuel is shifted or 'burnt off' prior to take-off to position the centre of gravity to one specific point. With no tailplane, the precise

*Track 'SM' is the westbound Atlantic supersonic track (see endpapers).

Tail view of Concorde G-BOAE at Terminal Four, Heathrow. The 'elevons' are drooped since, without the engines running, there is no hydraulic pressure; nor is any electric power generated. As Concorde is not fitted with an Auxiliary Power Unit to generate electric power, this has to be supplied from a source on the ground. Note the tailwheel, fitted to avoid the exhaust nozzles of the engines contacting the ground on take-off and landing following an 'over-rotation' (see page 69). The prototypes were fitted with a tail bumper

Executive, the tractor driver, the administrators . . . the list goes on. Their roles are vital, their aim identical – the successful flight of British Airways aircraft. That Concorde performs so well is proof that great pride in the job exists with this section of British Airways. Success breeds success; the 'Halo' effect of Concorde benefits all sections of the airline.

Familiar calls can now be heard.

'OK for boarding?'

'Fuel book,'

position of the centre of gravity on Concorde is more important than for an aircraft with a tailplane.

Finally: 'Start engines'. The inboards are started first. All four on, even at idle power, might damage the towbar on the tractor during the push-back. Hydraulic pressure from pumps driven by the engines at 4,000 lb per square inch (psi) is fed to the flying controls. They spring into life, ready for the comprehensive 'flying control check' that follows. The hydraulic jacks are signalled electrically, but have a mechanical back-up channel. The electrical signals are modified by an auto-stabilisation system which reacts similarly to the reflex actions in a human. The outboard engines are started, the tractor and towbar unhitched, communication with the ground engineer is cast off and Concorde taxis towards runway 28 left.

'Good morning, ladies and gentlemen. This is the First Officer adding my words of welcome to those of the Captain. I would like to describe the take-off, with an apology to those of you who already know our procedures so well. There is a greater thrust to weight ratio on Concorde than there is on subsonic aircraft so the take-off is a bit more sporty, if I can put it that way. One minute and twenty seconds after the start of the take-off run we shall be reducing the thrust and switching off the after-burners, which have been adding to that thrust. This reduces the noise near the airport. Inside the cabin you will notice both a reduction in noise and in the angle of climb. By about twelve minutes after take-off we shall be flying at 95 per cent of the speed of sound – Mach 0.95. Once we clear the coast of South Wales we shall accelerate to Mach 2. The weather in New York is perfectly satisfactory for aviators but not good for sunbathers – it is raining, but the forecast is for it to clear by our time of arrival.'

'Speedbird Concorde one nine three cleared for take-off runway two eight left,'* transmits the controller from the tower at Heathrow. 'Roger cleared for take-off, Speedbird Concorde one nine three,' replies the Captain.

All the checks are complete.

'Three, two, one, now.'

On the 'now' the throttles are opened and the stop watches started.

'Speed building,' calls the Captain, then 'One hundred knots.'

'Power checks,' responds the engineer. Each engine is using fuel at over 20 tonnes per hour and giving 38,000 lbs of thrust with after-burner.

'Vee one'. The First Officer moves his hand from the throttles, to the control column. There is no stopping now.

'Rotate', the control column comes back and the whole aircraft rotates to an angle of 13 degrees above the horizontal. Concorde becomes airborne at 217 knots.

'Vee two' – a safe climbing speed in event of engine failure.

*Due to the decrease in magnetic variation, the track with respect to magnetic north (°M) of what used to be runway 'two eight left', has reduced; now it is closer to 270°M than to 280°M. Therefore, since July 1987, it has been called 'two seven left'.

Captain Meadows, one of the original BA Concorde pilots, carrying out the preflight 'scan' checks. Each item is checked one after another following a strict pattern. Designed in the early 1970s, the instruments on Concorde are all electro-mechanical in contrast to the screens showing computer generated displays which began to feature in the 1980s

'Positive rate of climb.' Now there is at least 20 ft between the wheels and the ground.

'Gear up,' commands the First Officer. The Captain selects it up.

'Two forty knots', the pitch attitude is raised from 13 degrees to nearly 20 degrees to maintain 250 knots. Then looking to the stop watch the Captain calls 'Three, two, one, noise.'

On the word 'noise' the engineer switches the after-burners off and adjusts the throttles to a preset position on the throttle quadrant. To maintain 250 knots with less thrust the angle of climb must be reduced. The First Officer pushes the control column gently forward to maintain a new attitude of 12 degrees to the horizontal. The rate of climb reduces from 4,000 to 1,200 ft/min.

At 7 nm from London more power is applied and the speed is allowed to rise consistent with crossing a radio beacon called Woodley (close to Reading) at 4,000 ft or higher. Accelerating out of 250 knots the nose and visor are raised and as the view of the outside world diminishes, a glorious calm settles on the flight deck. By 300 knots the flight becomes smoother as the buffet from the 'vortex' lift disappears. There are no flaps and slats on Concorde, the same wing-shape serves throughout Concorde's 1,160 knot speed range.

''Speedbird Concorde one nine three, zero, climb and maintain flight level two eight zero', says the London Air Traffic Controller.

The clearance to climb is acknowledged by the Captain; 28,000 ft is programmed into the autopilot. The indicated airspeed during the climb is 400 knots. It is also as fast as the aircraft is allowed to fly between 6,000 and 32,000 ft, the limit being shown by a black and orange chequered pointer on the airspeed indicator. Climbing at a

A water colour by Roy Huxley of Concorde on a taxiway. The nose and visor are at 5° ready for take-off.

Below The initial cruising altitude out of London is 28,000 ft. Note Mach number: Mach 0.95. The compass shows TRUE course as opposed to magnetic. Note the drift about 7° right with a strong southerly wind

Overleaf Concorde at Waco in Texas during a charter visit between 12 and 15 June 1986, organised by Columbus World Wide Travel. James Hamilton (later Sir James), as Director General of the Concorde Division at the Ministry of Aviation from 1966 to 1970, feared that political pressure might force Concorde into service before being thoroughly tested. Such had been the fate, he noted, of the British Airship R 101 which crashed on 5 October 1930 at Beauvais in France on her maiden flight from Cardington (England) to India. Among those killed was Lord Thomson of Cardington, Secretary of State for Air, and possibly the next Viceroy of India. Mercifully the shadow of the past, in this case of the Goodyear Airship, did not come to haunt the Concorde project. Nevertheless, sales might have been far greater if the original in service year of 1969 had been achieved rather than 1976

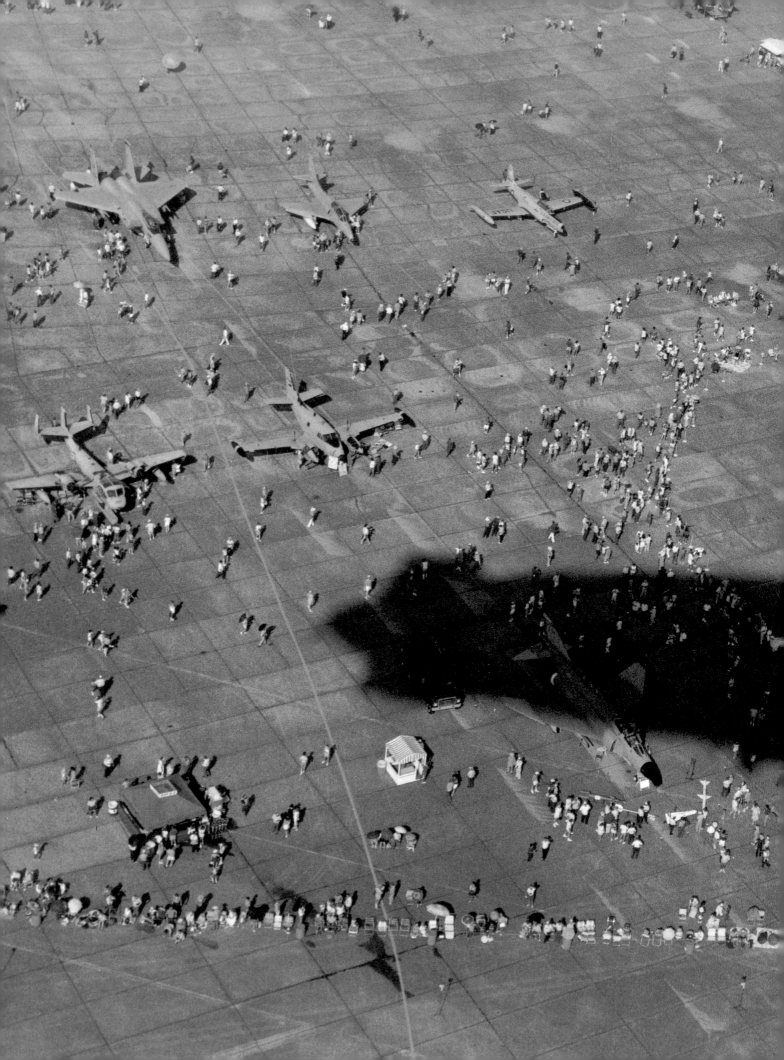

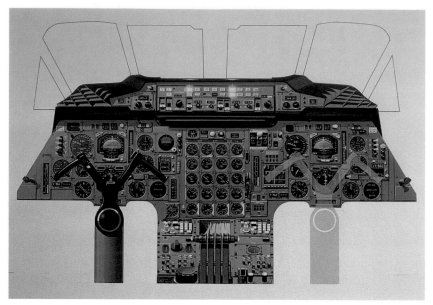

Instrument panel during supersonic cruise. Top centre, the selected autopilot modes are lit – horizontal path is defined by the Inertial Navigation System, vertical path by the combined 'Max Climb' and 'Max Cruise' (max of: Mach 2.04, 530 kts (indicated) or stagnation temp of 127°C). A sudden increase of Mach number due to air temperature decrease is contained by the autothrottle switching out of stand-by to decrease thrust (Painting by Roy Huxley)

The pilot's view of the instruments during Mach 2 cruise. At 53,000 ft the indicated airspeed is 501 knots although the true airspeed is 1.150 knots as evidenced by the Machmeter. Concorde climbs gently throughout the cruise as the weight reduces. The rate of climb in this picture is about 500 ft/min

constant indicated airspeed into the thinner air means that the Mach number will rise. At 25,000 ft it will have risen to Mach 0.93 - the limit for a subsonic climb. At that point there will still be about 70 nm to go before the coastline - the acceleration point. Once clear of the coastline, Concorde can accelerate to a Mach number which would cause the sonic boom to be heard. Usually the boom does not reach the surface until Mach 1.15 is achieved, a figure dependent on temperatures and wind.

'Centre of gravity steady at 55 per cent' the Engineer intones. As the Mach number builds the centre of lift starts to move to the rear. This has to be compensated for by the

rearward movement of the centre of gravity by about 2 ft, achieved by shifting the fuel. By the time Mach 2 is reached the centre of gravity will have been moved aft by a further 4 ft.

The autopilot 'acquires' 28,000 ft. As it does so the auto-throttles switch in and take responsibility for maintaining the speed – Mach 0.95 (385 knots indicated airspeed at this altitude), 100 mph faster than most subsonic aircraft.

'Speedbird Concorde one nine three cleared cruise climb, flight level four nine zero to six zero zero.' The message is acknowledged and 60,000 ft is programmed into the autopilot.

'Checks complete down to the after-burners; fuel is going aft; one mile to go,' says the Engineer. The First Officer pushes the throttle fully forward. A signal is sent to the engines, via their controlling computers, to give maximum climb power. The distance 'to go' shows zero.

'Inboard reheats' . . . a nudge as they light up increasing the thrust by about 20 per cent.

'Outboard reheats,' . . . another nudge. Each engine is now burning fuel at over 11 tonnes per hour. The Mach number climbs and hovers on Mach 1. The shock wave passes the static pressure-ports on the side of the fuselage causing a fluctuation on the pressure driven instruments, notably on the vertical speed indicator. Mach 1.01 is

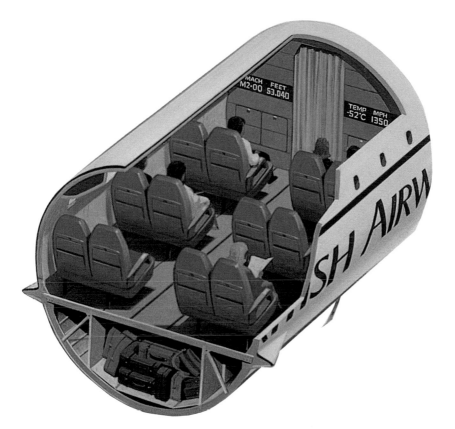

indicated and Concorde is supersonic.

At Mach 1.3 the variable ramps inside the engine air intakes begin to operate. They arrange the shock waves formed in the intake mouth in the most efficient pattern possible to compress and slow the airflow down prior to its entering the engine face.

The acceleration becomes more rapid as the Mach number builds. The passengers watch the progress on the 'Marilake' indicators at the front of each cabin. At Mach 1.7 a barely perceptible lurch indicates that the after-burners have been switched off. Reference to the cabin indicators shows the aircraft to be climbing through 43,500 ft, the outside air temperature to be minus 52°C (−62°F) and the ground speed 1,120 mph. There is a 20 mph headwind. Acceleration is now less rapid. Forty minutes from take-off Mach 2 is attained at an altitude of 50,200 ft and lunch is served.

'Ladies and gentlemen, at the risk of interrupting the Marriage of Figaro on the inflight entertainment – or worse still, your conversation,' says the First Officer, 'We are cruising at Mach 2 (a mile every $2\frac{3}{4}$ seconds) and climbing gently towards twice the height of Mount Everest – 58,000 ft. Here at the threshold of space, the sky above is far darker, almost black and the view of the Earth's horizon just betrays the Earth's curvature. Today it is very clear but big

volcanic eruptions in any part of the world, throwing up tons of minute fragments of debris into the upper atmosphere, can reduce the clarity.

'The sun is now climbing from the west. In winter it is possible to leave London after sunset, on the evening Concorde for New York, and watch the sun rise out of the west. Flying at Mach 2 in an easterly direction at these latitudes will cause the sun to set in the west at three times its normal rate, casting, as it does so, a vast curved shadow of the Earth, up and ahead of the aircraft.'

Mercifully the passengers do not choose Concorde solely to observe astronomical phenomena whilst eating haute cuisine served by the dedicated cabin crew. They fly on Concorde because it saves them days, not hours. West-bound, the critical working hours of the day are preserved; east-bound, the purgatory of the overnight sector is avoided. Concorde only flies between London and the United States during the waking hours of the Atlantic Seaboard dwellers.

Two hours out of London, Newfoundland is visible on the right-hand side. The passengers visit the flight deck. Foreign secretaries, famous people, chief executives, pop stars, owners of publishing empires, financiers and Concorde admirers, who have just come to experience 20th-century air travel at its most supreme, are among the

Newfoundland amid stretches of frozen sea from 55,000 ft. The earth's curvature is visible, albeit slightly exaggerated in this picture. The sky above is almost black here on the threshold of space

Senior Engineer Officer Bill Johnstone demonstrating that the gap to the rear of the engineer's panel is wide enough to accommodate a hand when the fuselage has expanded, due to its having been heated by airflow at Mach 2.

The radiation metre is visible on the lower right of the panel

passengers. All are treated as VIPs.

Some are stunned into silence. Then 'Do you know what each of these switches and dials do?' 'No,' replies the First Officer, 'We only have them to preserve the mystique,' laughter, then: 'Does Concorde really grow eight inches during the cruise?'

The engineer explains that due to the compression and friction of the air, the temperature of the outer surface of the fuselage rises to about 100°C (212°F), hence the expansion and increase in length. He puts his hand into a gap between his panel and bulkhead; it fits. 'Once the fuselage is cool there is no space to do that. If you want two flights on Concorde leave your hand there during the deceleration, it will become trapped. The only way then of removing it would be to wait for the next supersonic flight. It would be painful, but it might be worth it!' he adds with a grin.

Should the temperature on the nose, the hottest point, be about to exceed 127°C (260°F), then the Mach number has to be reduced. This occurs when the outside air temperature becomes warmer than minus 50°C (−58°F). The speed of sound is greater in warmer air so the reduced Mach number has little effect on the flight time.

'Boston this is Speedbird Concorde one nine three heavy flight level five six eight.' (56,800 feet.) A small cross with BA 193, FL 568 and 999 appears on the controllers radar screen. The 999 refers to Concorde's ground speed, the radar is calibrated no higher, so cannot show the 1,120 knots registered in the cockpit.

'Speedbird Concorde one nine three heavy. Roger. I have you radar identified. Omit position reports.' (The suffix 'heavy' serves to differentiate groups of aircraft, on the basis of maximum allowable take-off weight.)

Concorde is passing the south-western end of Nova Scotia now. The track is being precisely steered by the autopilot following instructions from the inertial navigation system (INS). A small yellow light captioned 'R Nav' illuminates in the top right hand corner of the Captain's instrument panel. Nantucket DME (distance measuring equipment – a radio pulse beacon), over 250 nm away, has just taken over the refinement of the almost impeccable accuracy of the inertial navigation system. Travelling at 1,900 ft per second the position is known to within about 2,000 ft.

The end of the supersonic cruise is near.

Engine instruments on the centre panel. Each vertical row of five gauges applies to one engine, there are yet more on the engineer's panel. Note the fuel flows, they total about 20 tonnes/hr. To the lower right, the INS shows the position in latitude and longitude. The left hand one shows distance to go to the next turning point and the time to go in minutes, 334 nm in 18.5 minutes. Gander DME, (refining the INS position) was 176.1 nm to the north when the picture was taken, as shown by the readout on the right of the picture. Note the readings of temperature, altitude, indicated airspeed and Mach number

CONCORDE

Concorde has a cabin crew of six, and their dedication to Concorde has been fundamental to the success of commercial supersonic flight. Here they are shown wearing the uniform current at Concorde's tenth anniversary with British Airways – 21st January 1986. The menu and Flight Certificate on the right are of the same date

MACH
2·00

Some of the snippets of information appearing in the 'Marilake' passenger display screens placed on the bulkhead to the front of each of the cabins. During the cruise the Mach number is 2.00; from time to time the plasma screens show the distance to go derived from the aircraft's navigation system (See top photograph on page 93)

WELCOME
TO
CONCORDE

TEMP
−11°C

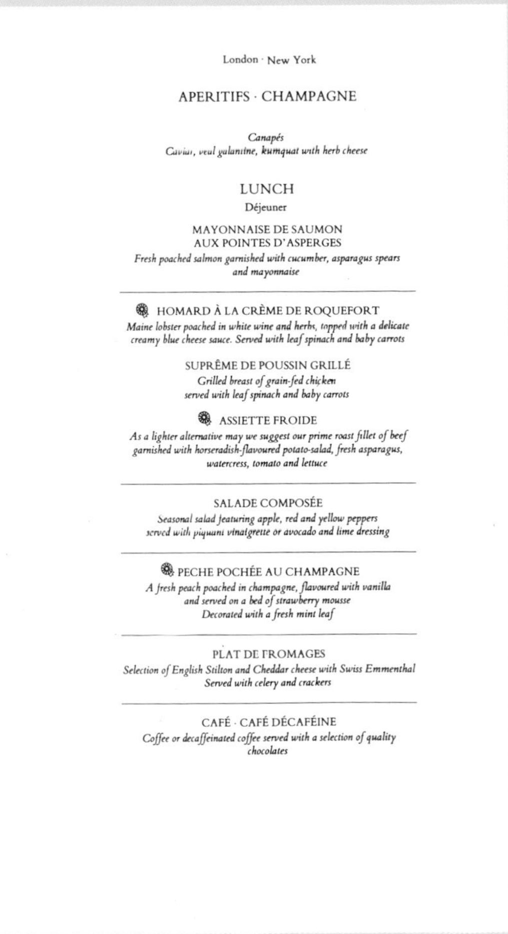

BRITISH AIRWAYS

LONDON—NEW YORK

3h40

MENU

APERITIFS & COCKTAILS
Sweet and Dry Vermouth
Campari Soda
Americano · Negroni
Medium Dry Sherry
Dry Martini · Gin · Vodka
Old Fashioned · Manhattan
Whisky · Gin · Brandy
Gin Fizz
Whisky · Brandy · Gin · Rum
Champagne Cocktail

SPIRITS
Bourbon · Rye

DRINKS

CONCORDE

London · New York

APERITIFS · CHAMPAGNE

Canapés
Caviar, veal galantine, kumquat with herb cheese

LUNCH
Déjeuner

MAYONNAISE DE SAUMON
AUX POINTES D'ASPERGES
Fresh poached salmon garnished with cucumber, asparagus spears and mayonnaise

HOMARD À LA CRÈME DE ROQUEFORT
Maine lobster poached in white wine and herbs, topped with a delicate creamy blue cheese sauce. Served with leaf spinach and baby carrots

SUPRÊME DE POUSSIN GRILLÉ
Grilled breast of grain-fed chicken served with leaf spinach and baby carrots

ASSIETTE FROIDE
As a lighter alternative may we suggest our prime roast fillet of beef garnished with horseradish-flavoured potato-salad, fresh asparagus, watercress, tomato and lettuce

SALADE COMPOSÉE
Seasonal salad featuring apple, red and yellow peppers served with piquant vinaigrette or avocado and lime dressing

PECHE POCHÉE AU CHAMPAGNE
A fresh peach poached in champagne, flavoured with vanilla and served on a bed of strawberry mousse Decorated with a fresh mint leaf

PLAT DE FROMAGES
Selection of English Stilton and Cheddar cheese with Swiss Emmenthal Served with celery and crackers

CAFÉ · CAFÉ DÉCAFÉINE
Coffee or decaffeinated coffee served with a selection of quality chocolates

Haute cuisine at high altitude and grande vitesse

The cabin interior in flight

MPH 1020

THANK YOU

FOR FLYING CONCORDE

CONCORDE

Flight Certificate

Presented to

_____

who flew supersonically on Concorde between

_____

on

_____

Colin M Marshall
Chief Executive.

Captain Brian Walpole
General Manager, Concorde Division.

The Flight – Deceleration

The view through the visor at speeds greater than 250 knots. Once the angle of attack is less than 9°, vision ahead is no longer obscured by the nose and visor in the fully up position, as shown here. The view is excellent in comparison to the view through the periscopic device fitted to the prototypes which only had a diminutive transparent visor as shown in the two upper illustrations on page 99

'Speedbird Concorde one nine three heavy, Boston, cross three nine four three north seven one zero seven west at flight level five two zero or above, cleared to cross Linnd flight level three nine zero or above. Descend and maintain flight level three nine zero.' The descent clearance is read back. Concorde must cross the boundary of a 'warning' area, dedicated to military flying, above 52,000 ft, before entering the regular airways system at a point over the ocean called Linnd at 39,000 ft or above, but no lower – yet.

The deceleration and descent distance is calculated; typically 120 nm are covered from Mach 2 to Mach 1. Decelerating over the ocean en route to New York, the point at which the deceleration is started is dictated by the distance required for nearly the whole descent. On most other routes it is fixed by the need to be subsonic 35 nm before any coastline sensitive to sonic booms; on those occasions Concorde decelerates through Mach 1 level at 41,000 ft;

into New York Concorde becomes subsonic during the descent through 35,000 ft.

There is a sharp noise: it is a microchip's rendering of a 'wake-up!' bugle call. The crew are carrying out the 'Deceleration and Descent Checklist'. The first item is to test the warnings associated with the autopilot disconnecting itself – hence the alerting audio warning. Next come the radio aids required for the landing and the procedure for climbing out again, if the landing is aborted for any reason. The altitude to which it is safe to descend and the whereabouts of the high ground or buildings are scrutinised. Finally the crew adjust their safety harnesses.

'Ladies and gentlemen, in 200 miles – 10 minutes in Concorde, but half an hour for the Boeing 747 in the 100 knot headwind which it is experiencing beneath us – we shall be commencing our deceleration. The time in New York is twenty past eight in the morning. We shall be landing at five past nine, on runway four right – the right hand of the two north-east facing runways. The rain has cleared and the temperature is 70°F.'

Thrust is reduced to an intermediate setting. Too low a value might cause the engines to surge (backfire); alarming, but not dangerous; also the racks of computers would overheat if the air conditioning supplied by the engines failed to supply a sufficient cooling draught.

There is a whiff of ozone. Between 40,000 ft and 60,000 ft Concorde has been flying in an ozone rich atmosphere. At 'cruise power' the compression of the air in the engines heats the air to over 400°C (750°F). This converts all the ozone present in the compressor into oxygen. The air bled from the engines prior to its being cooled in the air conditioning system is thus free of ozone. At reduced power, the compression and heating are less – hence the trace of ozone. In spite of the huge temperature drop in the supply of air to the air conditioning system, there is no temperature variation in the cabin.

At Mach 1.6 there is a further thrust reduction. Once the indicated airspeed has dropped to 350 knots the descent commences: 350 knots at 58,000 ft corresponds to a Mach number of 1.55 (890 knots true airspeed); by 35,000 ft it will correspond to Mach 1*.

The engineer moves the centre of gravity forward to keep the aircraft in trim. He pumps fuel from a tank in the rear of the

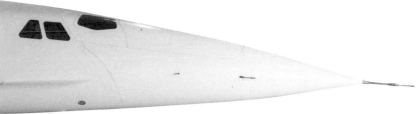

aircraft to tanks in the fuselage and wings. Eight or nine tonnes of fuel are moved forward at this stage. The gap between his panel and the bulkhead closes and the warmth radiating from the windows reduces as the fuselage cools.

Further descent clearance is acknowledged: 'Roger New York, cross three five miles south-east of Sates at one two thousand feet, altimeter two nine eight four.' The altimeters are adjusted to show altitude referenced to the pressure at sea level, 29.84 inches of

The author on the flight deck of Concorde 002, now at Yeovilton, showing the original visor/heat shield in the 'up' position. Even with a periscopic device to improve forward vision, the US Federal Aviation Administration would not have certificated this arrangement. Concorde subsequently benefited from improved glazing techniques

The three crew members at work. In the foreground is Senior Flight Engineer George Floyd

*See the 'Flight envelope' in Appendix.

mercury. Hitherto, they have shown altitude referenced to a standard pressure of 29.92 inches of mercury (1,013.25 millibars) – hence the instruction to maintain 'flight levels'. A flight level of 350 corresponds to 35,000 feet with the altimeter referenced to the standard pressure setting of 1013.25 millibars.

'Concorde one nine three, traffic eleven o'clock five miles south-west bound – one one thousand feet.' The crew peer slightly left and below. 'Contact, Speedbird Concorde one nine three.' 'Contact' means that the other aircraft has been seen – nothing worse. Although air traffic controllers are primarily responsible for the separation of aircraft under their charge, the crew include a careful lookout as part of their cockpit routine. The view ahead, although the visor is raised, is surprisingly good.

As the speed falls the angle of attack must be increased to maintain the lift. 'Angle of attack' is not some kind of refined military manoeuvre; it is the angle between the aircraft and the oncoming air (see page 11). As it is increased so the view of the airspace directly ahead of the pilots becomes progressively obscured by the nose. By 250 knots the visor and nose must be lowered for adequate vision ahead to be maintained. Initially the nose is lowered to five degrees. On final approach, where the angle of attack is 14 degrees, the nose is lowered to its fully down position (12.5 degrees).

'All secure aft,' the chief steward reports. This means that he has checked that all the passengers are strapped in and the cabin equipment is stowed ready for landing.

'Ladies and gentlemen, this is the First Officer. We are under the control of the New York radar controller and will be landing in eight minutes from now.'

'Speedbird Concorde one nine three, fly heading three five zero degrees to establish on the localiser runway four right, maintain 2,000 ft until established, reduce to two one zero knots.' The instruction is acknowledged, and the aircraft turns while 210 knots is dialled into the 'auto-throttles' and the 'IAS acq' button is pressed. As the speed falls below 220 knots the drag increases, calling for a thrust increase. Concorde is unique among airliners in flying at speeds below its minimum drag speed.

A short 'bugle call' is heard. The First Officer has disconnected the autopilot. Today he will carry out a manual landing. 'Localiser active,' calls the Captain. The radio beam defining the path to follow to the runway has been approached. The aircraft must be turned to the right from its heading of 350° M (referenced to Magnetic north) onto one that will let it track precisely along the radio beam transmitted from the ground. There is a crosswind from the right so the aircraft heads 48° M (3° east of north-east) to track 43° M along the localiser beam of runway 4 R.

By 12 miles to touchdown the speed has been stabilised at 190 knots. 'Glideslope active,' calls the Captain. There are 9 miles to touch down. 'Gear down and landing check-list please,' calls the First Officer. The engineer reads the checklist. There is a double thump as the main undercarriage legs lock down, almost simultaneously. Four green lights appear confirming that all four have been extended – two main, one nose and a tail gear.

'Nose,' says the engineer.

'Down and green,' replies the Captain, referring, not to the colour of the nose, but to a green light which confirms that the nose is locked down. The view of the runway is now quite unobscured.

'Glideslope engaged,' calls the Captain. Concorde will now follow a second radio beam, this one slopes towards the landing point making an angle of three degrees with the horizontal. Together the two radio beams, glideslope and localiser, are called the Instrument Landing System (ILS). The word 'glide' here is a misnomer. No jet aircraft could glide at such a shallow angle to the horizontal with all the drag from its flaps, least of all Concorde, with the high 'induced' drag found when the slender delta wings are asked to give lift at slow speed. It is a powered approach. A speed of 190 knots is maintained through use of the auto-throttles.

The First Officer follows two yellow bars which form a cross over his artificial horizon. The horizontal one commands him to pitch the aircraft either up or down to maintain the 'glideslope'; the vertical one, to turn either left or right to follow the 'localiser'. The bars are signalled by the automatic flight control system. Had the autopilot been engaged it would have pitched and turned the aircraft to follow the two radio beams.

'One thousand foot radio,' calls the Flight Engineer. This is the height of the main-wheels above the surface, determined by bouncing a radio wave off the surface. It is a far more precise measurement of height than that available through the pressure alti-meter; however, it only works below 2,500 ft. So well does it measure the height of the aircraft above the ground that the aircraft performs incredibly smooth automatic land-ings, somewhat to the chagrin of the pilots.

'Beep, Beep, BEEP, BEEP, Beep, Beep' in the headsets.

'Marker, height checks,' says the Captain. This is in response to this audible radio beacon being overflown at the correct height – 920 ft. The veracity of the glideslope has been checked – a little academic with the runway so clearly in view, but vital in conditions of low visibility.

'Eight hundred feet radio,' calls the Flight Engineer. Now the speed is reduced from 190 knots to the speed required just over the threshold of the runway, 163 knots at a landing weight of 103 tonnes. Concorde decelerates during the descent from 800 ft (2.34 nm before touchdown) to 500 ft (1.34 nm before touchdown). To maintain 163 knots, more power is required than was needed at 190 knots. The procedure is called the 'reduced noise approach', because less thrust is needed throughout the approach down to 500 ft. First because the drag is less

View of runway 4R
at JFK from about
1000 ft on final
approach over the
lowered nose and
visor

—200 feet —

—100 feet—

Crossing the runway threshold. The wheels are still at 50 ft above the ground with the pilots another 37 ft above them

at 190 knots than at 163 knots and secondly because less thrust is required during the period of deceleration. The noise generated by the engines is less with less thrust, and the fuel consumption is lower. Had an automatic landing been carried out, the final approach speed would have been achieved by 1,200 ft above the surface, so stabilising the descent rate for a longer period to allow the landing computer to make a smooth touchdown.

During final approach Concorde consumes fuel at ten times the rate per mile than is the case towards the latter end of the supersonic cruise. At the intermediate speeds the fuel consumption is also much higher; hence the requirement to arrive with 15 tonnes of spare fuel, enough for 50 minutes in the stacking pattern prior to a landing.

'Speedbird Concorde one nine three heavy, cleared to land four right wind zero seven zero at one five knots,' says the controller in the Kennedy tower. Rarely is Concorde held up by congestion at this hour in the morning.

'Cleared to land Speedbird Concorde one nine three heavy,' acknowledges the Captain.

'Five hundred feet,' calls the Flight Engineer. It is somewhat reminiscent of a 19th century sailor calling out the depths he has plumbed ('By the mark ten').

'Stabilised', confirms the Captain. The auto-throttles have captured the final approach speed – 163 knots and Concorde is established in the correct position for landing.

'Four hundred feet,'
'One hundred to go,' responds the Captain
'Three hundred feet,'
'Decision height,' calls the Captain.

Landing clearance has been received, the runway is visible and clear of obstacles. 'Continuing,' responds the First Officer. A 'go-around' is possible right up to the point of touchdown.

The approach lights on runway four right

protrude out of the water of Jamaica Bay. 'Two hundred feet,' and the pilots are 37 ft higher than the main wheels. 'One hundred feet'; over dry land now. 'Fifty', the auto-throttles are disconnected. 'Forty, thirty, twenty, fifteen.' The throttles are manually closed. At this point the aircraft would be pitched forward, both by the pressure of air trapped between it and the runway, referred to as 'ground effect', and by the reduction in thrust, but the First Officer gently checks this tendency by bringing the control column back to hold the attitude constant as the descent rate decays in the increasing ground effect. He also pushes the left rudder pedal to lose the remaining three degrees of drift required to fly down the centre of the runway, caused by the crosswind. Now the main wheels track along the runway for a moment before the touch.

A puff of smoke and dust whisks from each set of main-wheel tyres into the two vortices, one over each wing: a clear indication of the nature of the airflow that

has been supplying lift during the final stages of the approach. Reverse thrust is selected whilst the next manoeuvre is carried out - landing the nose wheel; during this manoeuvre the flight deck has to descend a further 17 ft.

'Stick forward,' calls the First Officer. The nose-wheel is down, and reverse thrust is selected. There is a roar in the cabin – noisier than at take-off. The brakes are applied. The stopping appears urgent, but all is normal. 'One hundred knots,' calls the Captain. Outboard engines are selected to idle reverse. 'Seventy five knots', and the inboards go to idle reverse. 'Forty knots groundspeed,' all engines are selected to forward idle thrust.

'After landing check, shut down two and three,' says the First Officer. The nose is selected to five degrees, unnecessary systems are switched off, the two inboard engines are shut down and the Engineer pumps four tonnes of fuel into the front tank to ensure that the aircraft will not tip tail down during unloading.

'Left at the end, cross one three left, right on the outer and call ground point nine,' says the controller. It is a kind of pidgin English, meaningless to the uniniated, but totally clear to the crew. Over the maze of concrete and tarmac that constitutes John F Kennedy Airport, New York, the crew find their way to the British Airways Terminal, at a speed no faster than a mile every two and three quarter minutes.

'Ladies and gentlemen, welcome to New York.' This time it is the Captain addressing the passengers.

'Our maximum altitude today was 58,000 ft and our maximum speed 1,320 mph, giving an average over the whole distance of close on 1,100 mph. On behalf of all the crew thank you for flying with us on Concorde; we look forward to seeing you all again. Finally, the Jumbo jet that left 10 minutes before us from Heathrow is very nearly, but not quite, half way here.'

A marshaller waving two fluorescent wands directs Concorde over the last few feet. The wands cross, the aircraft stops.

'Parking checklist,' says the First Officer.

'Brakes,' responds the Engineer.

'To park,' replies the First Officer.

The checklist continues, like some litany. The passengers disembark. 'Mind your head sir as you leave' cautions the Cabin Services Director, standing at the forward door to bid 'au revoir' to the passengers. They have had an excellent flight.

The landing sequence. Concorde G-BOAF landing on runway 4R at Kennedy. Note the vortices, the landing of the nosewheel and the buckets (secondary nozzles) closed over the jet pipes to deflect the jet efflux forward at an angle of about 50° to the horizontal to give reverse thrust. Since the aircraft tends to pitch up with reverse thrust selected the stick is held forward, thus the elevons move down, as can be seen. The nose is in its fully down (12½°) position for the landing, once the landing run is complete it is selected to 5°

Training
of the Concorde Pilot

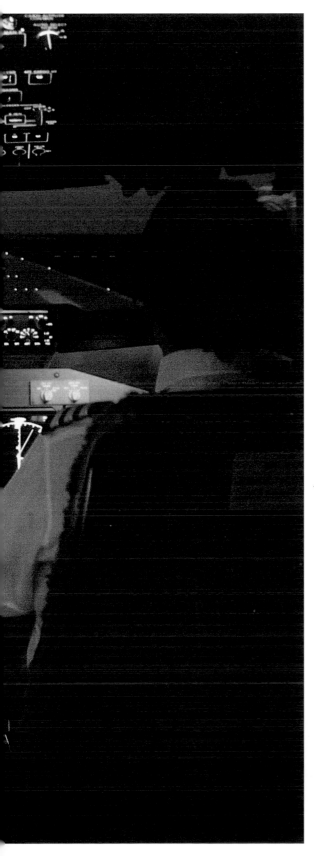

British Airways, like most of the world's airlines, only employs pilots who are already qualified. They must have at least a Commercial Pilot's Licence (CPL), be rated to fly a twin-engined aircraft and have an Instrument Rating. The latter allows a pilot to fly an appropriately equipped aircraft in cloud and into certain types of 'controlled' airspace, whether or not he can rely on visual reference. A private individual can pay for his (or her) own training at a CAA (Civil Aviation Authority) 'approved' flying college – a very expensive procedure (£55,000 1996 price at Prestwick). Or he can become qualified by acquiring 700 flying hours (200 hrs on the 'approved' course) and passing the relevant exams. Although cheaper, the 700-hour route to a professional licence can take several years.

If he (which includes 'she' in this chapter) is lucky, he may find that airlines in general, and BA in particular, are recruiting cadet pilots. If this is the case he can apply for BA sponsorship at one of the CAA 'approved' flying colleges. For this there are certain criteria: typically he must be between 18 and 24 years old at the start of training, be medically fit and be predicted to stay that way during his career (up to 55 in BA, but 60 is the UK upper age limit for most commercial flying). Furthermore, he must have the necessary exam qualifications and pass the interviews, along with co-ordination and aptitude tests. Usually, the exam qualifications include two 'A' levels, preferably physics and maths, but he must have passed at least maths and a science subject, along with English and two others at GCSE. A University degree may waive some of the specific requirements described above.

The next hurdle for the sponsored pilot is to successfully complete the 56-week CAA 'approved' course. Following the sale of the BA College of Air Training at Hamble, near Southampton, in 1987, BA has sent most of its cadet pilots to the British Aerospace

Training on the simulator of the two-crew Boeing 747-400. Concorde, in spite of being more complex, was developed just before information presented in cockpits via television screens became common place. Outside, the computer-generated image of the runway at night is stunningly realistic

Proof of motivation is essential for any pilot seeking training sponsorship from an airline. However, basic training does not include hang-gliding. Delta wing gliders of the 1920s were developed to reduce drag. On this descendant at the Grand Salève near Geneva, the upturned wing tips restore the stability normally provided by a tailplane. The effectiveness of swept wings for flight close to Mach 1 was not recognised until World War 2

*In 1996 the three main schools chosen by BA for their pilot training were: Cranfield, Oxford, and Adelaide. (Australia)

School at Prestwick in Scotland.*

Once in the airline, the BA pilot can choose, within certain constraints such as seniority, the type of aircraft that he wants to fly. If that aircraft should be Concorde certain extra rules apply. He must already have been qualified on one of BA's aircraft, which means in practice he would have been in the airline for at least three years. He must, in order to justify the extra training expense, be able to serve sufficient years before promotion or retirement.

There are four main parts to any conversion course: 1) the technical course, plus written examinations; 2) the simulator course, plus compulsory tests; 3) 'Base' training – flying the aircraft without passengers – also with tests; and 4) flying under supervision with passengers, plus the final 'route' check. The pilot then becomes fully qualified to fly as Captain or Co-pilot.

During the six-week Concorde technical course for pilots (eight for Flight Engineers), each system – hydraulics, electrics, flying controls and undercarriage – has to be thoroughly learnt. On the B747-400 this course lasts a mere three weeks. The information for most aircraft conversion courses in BA since the 1970s is presented through means of an 'audio visual' – slides accompanied by audio tapes. On Concorde the 'audio' part is taken by a lecturer, which allows dialogue that can highlight, for instance, how a system evolved – a helpful element in the learning process. During the Concorde technical course the simulator is

The model airport with a 'flying' TV camera like this one for the Concorde simulator at Filton has been superseded by a computer which can generate images of all the main airports. In the original Concorde simulator set up, data for the radio beacons around various airports included those of Novosibirsk, in Russia. Had the TU 144 been a success, a one-stop trans-Siberian route to Tokyo might have been negotiated for Concorde

The Concorde trainee on the simulator can find himself viewing a computer-generated image of the high rise blocks on the hills of Hong Kong (seen here) then, travelling apparently at a small percentage of the speed of light, arrive in New York, complete with a view of the World Trade Centre. Clever optics places the 165° panorama at infinity

used as a 'systems trainer', illustrating theory with simulated practice. Finally, the CAA-administered exam takes the form of a multichoice test on each system.

On Concorde the simulator training lasts 76 hours – 19 4-hour details (50 hours are spent on the B747-400). Every emergency procedure is practised until perfect. Single or double engine failure, pressurisation failure followed by emergency descent and failure of electrical signalling to the flying controls, are examples of some of the procedures. The trainee must pass several tests on the simulator. Finally, he has to renew his Instrument Rating – the general qualification which is not normally specific to a particular aircraft type.

The visual and motion systems on some aircraft simulators qualify the converting pilot to demonstrate his first landing on that aircraft for real with passengers on board – albeit under the supervision of a highly experienced training Captain. Originally the Concorde simulator (at Filton, Bristol) made use of a television camera 'flying' (suspended) over a model runway and environs within circuit distance. The image captured was projected onto a screen in front of the cockpit, but only with a limited horizontal field of vision, albeit collimated to infinity. By 1989 the original system had been replaced by a 165° field of view, colour, daylight, dusk or night computer-generated image. It is capable of showing individual airports, like Hong Kong with its famous curved approach path, or London Heathrow complete with gasometer to the north east as well as the airport buildings – to give realism during taxying. In addition, the Concorde trainee must carry out about 15 landings during 'base' training. On the B747-400, only if the pilot's previous type has been significantly different from the Boeing, must he land the real aircraft, usually a minimum of four times.

Take-off in the real Concorde, (like the simulator), is commenced with the call, 'Three, two, one, now' when the throttles are moved smoothly and swiftly from their idle position to fully open. The bank of engine gauges react with whirling digits and a single synchronised swing of 20 needles. Next, the four primary nozzle area gauges move into the white segment, proof that each reheat has lit. The brightness of the outside and the force of the acceleration are evidence that this is no simulator. Each Concorde pilot flies three 'details' totalling 2¾ hour (½ hour at night) and carries out at least 14 circuits. Most are 'touch and go's' (landing without stopping followed by immediate take-off), while a few will be 'go arounds' (approach to less than 200 ft above the runway followed by a climb out). On about half a dozen occasions there is a simulated loss of thrust from one engine on take-off. Once all the items are satisfactorily completed, the pilot is on to the final stage – route flying.

Now the trainee, under supervision and with an extra crew member to 'cover' for him, operates his first scheduled supersonic sectors. To begin with on the flight deck

there hardly seems to be enough time to fit in all the pre-departure tasks: Air Traffic Control clearance, take-off calculations, check lists, briefings, loadsheet, technical log, the problems caused by a late passenger, a minor technical defect – is there time to correct it, or does it limit performance? Relief at last, the door closes and it is time to depart. At least the flying is not so different from that received during training – confidence returns.

As the sectors clock up, so the tasks seem to require less time. Finally at the end of 20 sectors for a Captain and 16 for a First Officer the 'route' check is carried out. Once successfully over this last hurdle, the pilot suffers no more formal supervision. He is now qualified until the next six-month check on the simulator and the next annual 'route' check on the aircraft. On average six months elapse from the start to finish of a Concorde course, in comparison to about three-and-a-half months for the B747-400.

In April 1993 the first woman pilot ever to be qualified on Concorde took to the supersonic routes, Barbara Harmer, a former British Caledonia pilot, becoming a Concorde First Officer. By June 1996 108 BA pilots and 41 flight engineers had successfully completed the Concorde conversion course.

(See appendix)

Excellent though the simulator is, the trainee Concorde pilot must fly at least 14 circuits before his/her route training. At high angles of attack – 14° on final approach to landing – drag increases (demanding extra thrust) with reducing speed. Experiencing both the 'feel' of the actual aircraft, and the look of the runway in reality, arms the pilot with the confidence needed to tackle his/her first landing with passengers

Left *By the digital standards of the 21ˢᵗ Century the test equipment of the 1970s appears archaic yet it achieved its aim superbly. Seated are (nearest) Mike Addley, Peter Holding and Alan Driver.*

Below *The flight deck crew are equipped with 'quick-don' oxygen masks capable of supplying 100% oxygen under pressure. The donning of oxygen masks and the emergency descent is practised regularly in the flight simulator*

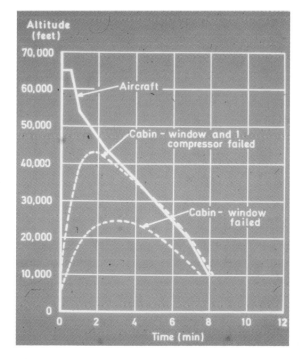

Above *Pressurisation. Should there be a problem with the pressurisation, the aircraft would carry out an emergency descent (continuous white line). Should a window fail, the cabin altitude would rise as indicated by the lower broken white line - unless an air conditioning group had been shut down*

The Future

Concorde represents a significant technological achievement. During development it extended the frontiers of aeronautical knowledge. In terms of supersonic hours flown it has comfortably outstripped the combined airforces of the world. Flying into its third decade of operation it still has a substantial portion of its life before it. Concorde has become, as the French say, 'engravé sur le marbre' (engraved on the marble). Concorde represents a real point on the graph of aeronautical progress, not an estimate of where an SST might have been, had one been developed in the 1960s. Such faith has British Airways in its flagship aircraft being in the forefront of the company's entry into the next millennium, that in 1994 a multimillion pounds refurbishment programme of Concorde was commenced.

The project also proved that international aeronautical collaboration could work, albeit somewhat ponderously. An evolved example of the Concorde experience is the Airbus Industrie consortium at Toulouse, producing a family of subsonic airliners, in which France plays a leading role. Concorde, as the French had hoped, restored their pre-eminence in aviation. Airbus consists of Aerospatiale (France 37.9%), Deutsche Aerospace Airbus (Germany 37.9%), BAe (UK 20%) and CASA (Spain 4.2%).

Concorde in 1962 was supposed to be Britain's entry ticket into the Common Market. Owing to the Polaris missile treaty, General de Gaulle (then President of France) vetoed Britain's entry, regarding its 'Special Relationship' with the United States as being contrary to the European ideal. Whether Britain's entry in 1971 caused the political problems that beset Concorde's entry into the US is open to question, but the UK seemed to have fallen between two political stools. Happily, since then Concorde flights to New York and Washington have enhanced the 'Special Relationship'. Nevertheless, there are lessons here for the future.

Whatever Concorde's technical merits, and they were legion, vast sales of the partner countries' cherished supersonic fledgling were not forthcoming. Only 14 aircraft were sold, and these were to Air France and

Concorde G-BOAG, The Red Arrows and the QE2 over the English Channel, Summer 1985. Captain John Hutchinson, noted for BBC television commentary for major British Air Shows, was on board on this occasion, with Captain Leney (Flight Manager, Technical) at the controls. Very many Concorde charters have been organised by Cunard – hence the publicity value of this association

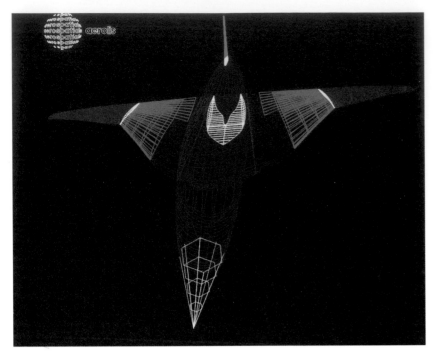

*Since the
development of
Concorde was started
in the early 1960s,
computers have
revolutionised design
techniques, replacing
armies of
draughtsmen. This
computer generated
image illustrates an
Aerospatiale
proposal, here
without a canard*

*Various American
AST designs based on
the 'Arrow' planform.
Note the preference
for a tailplane,
European designs
favour a canard*

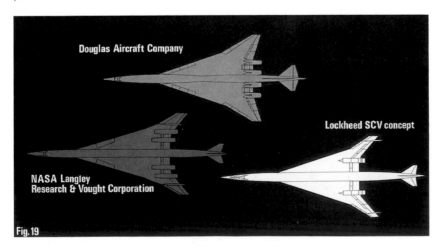

Fig. 19

British Airways. One contemporary cartoonist showed a wine glass being held aloft with the caption; 'Cheers, we have sold Concorde to ourselves'.

The failure to sell this technological wonder to the world's airlines has bestowed on British Airways and Air France a unique commercial advantage. The Concorde symbol has become a potent advertising tool for both the British and French flag carriers.

Concorde is exemplary in its prime role. By saving the trans-Atlantic business man the hours of the day, it saves him the days of the week. Westward Concorde beats the clock by an hour, and thus the whole of the first day can be devoted to useful work. Eastward it avoids the purgatory of the disturbed subsonic night, delivering him mentally refreshed for his first day's work in Europe.

The charter world was quick to spot Concorde's attractiveness. First, just as an end in itself – an individual could be wafted up to the threshold of space, all while enjoying champagne and caviare, before being returned to the point of origin. Secondly, as a time machine, transporting the traveller back 4000 years in just three hours from London or Paris, with, for example, a visit to the Pyramids at Giza in Eygpt. Cunard for another, noted that there are just two great ways of crossing the Atlantic, QE2 being one and Concorde the other. Roughly a tenth of Concorde's revenue in BA service comes from charter activities.

According to a 1991 Boeing forecast, the number of international passengers will increase from 1.09m per day in the year 2000 to 1.90m passengers per day in 2015. This suggests a potential of 315,000 supersonic passengers per day in 2000, rising to 607,000 by 2015. If each 300-seat Concorde successor flew two sectors per day, there would be a market for 500 aircraft, eventually rising to 1000. The pacific 'rim' is expected to exceed the average growth – an ideal area for a second generation Concorde with its long over water routes insensitive to the sonic boom. The journey time between, for instance, Los Angeles and Tokyo (c 4900 nms) would be reduced from over ten hours to just over four, a fact in itself that would stimulate the market. So what are the prospects for Concorde's successor?

Concorde's design would have evolved had more than 14 'production' aircraft been built. The successor, let us call it the AST (Advanced Supersonic Transport), will be a new design, based on the experience gained

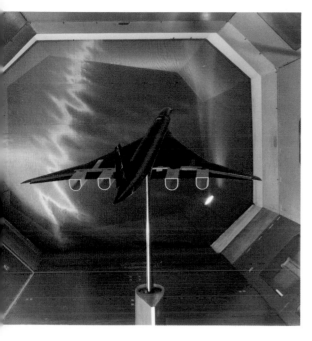

with Concorde, allied to the advances made since the mid 1970s. Although no metal has been cut, studies on how to build a better Concorde have been continual, and by the mid 1990s are beginning to look more practical. In April 1994 Aerospatiale, British Aerospace and Deutsche Aerospace announced their intention to work together on research into the possibility of a future supersonic airliner. The three key areas for improvement are aerodynamics, propulsion and structure.

The Breguet range equation (see appendix) states that the range of an aircraft is proportional to its aerodynamic efficiency (L/D – Lift to Drag ratio), the higher the bet-

In 1986 NASA, with US government funding, commenced High Speed commercial Transport (HSCT) studies- of speed, range, emission and noise requirements. In 1990 phase I of High Speed research (HSR) Program commenced. In 1994 phase II started with McDonnell Douglas and Boeing pooling their efforts. Phase II is critical for establishing the 'enabling technologies'. In parallel is the industry funded development effort. First flight of an HSCT prototype is scheduled for 2005... It might be that of McDonnell Douglas' Mach 2.4 HSCT concept. This one would carry 300 passengers 5,000 nautical miles with a take-off weight just twice that of Concorde.

A Lego representative and the author with a Lego model of Concorde beside Concorde G-BOAF at Billund, Denmark, 5 July 1985. Concorde is chartered to many places, this one was to 'Legoland', taking 60 children who had won prizes to see that famous village. One winning entry: 'A flight of my fancy to the land of fancy'

ter; its speed, the faster the better; divided by the rate of fuel that it must use to give a specified thrust (SFC – specific fuel consumption), the lower the better; all this is multiplied by its structural efficiency. The final term is a measure of how much fuel can be made available for the least structural weight of the aircraft, the greater the better.

The lift to drag ratio (L/D) must be improved across the whole speed range. During the Mach 2 cruise on Concorde it is 7.5 and at subsonic cruising speed, Mach 0.95, about 12. At take-off and landing speeds the L/D is a mere 4 in contrast to about 9 on a subsonic passenger jet. This poor L/D is thanks to the generation of lift by vortices over the delta wing – a very effective means of producing lift without flaps and slats, but bought at the expense of enormous drag. Concorde must carry 12-15 tonnes of reserve and diversion fuel for a 10 tonne payload. A Boeing 747 carries a similar reserve for a 50 tonne payload.

The supersonic L/D can be improved by reshaping the wing into an 'arrow delta' – bringing forward the centre rear portion of a standard delta wing. Control in pitch would be restored by having an extra aerodynamic surface – either a canard (foreplane) or a tailplane. All studies suggest that an L/D in excess of 10 is possible.

An improved low speed L/D would enhance the take-off performance and allow a steeper climb out with less thrust, resulting in less noise and lower fuel burn. On Concorde it costs a tonne of fuel to carry an extra tonne of payload and/or fuel. Requiring less fuel to carry the reserve fuel would translate into a highly favourable improvement in range and/or payload.

The improvement would come from high lift devices, retractable slats along the leading edge of the wing, as fitted to a subsonic airliner, and by making the elevons give flap effect. The 'pitch down' caused by the elevons giving flap effect would be counteracted by a combination of the extra aerodynamic surface (fore- or tail-plane), and by having the centre of gravity situated further

to the rear. A rearward centre of gravity decreases the stability of an aircraft. However 'active controls', pioneered on Concorde, which move the control surfaces independently of the pilot, can artificially restore the stability. This motion is actioned by computers fed with information from accelerometers, and by data concerning the aircraft's airspeed and altitude.

The Wright brothers first aircraft was unstable. It was controllable (just), thanks to the slowness of the unstable pitching. A jet propelled delta winged aircraft would not be so forgiving. Therefore, complete instability, as on the latest fighter aircraft, is not envisaged for the AST. However, absence of an emergency mechanical signalling channel to the flying controls, as on Concorde, would save weight. Thus at least two of, the say four, signalling channels would use fibre optic signalling ('fly-by-light'), which is less vulnerable from a lightning strike than an electrical channel ('fly-by-wire'). Incidentally, starting with a centre of gravity further aft, less fuel would

have to be pumped back to compensate for the rearward movement of the centre of lift during transonic acceleration, enabling the rear tank to be used for storing more fuel at the outset.

A side stick, replacing the conventional control column, was test flown on, but not retrofitted to, the production Concorde. However, it represented the prototype of the kind of controls found on the 'fly-by-wire' Airbus A320, A330 and A340. A European AST would be similarly equipped.

It may become practicable, by suction or other means, to remove the turbulent boundary layer from a wing surface and thus induce a laminar airflow. The nature and substance of the wing surface that would allow this, akin to the philosopher's stone in alchemy, does not, in the mid 1990s, exist. When it does, it will turn a base airflow into a golden one. On a subsonic wing at Mach 0.8, reducing the skin friction drag could reduce the overall drag by 45%, on Concorde at Mach 2, by 35%.

At higher Mach numbers the reduction is not so great: Mach 3, 20% and Mach 4 only 8%. Incidentally a laminar flow would also subdue the shock wave.

With no turbulent mixing, the maximum temperature of the structure at places other than the leading edge is dramatically reduced. On Concorde at the wing root near the trailing edge this reduction would be from 113°C to 51°C; on the Blackbird (SR-71) at Mach 4, the drop is estimated to be from 257°C to 104°C, but with the leading edge at 547°C. An aluminium alloy is quite comfortable at 104°C. An AST cruising at Mach 3 might after all be possible. However, the apparatus capable of sustaining laminar flow would add some weight and complexity to the wing of the resulting aircraft.

If that apparatus turned out to be nothing more than cryogenic fuel, then the design of the AST might be radically altered. Liquid hydrogen or methane could, by virtue of cooling the wing surface, diminish the boundary layer, thus creating a laminar airflow.

Liquid hydrogen has good calorific value per kilogram but bad per litre; its exhaust contains water, no carbon dioxide and, depending on the design of the combustion chamber, only traces of oxides of nitrogen (NO_x). However, it is not energy efficient to extract it from fossil fuels.

Concorde's four Rolls-Royce kerosene burning Olympus engines represent the pinnacle of turbojet development. They each have an intake system whose area constantly changes during supersonic flight according to ambient conditions and

engine demand, which then leads into the engines themselves followed by the re-heat system upstream of two variable nozzles. Must the successor engine achieve more and can it be made to do so? The answer is of course yes to both questions.

Although Concorde's engines are highly efficient at supersonic speeds, they are inefficient and noisy at low speeds. Compounded by the high drag, the rate of fuel usage at the terminal area manoeuvring speed of 250 kts is 50 kgs per mile. On final approach at 160 kts this increases to 150 kgs per mile. This compares with 15 kgs per mile used during the latter portion of the supersonic cruise.

Even if noise suppressors worked, they do not improve engine efficiency at low speed. The best choice for the AST would seem to be an engine with a variable cycle. This would reduce noise and the off-design fuel burn. For take-off, subsonic flight and landing, the new engine must be able to perform like a high by-pass engine (with high mass flow of air, but with low jet exhaust velocity), as on a Boeing 747. Then for supersonic flight, the engine would transform itself into a turbojet (with a low mass of air flow but with high jet exhaust velocity), as per Concorde. All this while it maintains the lowest specific fuel consumption possible.

Rolls-Royce and SNECMA (the Concorde powerplant partners) having pooled their ideas, are, in the mid 1990s, proposing a 'Mid Tandem Fan' engine for the AST. On take-off each engine would receive air from two intakes, the normal front intake leading to the first stages of the compressor, and side intakes with 'blow in' doors, to feed a mid fan turning on the same shaft. The mid

fan flow would by-pass the engine core, before surrounding the core exhaust flow and then exiting via the secondary nozzle. The amount of energy delivered to the low pressure spool (turning front compressors and the mid fan) would depend on the area of the primary nozzle (see page 121) – the greater the area the higher the by-pass flow.

After take-off the by-pass ratio will decrease (from about two to one) causing the jet velocity to increase as the Mach number increases. The jet velocity on take-off must not exceed 450 metres per second (Mach 1 = 340 m/s), otherwise the noise regulations (FAR part 36 Stage 3) will be infringed. The high by-pass (therefore quieter) engines, introduced in the 1970s, outlawed the preceding generation of noisier airliners and embarrassed Concorde's supporters. The AST is unlikely to meet a similar situation, as any future fan engines will exhibit only a small, but not revolutionary, noise reduction. Provided the noise rules governing the AST are established at the outset and achieved at the finish, all will be well.

The payload to weight ratio on Concorde is barely 6%. A subsonic airliner over a similar range (3,300 nm) can achieve 15%. For each passenger on Concorde there is about 1¾ tonnes of aircraft (and fuel) – on a B747 the figure is less than a tonne. Each passenger on Concorde accounts for just less than a tonne of fuel in crossing the Atlantic (17 passenger statute miles per gallon), whilst a Boeing 747 betters this by a factor of three and the smaller 767 by over four.

According to a Boeing study, high temperature thermoplastic or polyimide polymeric composites for speeds less than Mach 2.8 will be able to replace some of the alloy structures of the 1960s. Where metal is essential, techniques like the plastic forming and diffusion bonding of, for instance, Titanium can be employed to build matrices. Both methods reduce the structural mass. To repeat, on Concorde it costs a ton of fuel to carry an extra tonne. Such structural techniques reduce the mass, therefore the thrust requirement, therefore the engine size, thus the fuel burn and thus the take-off weight. By 1990 an AST of similar range and payload to Concorde would have weighed 125 tonnes, compared to Concorde's 185.

The AST must have an engine that can 'change gear'. It will then be able to cope with low speeds like the big fan engine on the B747's wing on the right, and for supersonic cruise like the Rolls-Royce Olympus engine as seen on Concorde taxying here to the British Airways terminal at New York's JFK International. The Rolls-Royce Mid Tandem Fan proposal could fulfil this exacting role

Turning now to the question of pollution from engine exhaust gases, oxides of nitrogen (NO_x) are formed when the combustion is close to stoichiometric – from the endothermic combination of atmospheric nitrogen and oxygen. There is a NO_x emission index, and it is a measure of the pollutant produced per unit of fuel burnt. On Concorde it is 19. A figure of 5 is both desirable and attainable without impairing the efficiency of a future engine, thanks to modifications carried out on the combustion chamber. One Pratt and Whitney proposal arranges the combustion to be rich, followed by a 'quick quench'.

Chloro-fluoro-carbons (CFCs) from aerosols, fire extinguishers and refrigerants, probably threaten the ozone layer more than the NO_x emitted in aircraft exhaust. NO_x possibly even destroys CFCs. The ozone layer is found between 30,000 and 150,000 ft above the earth's surface. Ozone (triatomic oxygen – O_3) filters out some of the ultra violet light which, in excess, can cause skin cancer. In the stratosphere above the tropopause (37,000 ft), less atmospheric mixing occurs. The higher the molecule

finds itself the longer it remains. One 'rogue' molecule can, by catalytic action, be responsible for the destruction of many ozone molecules. The wind blows even in the stratosphere, with the resultant mixing cleaning it out more quickly than was originally predicted.

Volcanoes are another source of pollution. During its eruption in June 1991, Mount Pinatubo (in the Philippines) hurled tons of pollutants into the atmosphere. Just prior to eruption, sulphur dioxide (a source of acid rain), was being emitted at the rate of 5000 tons per day. On eruption, a volume of 5-8 cubic kilometres of ash were spewed forth, some of which attained an altitude of over 100,000 ft. It has been estimated that debris in the atmosphere from this eruption alone will have caused global temperatures to have been depressed by over 1°C for up to five years. In calculating what level of pollution would be caused by a fleet of 1000 ASTs, all other possible sources should be examined and compared.

Even if NO_x generated by aeroengines is not a major threat to the ozone layer, it must, if possible, be suppressed. This, not least from the political point of view, caused Concorde's entry into the States to be delayed in 1976 while accusations, many of them false, of its committing environmental sins were being investigated.

Boeing is investigating a modified aerodynamic design which promises, at about Mach 1.7, some alleviation from the sonic boom by rounding off the N wave (see page 60). By reducing the rate of rise of the overpressure, the startle effect of the bang is diminished. If so it might become acceptable to fly at reduced supersonic speeds over 'boom sensitive' land. At about M 1.2, the shock wave is usually refracted away from the surface, thanks to the temperature differential between the aircraft's altitude and the surface. This effect is greater when there is a headwind at the aircraft's altitude compared to that on the surface; the other way round and the effect is reversed. But cruise Mach numbers less than about M 1.4 are inefficient, as the L/D is reduced without the compensating precompression effect in the intakes giving superior efficiency to the engines.

The propagation, by Concorde, of secondary shock waves (see page 58) caused some complaints from the ground. A modified track, or an earlier deceleration, alleviates the problem. That very low secondary disturbances are noticeable does suggest that any kind of primary boom over populated land may not be tolerable.

The only real option for the AST is to have sufficient range to avoid a surface sensitive to the sonic boom and, where this is not possible, to be as fuel efficient at Mach 0.95 as at Mach 2. Consider flying from London to Tokyo at Mach 2. The great circle (shortest) track via Scandinavia and eastern Russia (CIS is 5173 nautical miles (nm), flying time $5\frac{1}{4}$ hrs. Avoiding Scandinavia, but using a supersonic corridor between Lena and Okhotsk, the distance becomes 5550 nms ($5\frac{1}{2}$ hrs). Finally, avoiding all land, flying south west from the Bering Strait to Tokyo, 6311 nm ($3\frac{1}{4}$ hrs). Cruising in at Mach 0.85 via the great circle route, it takes about 11 hours.

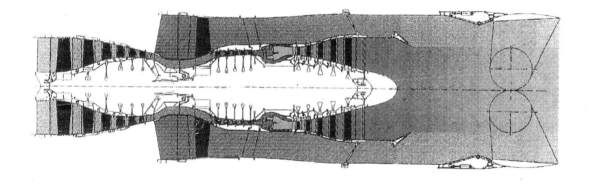

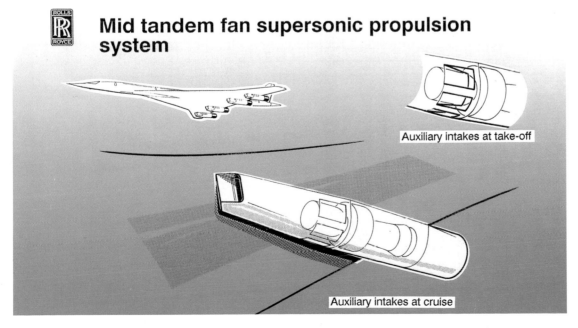

Mid tandem fan supersonic propulsion system

Auxiliary intakes at take-off

Auxiliary intakes at cruise

The Mid-Tandem-Fan engine proposal by Rolls-Royce and SNECMA, with an ultra-low emissions combustor and no reheat. For noise suppression and efficiency throughout the speed range, an engine whose by-pass ratio can be varied is virtually essential for the AST. An extra fan is placed around the 'waist' of the engine (in order to reduce frontal area) and driven by the same shaft that drives the low pressure compressor. High by-pass flow, for low forward speed, is achieved by opening the primary nozzle and arranging the fan inlet guide vanes for maximum flow; low by-pass, for supersonic cruise, by reducing primary nozzle area and adjusting the guide vanes for minimum flow

To accommodate the extra by-pass flow with low forward speed, extra 'blow-in' auxiliary intakes would be required. In this way the frontal area of the engine, vital for low drag, can be kept to a minimum

Left
One of the legacies of the B2707 was development of the 'glass cockpit' – the replacement of conventional electro-mechanical instruments with computer-generated depictions of instruments and aircraft situation. Here on a Boeing 767 the 'artificial horizon' looks like its mechanical predecessor, but the 'compass' can be made to show the predicted position of the aircraft, vertical and horizontal, as well as the actual. Accurate flying saves time and fuel – very apposite for an AST

Far left
18 May 1986. Concorde in formation with two Spitfires over Biggin Hill, which was an appropriate reunion as it was a Photo Reconnaissance Spitfire that paved the way to supersonic flight in 1943 (The Spitfire Society)

Below left
Concorde in the landing configuration. On a successor, synthetic vision-closed circuit TV- could replace 'direct' vision through a 'droop' nose and visor. A cockpit further aft, so in a wider section of fuselage, would be equipped with a projection system similar to one found in a flight simulator. Note the portion of the wings outboard of the engine. This was, in 1974, the subject of a possible redesign. The proposal would have included, from the 15th 'production' Concorde onward, extra fuel tanks and an improved engine, all to reduce noise and improve range. this was ruled out on cost . One of the misfortunes of the Concorde projection was that very little evolution could take place with such a small production run

Bottom left
Dawn Colorado Springs, midday London, 5 November 1985, prior to the return of the Concorde charter flight via New York

Many of the 1990s studies propose an AST with about 300 seats, with a maximum take-off weight of about 300 tonnes. This would improve the payload to weight ratio from Concorde's 6% to about 10% over a range of 5500 nautical miles roughly 2000 nms more than Concorde.

There is, however, a proposal from Lockheed for a 100 seater, 100 tonne supersonic transport of similar range. Although its engines are not of the variable cycle type (see above), it is said that it will be able to meet the FAR 36 Stage 3 noise rules. Lockheed, although not chosen for the original American SST project, have had considerable supersonic experience, notably with the Lockheed SR-71 Blackbird, which was capable of speeds well in excess of Mach 3.

A 1990 proposal for a supersonic business jet by Gulfstream (USA) with Sukhoi of the then Soviet Union and Rolls-Royce of the UK seems, by 1994, to have been shelved. For low supersonic drag an aircraft must have a high fitness ratio (length to maximum diameter) - hence Concorde's four-abreast seating arrangement. On an aircraft with a short fuselage the internal volume (for fuel and passengers) is therefore compromised. The operating costs of the AST might well exceed those of a subsonic airliner. The market would need to determine what level of surcharge would be acceptable in view of the time saved.

Mid-1990 studies suggest that a three class aircraft with a 15% surcharge over existing subsonic fares would be acceptable. Some caution must be registered here, however. Concorde was barely competitive pricewise when compared to the subsonic jets of the 1960s. Thus Concorde's delayed entry into service during the economic recession of 1976, and well after the debut of the highly economic Boeing 747, compounded its already difficult marketing position. The AST must not be compromised in a similar way.

Most studies favour a cruising speed of between Mach 1.7 and Mach 2.4. Higher speeds do not proportionally reduce flight times, as a substantial part of the flight must be spent in acceleration and deceleration. However, without laminar flow control, higher speeds add disproportionately to the difficulties. These mount as the temperature associated with the higher Mach numbers is reached. Not only must the materials and structure become more

Opposite
Avion de Grande Vitesse – a hypersonic proposal from Aerospatiale. Not exo-atmospheric, the AGV would still generate a sonic boom, experience high skin temperatures and be very expensive to develop. Evolving a Mach 2 successor built on the experience gained from Concorde could be preferable

Opposite below
A fitting descendant to Concorde in name – Alliance – implying continuing technological collaboration, could be this Aerospatiale proposal for un Avion de Transport Supersonique Futur (ATSF). Cruising with 200 passengers over 6500 nm between Mach 2 and 2.5, it would be propelled by variable cycle engines

Below
British Airways confidence and pride in its flag carrier Concorde is exemplified by the multi-million pound refurbishment programme instituted in 1993. The picture illustrates the third example of Concorde's cabin furnishings since entry into service in 1976

sophisticated, but also the fluids - fuel, oil and hydraulic. Stagnation temperature at Mach 1.7 in ISA (International Standard Atmosphere) conditions is 68°C, at Mach 2 is 116°C, at Mach 2.4 is 192°C and at Mach 3 it is 332°C (see appendix for formula).There is an alternative to the AST described above. That is to wait, perhaps over 50 years, for a derivative of the space launch vehicle that could have been developed by mid-21st century.

21 Years In Service

Concorde G-BOAF departs Bournemouth International Airport (Hurn) from runway 08/26. The newly extended strip has allowed the airport to become another starting point for Concorde charters 18th August 1996

In 1903, man achieved the 'impossible' flight in a heavier than air machine. Then, in spite of enthusiastic conjecture to the contrary, most serious commentators foresaw neither supersonic nor space flight. Yet only 66 years after the Wright Brothers feat at Kitty Hawk, a supersonic airliner had flown and man had landed on the moon. Next it seemed as if all long range flight would be supersonic and that the moon would be colonised by the turn of the century. In 1976, when Concorde entered into service, its prospects appeared gloomy. By 1986 improvements were apparent. This chapter is about how Concorde fared in the ten years since this book was originally published, and takes a glimpse at its future.

In 1996 Concorde operates in a commercial aviation arena which consists of a perpetually increasing number of airline passengers travelling ever further and in larger machines. But they fly, in the main, at the same speed as 35 years earlier.

This passenger growth has stretched resources. Reformed administration benefited by computers has enhanced Air Traffic Control and airports have expanded. Nevertheless Heathrow is, in 1996, in urgent need of the proposed fifth terminal. In the year 1995-96 fifty-four million passengers were in transit through Heathrow almost 30 million of them with British Airways.

By 2010, assuming that Terminal 5 will be in use, the forecast figure is eighty million

with British Airways maintaining its share. Without this expansion, Heathrow, in spite of having celebrated 50 years of pre-eminence, could lose business to a rival continental airport.

Heathrow's 50th birthday was celebrated with a fly past of historic and present day aircraft. For half an hour during the afternoon of 2nd June 1996, the business of transporting passengers was halted. Leading the assortment of aircraft was the Avro Lancaster, followed, amongst others, by two diminutive De Havilland Dragon Rapides; the elegant Comet, representing the first of the jet airliners; Concorde, in formation with BAe Hawks of the Red Arrows and finally the most recent subsonic jet airliner, the massive twin-engined Boeing 777 of British Airways.

After nearly 21 years in service at the time of writing, Concorde still evokes wonder. For the celebration described above, the British Airways' flagship was under the command of Captain Michael Bannister, the

The Captains' control panel seen from his vacated seat. The visor is in position as the aircraft climbs to cruising altitude and Mach 2. In spite of intertial navigation systems there is still a basic stand by compass seen here on the centre pillar of the windscreen

The graceful lines of Concorde still turn heads even after 21 years in airline service

Captain Mike Bannister who commanded the first charter flights to and from Bournemouth International Airport (Hurn) on 18th August 1996 and commanded Concorde during the flypast to celebrate Heathrow's 50th anniversary 2nd June 1996

Concorde's principle scheduled services are from London or Paris to New York. Over the winter months there is, for British Airways, a once, sometimes twice, weekly scheduled service to Barbados. In 1980 British Airways in association with Singapore Airlines discontinued the London/Bahrain/Singapore route. In 1982 Air France ceased Concorde flights to Rio de Janeiro, Caracas, Mexico City and Washington. In October 1994, after 18 years, British Airways dropped their London to Washington service, the Miami extension to that route having been discontinued by March 1991. The cutting of the latter two

The fuselage section around a cabin window is made by integral machining. The skin and its supporting framework have all be 'carved' out of a single piece of aluminium alloy. The pipework leading to and from the window supplies cooling air between the inner and outer transparencies

Flight Technical Manager, but was flown from the lefthand seat by Captain David Ross, himself a former RAF pilot. As such displays require exact navigation and precise timing, especially the link up with the Red Arrows (the first for ten years) the operation was closely monitored by Senior First Officer Tim Orchard; whilst the flight engineer's panel was operated by Ian Smith - himself a long serving Senior Flight Engineer on Concorde.

The British Airways Concorde operation accounts for a small proportion of the 150,000 passengers passing daily through Heathrow. But Concorde carries a significant group of people. It has been noted by some observers that the performance of the UK economy can be almost predicted by an analysis of Concorde's revenue.

One of the many Concorde charter destinations of Goodwood Travel is Petra in Jordan. Known as the Rose Red City, it was sculpted out of the living rock. A similar technique was used 20 centuries later in the construction of Concorde

routes, British Airways saved six hundred supersonic sectors per year thus prolonging Concorde's useful years of service.

With the cessation of the direct three times weekly Concorde service to Washington Dulles, a daily morning connecting flight was established between New York and Washington National. This takes about ninety minutes longer than the old direct flight. In compensation 'National' is forty-five minutes closer by road to the US capital than 'Dulles'.

In good economic years Concorde is extremely profitable. It even survived the

recessions of the mid-80s and early 90s. In 1996 British Airways' twice daily service between London and New York, at normal Concorde fare levels, was achieving load factors west bound of 70-80% and east bound 50-60% (In June 1996 the return fare was £5,774 or £4,772 with $70 cancellation charge, versus £4,314 subsonic First Class; the cheapest Concorde charter ticket being £225 for a thirty minute subsonic and £545 for a one hundred minute supersonic flight). For Air France the single daily service between Paris and New York achieves an overall load factor of over sixty percent. By October 1987 the British Airways Concorde had carried its one millionth scheduled trans-Atlantic passenger; the figure for Air France being 677,000. By the 20th anniversary of Concorde operations (21st January 1996), Air France had carried a total, including charter passengers, of over 1.1 million; for British Airways this total approached two million.

Concorde carries more passengers west than east bound. The supersonic traveller from Europe arrives in New York one hour, from UK, or two hours, from France, before he has left. West bound the time change is subtracted from the flight time; east bound it is added. It would in theory be possible to start a round the world supersonic west

Pipes and wiring beneath the cabin floor. Note the elongated bracket holes beneath the seat rails (black and white running parallel across the picture) - designed to cope with the differential expansion of the fuselage (at 100°C) when supersonic compared to the cooler cabin

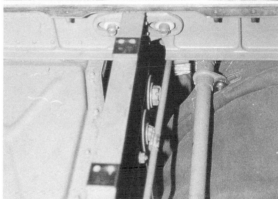

Below
The interior of G-BOAG reminiscent of a 'tube tunnel' on the London Underground. For a thorough inspection and completion of the Crown Area Modification the removal of all cabin furnishing is essential

Concorde heads the BAe Hawks of the Red Arrows, the Royal Air Force display team, on their run in to Heathrow on the occasion of the airport's 50th anniversary on the 2nd June 1996. Concorde was commanded on this flight by Captain Mike Bannister (John M. Dibbs)

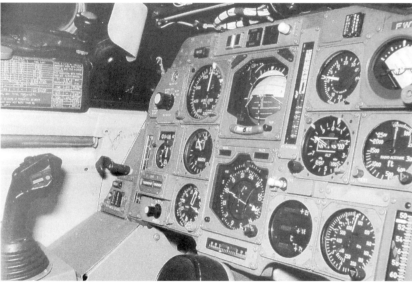

Concorde is constrained by 'night jet bans'. At Heathrow no aircraft 'movements' are allowed between 11:30pm and 7:00am, at New York between 10:00pm and 7:00am. Theoretically it is possible to avoid the ban at each end, nevertheless an overnight supersonic east bound flight is impracticable. A 9:45pm take-off from New York (leaving very little margin for error) could often arrive at Heathrow before 7:00am. Reducing speed to arrive at, say, 7:30am, would defeat the object of Concorde, furthermore there could still be complaints about early morning jet noise. In any case, having suffered a very short night's sleep and paid more for the privilege, the passenger could be less comfortable than his subsonic counterpart. For a Concorde successor flying east bound, there is a potential conflict of night jet bans with the short flight times. This conflict lessens as the local hour change between points increases. An eight hour time change between two places with a five hour flight, would make for an east bound journey equivalent to thirteen hours. So a flight departing at 8pm would arrive at 9am the following day, both times being well within jet ban tolerances.

Top The TCAS instrument is a modified vertical speed indicator, in the unlikely event of there being a collision risk, it commands climb or descent to avoid the other 'traffic'. The 'traffic' or other aircraft, is shown relative to Concorde within the centre of the dial

Above Concorde 201 was used to test the feasibility of side stick control. Airbus, also using 'fly-by-wire', have successfully applied this system of control to the A320 and subsequent airliners

bound service with a single aircraft that always left at the same local time.

The reason for the disparity is as follows. Having arrived in New York on the morning supersonic flight, many business men complete a full day's work. Then despite the jet lag, they return on the overnight subsonic flight, to be ready (or so they think) for work the next European morning.

A less tiring option, although involving an overnight stay, is to return on the following morning or afternoon supersonic New York to Europe flight. Leaving at 8:45am (local time), on flight BA002 the executive returns to London at 5:25pm (BA004: 1:45pm-10:25pm; Air France New York-Paris on AF001: 8:00am-5:45pm).

For the passenger who originates his trip in the United States, the supersonic day flight is very attractive. This delivers him fresh in Europe allowing easy adjustment to the new time zone.

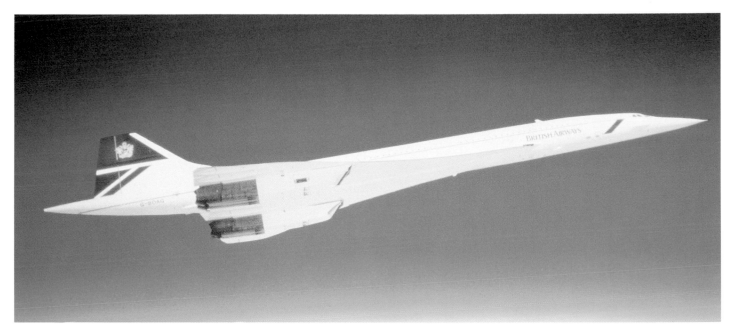

When Concorde services started, a cartoon was published showing a very jet-lagged top executive being consoled by his secretary. She was saying to him: "Look at it this way, you may have lost the multi-million dollar deal, but you did save one hundred and sixty-two pounds and twenty pence by not taking Concorde."

A tenth of the supersonic business, in British Airways' case, consists of charter flights, a point touched on in the chapter 'The Future'. In 1996 there were six main charterers:Cunard, Goodwood Travel with Spirit Tours, Superlative, Intrav, David Gladwin Concorde Limited and Yorkshire Charters.

Cunard combine Concorde flights with

Above *Climbing to cruise altitude and Mach 2*

Below *Concorde G-BOAA in take off configuration*

On the London/
Bahrain sector, the
first chart shows the
supersonic track over
the Adriatic. It is
carefully routed to
avoid placing a sonic
boom on either Italy
or Albania, a mini-
mum of 30 nautical
miles (nms) from the
coastline is required
on the inside of a
turn and 20 nms fly-
ing straight. The
track fits precisely
within the limits.
During the troubles
in former Yugoslavia,
the route was tem-
porarily suspended.
The second chart
shows the east and
west bound tracks to
the south of Cyprus
and over the coast
north of Beirut. Until
1980 supersonic
flight was permitted
over North Lebanon.
Subsequently Egypt
permitted supersonic
flight over the Nile to
the south of Cairo;
the new route then
crossed Saudi Arabia
to Bahrain. Later,
approval of super-
sonic flight over
Saudi was with-
drawn, another fac-
tor in the decision to
discontinue the
Singapore service
which had operated,
off and on, for barely
two years

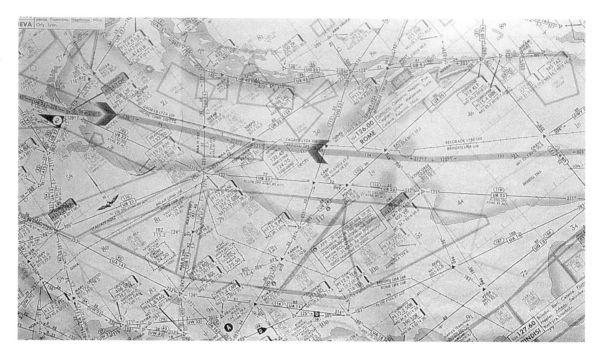

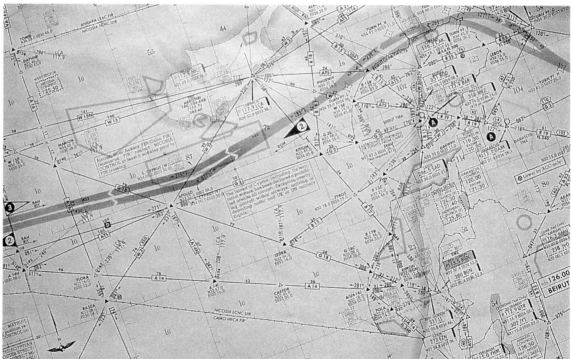

the QE2 voyages. They frequently invite a crew member from the Concorde fleet as guest speaker who naturally extols the virtues of the only other way of crossing the Atlantic...

Goodwood were formed in 1981 by Jan Nott, Colin Mitchell and George Stevens. Based at Canterbury they chartered their first 'Flight of Fantasy' Concorde to Nice for the 1983 Monaco Grand Prix. In October 1992 Goodwood broke the record for a circumnavigation of the world using an Air France Concorde, completing the trip in 33 hours and 1 minute. In June 1994 Goodwood

in conjunction with Cunard's QE2 combined two anniversaries: the 25th of Concorde's maiden flight and the 50th of the D-Day landings on Normandy. By August 1995 Goodwood had carried 70,000 passengers on Concorde. By June 1996 they had taken Concorde to no less than forty-seven destinations (see appendix for all Concorde destinations). In particular Goodwood are famous for the 'Father Christmas' Concorde flight to Rovaniemi, Finland. They are noted for their superb brochure and the imaginative way they have rekindled the romance of travel. They offer such combinations as:

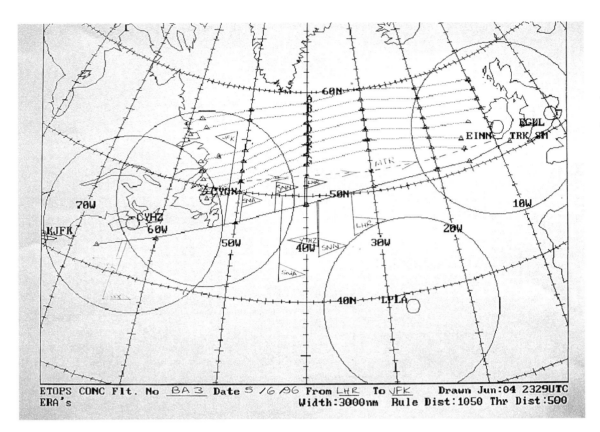

ETOPS CONC Flt. No __BA 3__ Date _5/6/96_ From _LHR_ To _JFK_   Drawn Jun:04 2329UTC
ERA's   Width:3000nm Rule Dist:1050 Thr Dist:500

The point of no return chart shows which alternates can be reached following either a single (upper flags) or double engine failure (lower flags) along Concorde's west-bound route. JFK (New York) is in range on three engines (Mach 0.93 cruise) by 52° W; while Santa Maria in the Azores (SMA) is out of range on two engines (Mach 0.80) by 43½° W. Here the seven subsonic tracks and the minimum time east bound route are well to the north; but must be considered, since an engine failure would force Concorde to descend through their altitudes

Concorde to Istanbul with a return on the Orient express, Concorde in conjunction with the Golden Arrow and Concorde to Jordan with an excursion on the train used by Lawrence of Arabia. Also on that tour is a visit to Petra - The Rose Red City - which was carved out of the living rock. Twenty centuries later a similar technique was used in the construction of Concorde - instead of rock the medium was the carefully developed Hiduminium RR58 aluminium alloy out of which were carved pieces of fuselage by integral machining.

Superlative Travel, based in London, have also featured the exotic factor of Concorde travel to romantic destinations - Voyage to Monte Carlo, Mediterranean Magic and Caribbean Christmas. Both they and Goodwood Travel liaise with Cunard's QE2.

Intrav are based in St Louis, Missouri. There speciality is in organising round the world Concorde charters at the rate of two or three per year.

David Gladwin Concorde Limited is based in Nottingham. A former British Airways VC10 pilot, Gladwin was scheduled for a Concorde conversion course in 1978. Difficulties within BA caused the course to be cancelled. In 1986, instead of becoming a Concorde pilot, he started chartering Concorde. Ten years later his firm had carried almost 40,000 passengers. Included have been special flights, one to inaugurate

Manchester's new Terminal and others marking the 25th anniversary of Concorde from Filton, Bristol - Concorde's birthplace.

The smaller end of the Concorde charter business is, in 1996, being conducted by an enthusiastic company - Yorkshire Charters managed by Keith Walker and based in Ossett. In April 1987, they arranged the first visit of Concorde to Leeds Bradford. This proved so successful that it has been repeated several times each year; with Newcastle and Teesside being included on other occasions.

How is Concorde performing technically? Brian Calvert, in his book 'Flying Concorde', likened the building of Concorde to watch making in a hangar. The servicing of the 'time machine' is somewhat similar.

At specific intervals, Concorde undergoes

```
PAGE 1  BAW003    LHR-JFK  ROUTE 008  C/S BAW3   05JUN96 G-BOAC

   10.0 PL/PAX .....  ZFCG    .....  T/U SLOT .....  TNKS   .....
   91.0 ZFW    .....  TOCG    .....  2150 ATA .....  TAXI   .....
   90.2 FPF    .....  PTBO/TR .....  1800 ATD .....  T OFF  .....
  181.3 TOW    .....  FNL11   .....  0350 IOT .....  TRIP   .....
  103.6 LW     .....  SG      .....  LIMIT CAP       LAND   .....

TIF    77630    3.25  TL P0.00                       TAXI   .....
CONT    2500    0.12      NEWARK
DIV     3660    0.20  DIV EWR FRM FL100              RAMP   .....
RSRV    6500    0.30  PLAN REMAIN 12660
ADDNL      0    0.00                                 WX ATC .....
REQD   (90290)  4.27                                 05JUN96 1647
EXTRA  .....    ....
FPF    .....    ....
TAXI   .....    ....
TANKS  .....

 TOW CHANGE 1000 KG PLUS/MINUS 460 KG TRIP FUEL

RMKS : T/O R/W 09 340KG/1MIN LAND R/W 13/31 400KG R/W 22 800KG
       STD VIA KENDA DIVN EWR TACT 1
```

The computer generated flight plan showing fuel required from London to New York (highlighted), total fuel (circled) and fuel required for take-off-weight (TOW) change (highlighted) - the fuel used on the crossing increases by about half of the increased take-off weight. Note, in contrast to a B747, the total reserve fuel exceeds the payload (by 2660 kgs in this case)

checks, every 12,000 flying hours each aircraft is submitted for the 'major' check. In British Airways the last aircraft in the fleet to achieve 12,000 hours was G-BOAG (aircraft 214). By 2004 the series of 'majors' will come round again. A 'major' on Concorde lasts for about five months, which includes a month for the structural work associated with the Crown Area Modification.

The Crown Area Modification strengthens the top of the fuselage. At 'rotate', during take-off, the elevons move up placing a down force at the tail. The reaction to this stretches the top of the fuselage as the aircraft is pitched up. Calculations suggested the need for minor reinforcements along this section. In spite of this, a computer model was made of the structure of 'G-BOAF'. About forty strain sensors were fitted and the data they gathered over several flights was analysed. A far more accurate picture of the structure was formed than was possible when Concorde entered service. This proved that the designers had erred on the right side. Concorde is exceedingly strong, albeit at the cost of a small weight penalty.

Before the Crown Area Modification can begin, the aircraft has to be 'candlesticked'. This involves being jacked up in such a way that the skin experiences zero stress; adjustments are even made for diurnal temperature variation. Then at two positions over the top circumference of the fuselage a double row of fasteners is removed. Into each resulting hole is forced a mandril. The ensuing stress strengthens the surrounding metal. The mandril is removed and a new fastener put in place. Since all this takes place at room (hangar) temperature, it is called 'cold working'. Included in the modification is the addition of one strap over the top surface of the fuselage just to the rear of the centre door.

To keep Concorde flying well into the future there is the Life Extension

Programme. Bitter had been the experience of the builders of the early Comets - at least two of which, in the early 1950s, had suffered explosive decompression. Hence the requirement, already mentioned in the chapter 'The Turn of the Tide', to build two Concorde fatigue specimens and subject them to forces, vibrations, heating and cooling to an excess of that expected during normal service. Before being shut down in 1985, the test rig at Farnborough achieved 20,000 'supersonic flight cycles'. After 6,700 cycles - a third of the total - it was agreed that more stringent airframe inspection procedures would have to be established. These constitute the Life Extension programme.

Rather than the Supersonic Flight Cycle, the yardstick established for measuring Concorde life subsequently became the Reference Flight (RF). Every flight is counted but the figure is modified in proportion to the take-off weight. A flight at over 170 tonnes take-off weight counts as one RF and less than 120 tonnes as half an RF. As of 14th June 1996 the oldest British Airways

Below In 1985 the original Concorde cabin decor was superseded by the 'Landor' version (see page 96). In 1993 it was refurbished again to the version shown opposite

Concorde had achieved 6,042 RFs and the youngest 3,792 RFs. The initial Life Extension will allow for 8,500 RFs. Three years before this total is reached, a review will take place, modifications made (if necessary) and different inspection procedures (if required) established to take the life up to 10,000 RFs. The oldest Concorde could achieve 8,500 RFs by the year 2004 and the youngest by 2012. With an extension to 10,000 RFs and assuming no other limitation, Concorde could still be flying up to 2020. A minimum of four Concordes would be needed to support the New York service.

To make the various inspections required by the Life Extension programme simple, modified aircraft will be fitted with borescopes. These are visual devices - using fibre optics or even micro TV - capable of seeing round corners to examine the more inaccessible parts of the fuselage without dismantling internal structures such as galleys.

Due to thermal heating during the supersonic cruise, Concorde's fuselage is less prone to corrosion than that of a subsonic aircraft. Fluids evaporate from the inside of an aircraft skin regularly heated to 100°C; in contrast they condense on the inside at minus 30°C. On Concorde it is areas where fluids can be spilt onto the structure at room temperature, for instance around the galleys,

that need to be subject to greater scrutiny. During checks very minor blemishes are 'blended out' by careful metal polishing; if larger, then the piece is completely renewed.

Will there always be a sufficient supply of spare parts over the projected life time of the

The Crown Area Modification called for an extra strap over the top of the fuselage and the removal of a double row of fasteners (in two positions over the fuselage) for strengthening through 'cold working' prior to the refitting of the fasteners

140

Left *Concorde in the attractive colour scheme of Air France*

Below *The floor looking aft in the vicinity of the forward galley. Even the most minute blemishes caused by corrosion are replaced. The section on the right with the circled area, where the corrosion has been removed, is to be substituted with the one on the left which has been newly assembled*

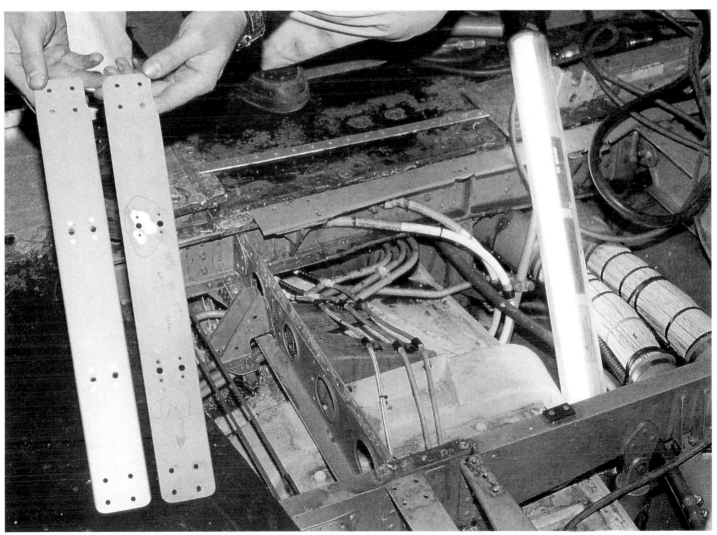

Below centre
Wherever Concorde goes it always attracts crowds. The roads skirting the boundaries of Bournemouth International Airport were brought to a standstill by sightseers

Below *Concorde G-BOAF touches down for the first time on Bournemouth International's newly extended main runway 18th August 1996*

Left
The Red Arrows formate on Concorde as they approach London Heathrow for the airport's 50th anniversary fly-past (John M. Dibbs)

Below *Concorde manoeuvres on to the apron at Bournemouth. In the foreground is a Douglas DC 3, of Air Atlantique, probably the most significant aircraft in the history of passenger air transport* (Evening Echo Bournemouth)

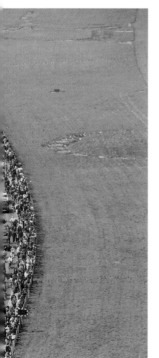

143

On 2nd April 1996 Pepsi Cola launched their new 'livery'. Air France Concorde 'F-BTSD' in the new Pepsi colours visited ten European and Middle Eastern cities. Celebrities Claudia Schieffer, André Agassi and Cindy Crawford assisted at the launch held at London Gatwick Airport. Contrary to press reports, the paint withstood supersonic flight. The aircraft was restored to Air France colours after two weeks

Below *March 2nd 1989, Concorde's 20th Anniversary (since first flight of the prototype) party in Toulouse; General Henri Ziegler, Chief Executive of Sud Aviation in 1968, and Concorde enthusiast, with Sir Keith Granville who, in 1972, ordered five Concordes for BOAC*

aircraft? When necessary new parts have to be built from scratch. For instance new rubber sheathing to the weather radar cable guides had to be made out of a non-carcinogenic material and electronic circuit boards for the air intake computer units have been constructed as new items.

When the rudder surfaces on the fin showed a tendency to delaminate, new sets had to be manufactured. The £7million bill included the construction of new manufacturing jigs as the original jigs had, in 1981, been scrapped. The new jigs are kept with Concorde 202 in a hangar at Filton.

Just after Concorde went into service three important modifications were made: thinning of the lower intake lip, approval of a further aft centre of gravity for take-off and stiffening of the main undercarriage oleo legs. The first modification improved supersonic range enabling the Bahrain/Singapore sector, at the time routed to the south of Sri Lanka, to be flown direct. The second allowed more fuel to be carried in the rear fuel tank thus improving take-off performance; this is due to the increased 'flap effect' of the elevons (angled further down to compensate for the more rearward centre of gravity). The third, a modification to the undercarriage, allowed Concorde to use some of the more undulating runways around the world. During the route proving phase (prior to entry into service), violent oscillations had been experienced on take-off at Singapore.

A later modification involved fitting strain sensors to the main undercarriage bogey beams. Should a tyre deflate below a certain speed during take-off, the twist on the beam causes a warning light to illuminate calling for the take-off to be abandoned. This avoids overstressing the neighbouring tyre, risking a burst and debris entering the engines.

Apart from an improvement in the computer software of the Inertial Navigation

Below *March 2nd 1989, Concorde's 20th birthday cake. Expansive celebrations were held at Toulouse to celebrate this event. Nevertheless there is a certain ambivalence... should one be proud or secretive on the question of the age of what is still, in 1996, the most beautiful and advanced airliner yet built?*

System (INS) and the fitting of the Traffic Alert and Collision Avoidance System (TCAS) no other significant modifications have been made.

Occasionally changing legislation means that airliners must be fitted with new avionics. After a specified date without TCAS, the United States would not accept an airliner, even Concorde, into its airspace. First somewhere had to be found on Concorde's densely packed instrument panel for the display; then the detector aerials had to be fitted. A solution was found for the former; but due to becoming overheated during supersonic cruise, the aerials refused to work. The deadline passed... Months of special exemption were in fact allowed before the problem was finally solved.

Could the electromechanical instruments (artificial horizon, compass etc.) on Concorde be replaced with television screens? These are found on later airliners with computer generated display images of similar but improved instruments. This is possible; but very expensive. The expense lies not so much in the purchase and fitting of the equipment; but in the necessary certification process - six months of static testing, six months of test flying without passengers followed by one to two years of revenue flying.

British Airways uses all seven of its Concordes, while Air France, which origi-

nally had seven, uses five out of its six on a rotational basis. In November 1977, F-BVFD (211) was involved in a heavy landing at Dakar - 14 feet per second (fps) at touchdown (10 fps is the standard limit). Only minor repairs were required, further evidence of the immense strength of the structure. In 1982 Air France finally grounded 'FD'. Out of service for 12 years the aircraft had suffered serious corrosion and was dismantled in 1994.

Improvements have been made in flight planning. Once determined manually, the fuel calculation is now made by computer. This more accurately accounts for the forecast winds and temperatures of the day. The Point of No Return (PNR) chart has been similarly treated. Concorde would lose twenty-five percent of range if some failure, such as an engine shut down, forced a deceleration to subsonic speeds. Unable to make the destination or return to the departure airport, the chart shows the alternates that can be safely reached from various points across the Atlantic.

The routes to and from the United States have, over the years, remained essentially the same and are shown on the endpapers of this book. As data has been accumulated about the propagation of the secondary boom and its variance with the strength of the upper winds, deceleration points have become increasingly subject to seasonal modification.

When Concorde entered service, critics were quick to point out that the equivalent of half the flight time was 'wasted' in airport procedures. Although there were many subsonic flights of similar duration to Concorde's, supersonic flight seemed to

Below Concorde decelerates after landing using reverse thrust. Note the fully-drooped nose allowing the crew maximum visibility on final approach to landing. In contrast to her one time Russian rival, seen opposite, there is no 'canard' or foreplane. Furthermore advanced tyre and brake technology allowed the Concorde undercarriage to consist of eight rather than the sixteen wheels of the TU-144, although the maximum take-off weights of each aircraft are similar

emphasise the incongruity. With this in mind, the British Airways Concorde Brand Management Team arrange everything to cut the red tape. There is a dedicated fast track channel, a telephone check-in, for those who carry only hand luggage and a suiter service. This ensures the suit carrier reaches the baggage hall within eight minutes of arrival. Finally there is the famous Concorde lounge which is remote from the ceaseless commotion of the airport.

On board there are six cabin crew members, all of whom have been especially selected for their suitability and dedication to operating Concorde. All, two hundred and thirty-six Concorde qualified personnel, also serve on British Airways' narrow body fleet aircraft (Boeing's 737 and 757 and the Airbus A320), sixty percent are seconded for two years, the remainder for longer periods. This mix achieves enthusiasm tempered with experience.

The 'technical crew' consists of two pilots and a flight engineer. In 1996, to fulfil all the planned flying, about two and a half crews per aircraft were needed. The list in the appendix shows more Captains 'current' than First Officers. This is due to a retirement bulge having (in June 1996) called for an increase of Captains to cover for the imminent retirement of some of their colleagues. On average a flight deck crew flies eight trips (of two days) per month, has stand-by duties, ground training and also public relations duty days. The allocation of scheduled flights is decided on a seniority basis, while the charter flights are shared out. Six days per year are spent on the simulator for checks and refresher training.

Concorde's role continues to evolve. The scheduled routes of both its airlines have been gradually pared down and are, in 1996, at a minimum consistent with profitability. The charter market, for which Concorde was not originally designed, but in which it has been notably successful, remains buoyant. Before the end of its life Concorde could be flown by pilots born long after it entered service.

Although older in years than most of the rest of the British Airways fleet, Concorde is not old in terms of utilisation. In 1996 the average Concorde had flown the same number of hours as a four year old Boeing 747, achieved the same number of flights as a two and a half year old Boeing 737 and was in the same condition as a three year old Boeing 757. That Concorde is kept in such superb condition is due, in particular, to the dedication and expertise of the ground engineers of both British Airways and Air France.

Above *On 29 November 1996 the TU-144LL (RA-77114) flew again from the Zhukovsky flight test centre, near Moscow. A series of thirty two joint Russian-US test flights in the High Speed Research study program were originally proposed. Out of storage after ten years this aircraft, one of the seventeen originally built, was re-engined with Kuznetsov NK-321, two-shaft turbofans, replacing the Koliesov design bureau engines, which were fitted to only 5 of the TU-144s for longer range* (Quadrant/Flight)

Sub-Orbital Travel

At a speed of 15,000 kts (Mach 26 in the atmosphere), an object would be capable of orbiting the earth. Providing there was no aerodynamic drag it would require no thrust and, being weightless (but not massless), no lift. Until sometime during the next century vehicles will need several stages to achieve Low Earth Orbit (LEO – 300 kms). Even the US Space Shuttle is assisted by two solid fuelled rocket boosters. These are reusable, unlike its vast external fuel tank which is sacrificed on every launch. To fractionalise the cost of placing a payload into LEO a vehicle must be developed that is capable of Single Stage To Orbit (SSTO) and return, in its entirety.

A variation of such a vehicle could 'fly' from London to Australia in about an hour. During the early 1980s in America, President Reagan announced, after a particularly tiring trip to the Far East, that something quicker than a Jumbo jet should be developed. Hence the US NASP (National Aero Space Plane) project, dubbed, thanks to the President, 'The Orient Express' – this, in spite of it being supposedly an orbital vehicle. The contender for SSTO on the other side of the Atlantic, but not conceived by a jet-lagged British head of state, was HOTOL.

A rocket using oxygen and hydrogen must carry these in a mass ratio of six to one – the burn is slightly rich. So, to avoid weighing the vehicle down with oxygen, it would be better to collect it from the atmosphere during the flight into orbit. On NASP a SCRamJet (Supersonic Combustion Ram Jet) is being investigated, in the hope of it eventually being able to thrust a 'demonstrator' into LEO.

Air compressed in an intake heats up. By avoiding the need to decelerate the air to subsonic speed during hypersonic flight (Mach 5+), the temperature rise can be contained. This allows a greater margin for adding heat during combustion. However, NASP has encountered problems and, in 1994, is on 'hold' at the time of writing. First, NASP needs an engine (turbojet or rocket) for take-off – ram jets cannot operate from rest. Secondly, above Mach 15 it requires a rocket, otherwise the intake would have become huge and the exhaust

Opposite page
Impression of HOTOL in airbreathing mode. The two glowing orifices beneath the four main chambers indicate that some of the excess cooling hydrogen instead of being dumped, is being put to work in the 'Spill ramjet', usable up to Mach 4.5

The launch trolley (possibly rocket propelled) proposal for the air-breathing HOTOL would have to be capable of stopping its 250 tonne payload in the event of an aborted take-off

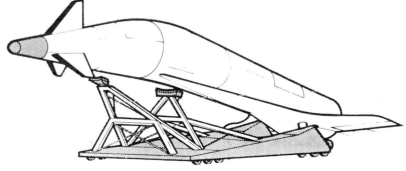

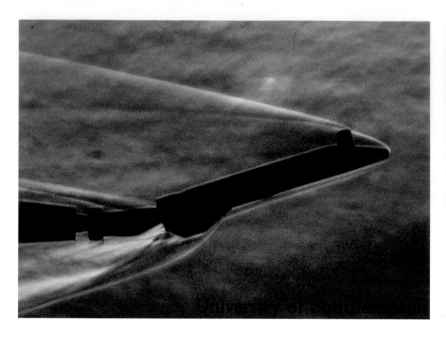

View of a HOTOL scale model at Mach 8 being studied in a wind tunnel at Southampton University. A passenger on a suborbital flight would experience 30 minutes of acceleration, a short period of weightlessness (but not masslessness), followed by 30 minutes of deceleration. Total flight time from London to Sydney would be about 70 minutes! (Southampton University)

HOTOL would rely on separated airflow for lift at low speeds, seen here in a wind tunnel test with engine intake closed. As with the US Space Shuttle, it would land from a glide approach, with no ability to 'go-around'

temperature excessive. Thirdly, to operate in accelerating flight, internal variable geometry is required – expensive. Fourthly, for ideal combustion the necessarily very smooth airflow must, at the combustion point, be made suddenly turbulent to ensure mixing with the hydrogen – conflicting requirements. One engineer has dubbed NASP as 'the Smithsonian in orbit' (Aeronautical Museum in Washington). An alternative solution is to design a rocket engine which can first use atmospheric oxygen then, for Mach 5+, onboard liquid oxygen combusted with hydrogen fuel.

The RB545, whose patent was acquired by Rolls-Royce from its inventor Alan Bond, is such an engine and was designed for the British HOTOL (HOrizontal Take-Off and Landing). For take-off, from a rocket-propelled trolley, and initial wing borne climb, the engine 'breathes' air. Air, compressed in the intake, is cooled by a heat exchanger through which liquid hydrogen fuel is circulating. Then two-thirds of the hydrogen, before being dumped, drives a turbine to compress the air further, prior to combustion with the remaining one-third of the hydrogen in the rocket chambers.

By Mach 6, momentum drag in the intake about equals the thrust, excessive energy then being needed to remove heat at the exchanger and the speed becomes too great for an intake of practical size. Therefore nine minutes after take-off at 85,000 ft and Mach 5, the engine would be switched to rocket mode, using liquid oxygen. This would continue until the craft reaches a speed of 15,350 kts at an altitude of 300,000 ft. It would then coast under its

own momentum into LEO, at nearly 1,000,000 ft (300 kms) above the earth's surface.

The HOTOL design suffered from one major aerodynamic defect. Although the centre of lift moves rearwards during transonic acceleration it moves forward again at the higher Mach numbers. Excessive quantities of hydraulic power would have been necessary to apply a compensating 'down' aerodynamic force – this despite maximum movement of the centre of gravity.

The engine cycle of the RB545 is more intricate than described above and would have been expensive to develop. Private money might have been forthcoming, but Rolls-Royce was not prepared to go ahead with anything less than British Government involvement. As a result a rocket-propelled 'interim' HOTOL was proposed, to be launched at 30,000 ft from the back of the six-engined Russian transport aircraft, the Antonov An-225. British Aerospace was still involved in 1994.

In 1991, Alan Bond, unable to hawk his original idea around foreign financiers (it was then an Official Secret), invented another engine – SABRE. This is not patented, and thus not liable to be constrained by the Official Secrets Act.

SABRE stands for the Synergetic Air Breathing and Rocket Engine. Two such engines are proposed on Alan Bond's SKYLON, which is a refined version of HOTOL. SKYLON could become the choice of FESTIP (Future European Space Transportation Investigations Programme), and might, by 2005, be carrying 12 ton payloads (cf 7 tons on HOTOL, 28 tons on Shuttle) into LEO. It is estimated that the cost per launch could be as little as $(US)10.7m. The Space Shuttle's recurring costs per launch are $615m, but are of course much more if the development cost is included.

During late 1993 configuration C1 of SKYLON was under consideration. Weighing 275 tonnes it would take-off towards the east from an equatorial runway (to gain maximum benefit from the earth's spin) using its own undercarriage. It has the ability to reject take-off. Having covered 2.8 kms during a 36 second $\frac{1}{2}$g acceleration to 'rotate' speed (about 350 mph, Mach 0.5), SKYLON would become airborne. In airbreathing mode the total thrust would be 220 tons. SKYLON would then switch to rocket mode (300 tons thrust) in a similar manner to HOTOL, for transition into LEO.

The configuration of SKYLON allows for better centre of gravity control than was possible with HOTOL. Centrally mounted wings and engines allow usage of liquid hydrogen fuel from tanks at the fore and aft extremities of the fuselage. Pitch control would be enhanced with a canard surface, whereas the fin, in configuration C1, is placed aft.

After a $1m kick off fee, SKYLON would need investment from public funds. Alan Bond was hoping that $200m would be forthcoming as a government high risk investment, repayable if SKYLON worked. Once the concept had been proved, some kind of Venture Capital would be sought. Bearing in mind the financial lessons from the Concorde project, Bond insists that: 1) a truthful initial estimate of the cost of SKYLON should be submitted, no matter how great; 2) the size of SKYLON should be established before starting; so that 3) only one version of SKYLON is built, not three as in the case of Concorde. The first flight into orbit should be within seven years of the start of the project, with return on investment within ten. This reflects the theory that longer time scales are financially unattractive. However, in May 1994 further cuts in Britain's space budget made the choice of SKYLON to fulfil the FESTIP requirement appear unlikely.

That the next step in aerospace engineering is being proposed and researched by a few dedicated enthusiasts, and not by a multi-national company, says volumes about human innovation. The Wright brothers, von Braun and Sir Frank Whittle are examples of independent innovators. The great multi-national companies, with so much to lose if things go wrong, are possibly not the ideal oysters in which to attempt to culture revolutionary pearls. Nevertheless, they have a vital part to play once theory has become practice. Just when it seemed that space exploration had to be dominated by the great battalions, the home computer, itself spawned by the space age, became powerful enough to allow one individual to replace the ranks of draughtsmen without whom, it must be

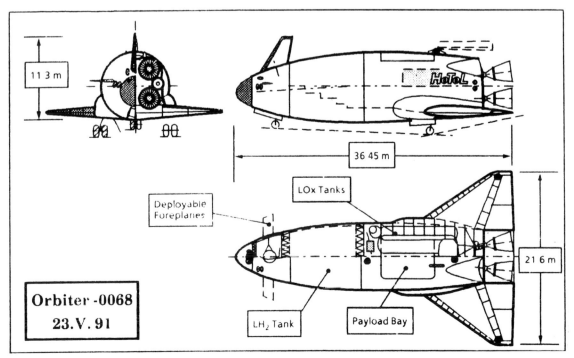

Orbiter -0068
23.V.91

113 m
36 45 m
216 m

Deployable Foreplanes
LOx Tanks
LH₂ Tank
Payload Bay

Interim HOTOL. Drag at low altitude being of less consideration, this version is more bulbous than air breathing HOTOL. Other studies have placed the fin at the rear

The launch technique from the An-225 would require a pull up to give HOTOL lift for separation, followed immediately by a dive to avoid the flame plumes from the orbiter's four pure rocket engines (total thrust about 200,000 lbs). Only from a surface launched airbreathing derivative of HOTOL could there be evolved an economic sub-orbital transport

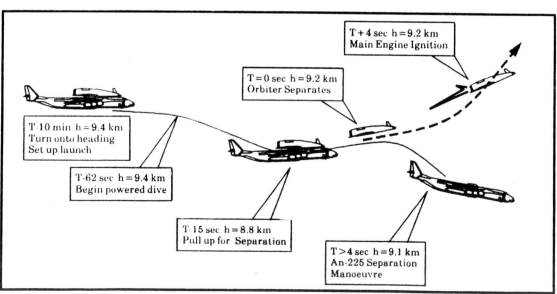

T + 4 sec h = 9.2 km
Main Engine Ignition

T = 0 sec h = 9.2 km
Orbiter Separates

T-10 min h = 9.4 km
Turn onto heading
Set up launch

T-62 sec h = 9.4 km
Begin powered dive

T-15 sec h = 8.8 km
Pull up for Separation

T > 4 sec h = 9.1 km
An-225 Separation
Manoeuvre

Left

The rocket-powered 'Interim' HOTOL proposal, being launched at Mach 0.8 from 31,000 ft off the back of the giant Russian An-225 – capable of lifting a 250t HOTOL complete with 7t payload – shown here with eight engines. In 1990, with lack of funds to develop the RB545 hybrid (capable of using either atmospheric or liquid oxygen) engine, BAe began exploring this way of providing a cheap satellite launch system for Europe

Right

The US National Aerospace Plane (NASP), or X-30, proposal. During the 1960s, rocket propelled X-15s attained 354,000 ft and Mach 6.7.

However, the programme was cancelled before a ramjet propelled version could be fully tested. In the 1980s, under the auspices of NASA, a team of several contractors was formed to research and develop a craft capable of 'Single Stage To Orbit'. The main thruster of NASP should be the Supersonic Combustion Ram Jet. However, to work it must have sufficient forward speed, say Mach 1+, then from Mach 15 up to Mach 25 (necessary for orbital flight) there is little room to add heat to the super heated intake flow. Furthermore, the huge intake (itself a major structural headache) required at Mach 15 makes slower flight extremely inefficient

SKYLON (after a similarly named and looking structure at the 1951 'Festival of Britain') – an evolution of the HOTOL concept. Propulsion would be by two pairs of four SABRE hybrid engines. It is designed to be capable of take-off from its own undercarriage, flight into Low Earth Orbit and return without shedding any rocket assisted stages. The movement of centre of gravity, through propellant usage, to compensate for the variation of centre of pressure with speed, is not compromised by a rear-mounted engine

The Two Stage to Orbit (TSTO) proposal from Aerospatiale

Aerospatiale's version of a Single Stage to Orbit (SSTO) vehicle would be propelled by a turbo-rocket-ramjet unit

admitted, there would have been neither Concorde, nor a manned trip to the moon.

The French and German proposals for the next generation of space launch vehicles are (like NASP) still the children of the great companies. However, they envisage two stages. The first, a hypersonic air-breathing vehicle from which the second stage, a rocket propelled orbiter, would be launched, with both stages being reusable. It would be from the first stage that a hypersonic transporter could be developed.

Incidentally, the German proposal derives its name from an engineer called Sänger. While working during World War 2, he designed a vehicle that, launched from Germany, would bounce along the upper atmosphere, bomb New York, complete the earth orbit then return to Germany. It was not built.

If resources for aerospace projects are finite, what kind of project most merits investment? The Ultra High Capacity Transport (UHCT) to replace the Jumbo, a reusable SSTO vehicle or the AST? Airports would need radical alterations to accommodate a 600 tonnes UHCT modified buildings, wider taxiways and stronger runway construction. Perhaps the distance between a landing UHCT and a smaller aircraft would have to be increased to allow time for the powerful vortices to dissipate, thus reducing the number of landings per hour. An SSTO would open up the infinite resource of space, but at some economic risk. Almost as risky is the AST. But the latter two are infinitely more exciting, and people do pay for excitement. Space tourism - a week in orbit - may become an economic reality.

Should major projects be collaborative? World-wide collaboration has the advantage of ensuring universal acceptance, a well spread risk and the building of fewer versions. Competition, on the other hand, is a great spur. Without the Soviets taking an early lead in space, it is doubtful whether the US would have gone to the moon so quickly. In the 1960s, Europe wanted to retrieve her pre-eminent place in aviation – hence, among other things, Concorde.

Without the competitive element two things happen: the proposal to build can be more dispassionately analysed, but the urgency to start diminishes. However, as soon as it appears that an AST and/or

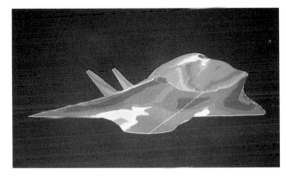

space plane will have attractive economic prospects, then the building of only one collaborative version will become inevitable.

Man is by nature an innovator. Technology is his plaything and economics the measure of his efforts. What is inevitable is that the next aerospace projects will still need men of the stature of Sir George Edwards and André Puget, the former's opposite number in Sud Aviation, to guide them to fruition.

In 1992 Robert McKinlay, former Concorde engineer and Chairman of British Aerospace Airbus Ltd said, in a lecture entitled *Concorde First or Last*: 'In the year 2010 grandfathers are not going to want to say to their grandchildren, "We used to cross the Atlantic in three and a half hours".'

A 1990s concept for space transportation – Sänger. Here, at 115,000 ft and Mach 6.8, the rocket-propelled orbiter 'Horus' is seen separating from the hypersonic ascent stage propelled, in one study, by a concentrically arranged turbo ramjet engine. Above Mach 3.5 only the ramjet would be in operation. A commercial hypersonic vehicle might be developed from this. 'Sänger' is named after the World War 2 engineer who proposed bombing America from Germany. Once launched, his craft would have bounced in and out of the atmosphere, released its load over New York, completed its earth orbit with diminishing skips, and finally glided back to Germany

Above left Powerful computers capable of complex calculations have revolutionised design. By 1845 the Navier-Stokes equations for the computation of fluid dynamics had been formulated. They remained virtually unsolvable until the era of the supercomputer over 100 years later. Here, a temperature plot of the hypersonic Sänger/Horus combination is shown.

Tragedy at Gonesse

It was Tuesday of Air Show Week at Farnborough. I had left the show early, and was walking to the station to catch a train to London for a reception at the Royal Aeronautical Society. My daughter, who happened to be watching BBC News 24 at the time, phoned me to say that a Concorde had crashed. With only 12 examples flying, it was an accident that statistically was never supposed to happen. Were there any survivors? Where did it happen? Which airline was it? Possibly, Paris, Air France came the replies.

On 25 July 2000 at 14:43 GMT, the tyre of the number 2 wheel of Concorde F-BTSC burst during take-off. This set in motion a train of events that resulted in the destruction of Concorde 203. Two minutes after starting the take-off roll, the aircraft crashed on to a hotel at Gonesse, 8 kilometres to the west of Charles de Gaulle airport, with the tragic loss of all 109 people on board, four on the ground and injury to six others.

Early reports had spoken of survivors; these turned out to be hotel staff and guests. One girl had had a miraculous escape. The owner of the burnt-out hotel spoke of the extraordinary sound that Concorde had been making: '...really overdoing it.' Other observers referred to the bravery of the

Captain who turned his burning aircraft away from a more densely populated area. *The Times* reported how the crash was witnessed by a group of 65 young musicians from Suffolk travelling to the hotel.

News of the accident reverberated around the world. Journalists gave instant analyses, while Jim Naughtie of BBC Radio 4's Today programme was sent to Paris. At Farnborough the flags were lowered to half-mast.

British Airways cancelled that evening's service to New York and agonised about continuing Concorde flights. It resumed flights the following day, while Air France did not.

In the days that followed, details were revealed about those on board. Of the 100 passengers on Special Flight AF4590, one was an American, one an Austrian, two were Danish and 96 were German. All were en route to New York where they were to join their cruise ship, the MS *Deutschland.*

On Thursday 27 July, a memorial service was held at L'Eglise Madeleine in Paris, the same church where, three years earlier, people had paid their last respects to Diana, Princess of Wales.

At first Concorde's Certificate of Airworthiness (CofA) remained valid. The aviation authority of the country where the aircraft is registered issues a Certificate of Airworthiness. In the UK it is the Civil Aviation Authority, in France the Direction Générale de l'Aviation Civile. Since Concorde is a joint project between Britain and France, both authorities are responsible for its airworthiness. For Concorde, being the first SST, a new set of standards had been established, known as the TSS (Transport Supersonique Standards). Because of Concorde's revolutionary aerodynamics and speed range, these require-

ments were often more stringent than those for a subsonic aircraft. For instance, following an engine failure on take-off, an SST has a climb gradient that is more sensitive to speed variations than that of a subsonic airliner.

This short synopsis of Concorde's performance is relevant to what follows.

All aircraft have structural and performance weight limits. The latter assumes an engine failure at the most critical point on take-off; it varies depending on the length of runway available, the meteorological conditions and how steeply the aircraft must climb to avoid obstacles (hills, tall buildings). Furthermore, Concorde has a tyre speed limit of 250 mph (220 knots). This limit can be a factor when the ground speed on take-off is high, due to heavy weight, flying from a high-altitude airport or when there is a tailwind.

Weight restrictions due to performance considerations could reduce range and/or payload. Should the wind suddenly change, causing a take-off weight restriction, an alternative runway might have to be requested. At Charles de Gaulle, this could entail a 4.2 kilometre taxi from 26R to 08L. A small weight reduction can be achieved by burning off the excess fuel before take-off.

Using the actual take-off weight from the load sheet, the 'V' speeds are confirmed. V_1 is 'decision' speed. If there is an engine failure at, or less than, V_1, the take-off must be safely abandoned. Once at V_1 or above, the take-off must be continued, there being sufficient runway from which to get airborne. V_1 for Concorde is typically 160 knots.

The next speed is V_R (typically 190 knots) when the control column is pulled back to 'rotate', that is, pitch up the aircraft with respect to the horizontal. On Concorde with

The two southern runways at Charles de Gaulle, Paris; 26R is 4.2 kms long. The B747 was waiting on the south side at the final taxiway to the west. Normally r/w 27 (on the north side and not shown here) would be used by Concorde, but some of it was closed due to maintenance

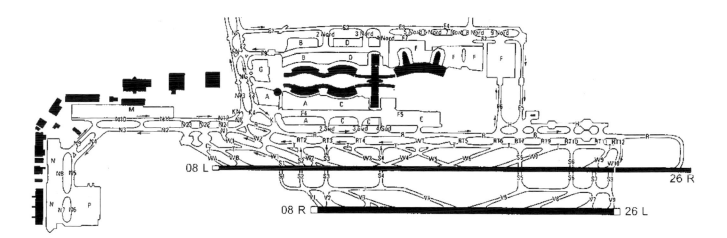

The incidence vane senses the angle of attack. The air data computer relays this to the 'anti stall' system and the engine air intake computers as well as to an angle of attack indicator

The angle of attack indicator showing 3°. On final approach it reads 14°, so with a pitch attitude of 11° the descent angle is 3°. At the final stages of the accident the reading was well over 16° where there is huge aerodynamic drag. The pointer on the left side shows vertical 'g'

all engines operating, the rate of rotation required is $2\frac{1}{2}°$ per second to a pre-set angle of pitch - θ_2 (typically about 13°). Approaching 250 knots the aircraft is pitched up again to maintain that speed, for the noise abatement procedure. Should an engine have failed at V_1, the rotation rate (still initiated at V_R) is slightly reduced. The aim now is to achieve V_2 (the engine failed climb speed, typically 220 knots) and a pitch of θ_2 simultaneously. V_1, V_R, V_2 and θ_2 are determined for each departure. Flight AF4590 from runway 26R, dry surface, calm wind, temperature 19°C, pressure 1008 millibars, was limited by the maximum permitted structural weight of 185,070 kilograms; V_1 was 150 knots, V_R 199 knots, V_2 220 knots and θ_2 was 13°.

Concorde generates lift at high angles of attack (in excess of 7°) due to the formation

The artificial horizon on Concorde has a white 'bug', here set at $4\frac{1}{2}°$ and just visible behind the yellow flight director bars. On take-off it is set to θ_2 by a thumb wheel on the control column, on final approach to 11°. The minimum pitch when supersonic is -5.5°, indicated by orange marks

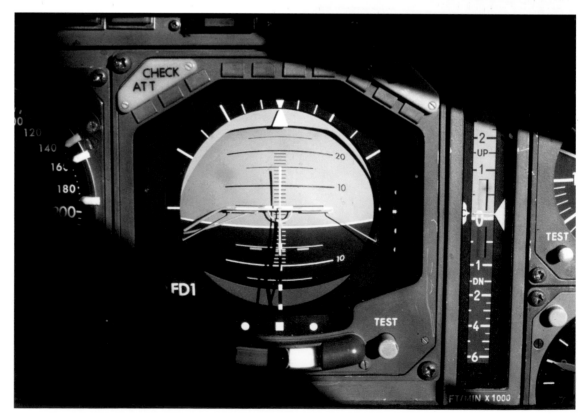

To fly with minimum drag the side slip should be zero. The indicator moves to the right if a left engine loses thrust and vice versa. The sensing vane is beneath the flight deck

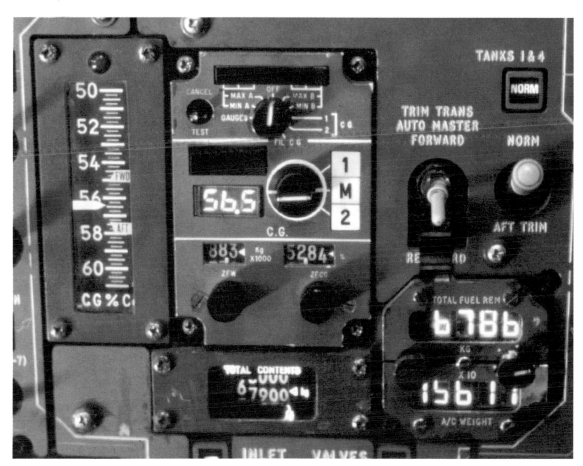

The zero fuel weight and zero fuel centre of gravity are entered before the flight, on this occasion, 88.3 tonnes and 52.84%. Just above, displayed in lit digits, is 56.5% - the actual c of g computed from the quantity of fuel in each tank. The vertical instrument to the left shows the range of c of g available at a given Mach number, indicated by the yellow bugs 'fwd' and 'aft'. The instantaneous weight of the aircraft and the fuel remaining is displayed as well. The fuel was being transferred reward (see selector) when this picture was taken

V_{ZRC} knots at 185 tonnes	3 engines operating	2 engines operating
Gear retracted	193 knots	262 knots
Gear extended	205 knots	>300 knots

There are 13 fuel tanks; numbers 9, 10, and 11 are used to trim the aircraft, numbers 1, 2, 3 and 4 are the feeder tanks for their respective engines. Tank 5 was ruptured during take-off from Paris

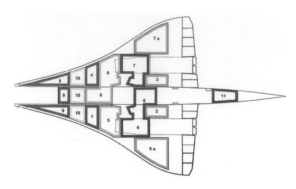

*subsequently proved to be just one.

The secondary nozzles set for noise reduction: they open for supersonic flight (see Appendix), then close for reverse thrust. The nozzle motor on the number 2 engine was changed on F-BTSC just before departure. After the accident, it was suspected of having caused the fire

of vortices over the wings. These give lift at the expense of increasing induced drag (drag due to lift). The slender delta wing, at even higher angles of attack (over 16°), does not stall conventionally but exhibits another phenomenon – it can generate more drag than there is thrust available. When thrust and drag are equal, the aircraft flies level, in other words it has a zero rate of climb. With maximum available thrust, the speed at which this occurs is known as V_{ZRC} – the zero rate of climb speed.

Following an engine failure at V_1 the subsequent climb profile is fixed using a compromise between climbing to clear immediate obstacles (using extra or 'contingency' thrust) and accelerating the aircraft to a speed well in excess of V_{ZRC}. Inability to accelerate was a major factor in the Gonesse accident. The following table gives the figures for V_{ZRC} at a weight of 185 tonnes:

Concorde crews are very conscious of this phenomenon.

For optimum climb performance on three engines, Concorde must be flown with zero sideslip, in other words straight into the oncoming airflow. There is a sideslip indicator beneath the compass (horizontal situa-

tion indicator). If a left-hand engine fails, the aircraft points to the left and, without rudder input, slips (or crabs) to the right. Application of right rudder stops the slip, but due to asymmetric thrust there is a small residual turn to the left. This is arrested by applying about $2\frac{1}{2}°$ of right bank

The centre of gravity for take-off is usually at 53.5% along the wing root chord. 1% is roughly 30 centimetres. The position of the 'zero fuel centre of gravity' is entered on the computer on the Flight Engineer's panel. This figure is derived from the disposition of the payload, pantry (meals) and crew. The computer now sums the fuel from the 13 tanks (numbered 1 to 11 – there is a 5A and a 7A) and produces the actual centre of gravity. Most often this is at variance with the 53.5% required. If it is forward of 53.5% then fuel is transferred to the rear tank 11; to the rear of 53.5% then fuel must be transferred forward. In this condition all the forward tanks are full so there is space to complete the transfer only after the engines have used some fuel during taxi. Therefore a pre-calculated amount of fuel has to be burnt off. Should the centre of gravity be in excess of 54% on engine start-up, it is allowable to use 54% for take-off. As has been alluded to already in this book, a rearward centre of gravity gives 'flap' effect at the expense of making the aircraft less stable. Stability with full tanks (apart from 11) is not compromised. The flap effect is put to use since it improves a performance limited take-off weight by about a tonne.

On the morning of 25 July 2000, the number 2 engine of F-BTSC had an unserviceable thrust reverser unit. Although Concorde is allowed to depart, once the unit has been safely locked, it incurs a performance penalty, which reduces the range. The Captain requested that the unit be changed in spite of the delay. It all became part of the intense media speculation over what caused the ensuing tragedy.

The following day, British Airways resumed its Concorde flights. Even tiny events of no consequence became the focus of enormous press interest. Because the cabin crew detected a faint smell of kerosene in the galley, one New York-bound Concorde diverted to Gander in Newfoundland. It was a false alarm.

Questions were already being asked. Had the recently reported hairline cracks in the wing caused the disaster? Did the last-minute change of the thrust reverser cause an engine to catch fire? Study of the photo-

graphs taken of F-BTSC on departure revealed a burning wing. How had a fuel tank been penetrated? The subsequent investigation was to produce four reports and take 18 months to complete.

On 27 July the Bureau Enquêtes Accidents (BEA) issued the first of 14 bulletins or *Comuniqués de presse*.

Paraphrased and translated from French it stated:

Shortly after V₁, the 'Tower' (Control Tower) reported seeing flames coming from the rear of the aircraft. Engine no. 2 appears to have lost thrust (noted by the crew) followed later by no. 1. The undercarriage would not retract. Speed and altitude remained constant and the flight lasted for about a minute. After banking sharply to the left, the aircraft crashed. The remains of tyres were found on the runway, debris was found along the flight path and in a small area at the crash site. A Preliminary Report would follow at the end of August.

The bulletin made two further points. The first mentioned that British, German and American investigators would be included under the auspices of the BEA. The British equivalent to the BEA is the Air Accident Investigation Branch (AAIB).

The second point acknowledged the role of the French judiciary, whose task is to take

Left *The piece of tank 5 sealed in a polythene bag which prevented the investigators getting sufficient access*

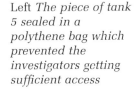

Below left *The metallic strip which fell from the DC10 shortly before F-BTSC's departure. The shape of the strip prevented it from being flattened by the tyre. Instead it was 'locked' at right angles to the tread and cut the tyre from shoulder to shoulder*

Above centre *The cut in the tyre corresponded to the shape of the metallic strip. Half the circumference of the tyre became detached and hit the tank above*

Above *The portion of tank 5 found on the runway after the accident showed no signs of having been impacted. It measured 30 cm x 30 cm which allowed an initial leak rate of 100 litres per second.*

Left *The interior of tank 5; the black ribbing on the left shows the bottom of the tank. The red mat is for the maintenance engineer*

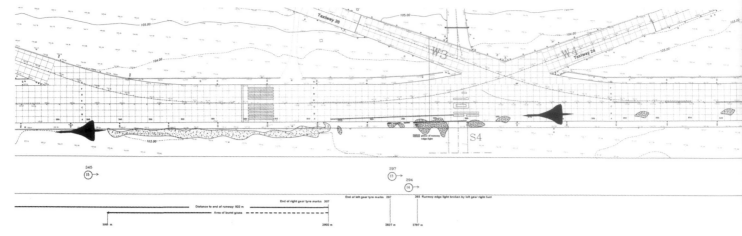

Various labels on the plan: Taxiway 20, 105.00, W3, 104.00, 105.00, W4, Taxiway 24, 105.00, 103.00, 104.00, S4, place of runway edge light

345 ⑮→   297 ⑬→ 294 ⑭→

Distance to end of runway: 922 m   End of right gear tyre marks 307   End of left gear tyre marks 297   263 Runway edge light broken by left gear right fuel

Area of burnt grass

1585 m   2802 m   2827 m   2797 m

action should the law have been broken. In France any evidence is 'owned' by the judiciary which can take advice from the investigators. In the UK the evidence is 'owned' by the investigators who work in parallel with the Coroner or Board of Inquiry. The investigator's remit is not to apportion praise or blame. By preventing early analysis of some parts of the wreck, the AAIB felt that the French judiciary had impeded the investigation. This represented a contravention of ICAO Annex 13 to which France is a signatory.

On 28 July the second bulletin appeared. Paraphrased it stated that:

… debris found on runway 26R came from the Concorde's left hand side including remains of two* (of the four) tyres from the left gear leg. No engine debris was found and evidence suggested that the fire was external to the engines.

On 30 July the third BEA bulletin released more details, including that of the discovery of a portion of fuel tank on the runway. The judicial authority retained this piece. The polythene bag in which they had sealed it became opaque from being handled. Things like this, said the AAIB, had delayed the investigation.

A tyre burst causing a fuel leak, which was somehow ignited, now appeared as the most likely explanation for the accident.

The fourth BEA bulletin, on 1 August, defined the seven areas of investigation for the Commission of Enquiry (presided over by M Alain Monnier):

- site and wreckage
- aircraft, systems and engines
- preparation and conduct of the flight, personnel information
- flight recorders

- aircraft performance
- witness testimony
- examination of previous events.

From the fifth bulletin on 4 August came the announcement that a metal strip about 40 centimeters long, not belonging to the Concorde, had been found among the debris on the runway.

Was this the cause of the tragedy? How did such an object come to be on the runway in the first place?

The answer to the first question appeared to be 'more than likely'. The second question was not answered immediately, but started a debate about runway inspections. The requirement was three times daily. Then it transpired that, due to a fire practice on 26R (runway used by F-BTSC) and 26L, the second inspection had been delayed.

On 16 August the eighth bulletin announced that Concorde's Certificate of Airworthiness had been suspended:

… Le BEA et son homologue britannique, l'Air Accidents Investigation Branch, ont émis une recommandation de sécurité visant à la suspension des certificats de navigabilité des Concorde…

On the grounds that such an event might easily happen again:

…le BEA a déterminé que c'est la destruction d'un pneu - événement simple dont on ne peut affirmer qu'il ne puisse se reproduire …

The previous day British Airways had been warned by the CAA of the imminent suspension of the Certificate of Airworthiness. For everyone involved with Concorde, having operated it safely for nearly 25 years, this was a bitter blow. A

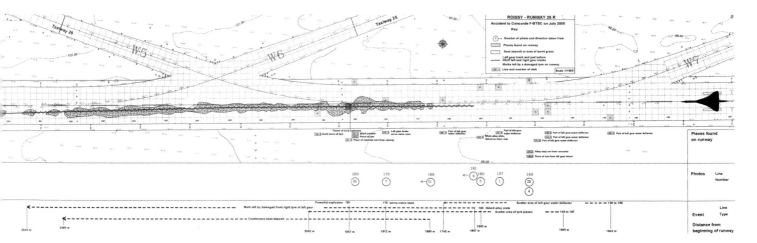

New York-bound BA Concorde flight had just commenced taxiing for take-off at Heathrow when it was recalled to the stand. John Tye, the First Officer, remembers acknowledging the instruction to return and the gloom that ensued at what seemed to be Concorde's finale.

There had been occasions involving tyre deflations, but following the incident described below, these had been satisfactorily addressed. By 1993, following further modifications, tyre incidents were practically eliminated.

What had been the most notable tyre burst happened to AF Concorde F-BVFC on 14 June 1979 at Washington Dulles. The cause was not established. During taxiing before take-off, a main wheel tyre deflated probably due to faulty 'fusible plugs'. These are fitted to prevent an overheated tyre from exploding. The neighbouring tyre on the same axle now bore twice its normal load for the whole of the take-off run (there are two axles and four wheels on each of Concorde's two main legs). According to TSS the overloaded tyre should have coped. In this case V_R (rotate) speed would have been about 190 knots. On take-off, the slender delta wing does not give lift until there is a distinct angle of attack. On take-off the conventional swept wing starts to give lift as soon as the speed builds. It is possible to notice this phenomenon since the wings increasingly curve upwards as they start to generate lift prior to rotation. With Concorde at V_R, the wheels are momentarily forced into the ground so bear a force somewhat greater than the weight of the aircraft. This resulted in the extra-loaded tyre bursting. Debris from the wheel rim penetrated the tanks, damaged some hydraulic piping and caused a fuel leak of 6 litres per second (one tenth of the average rate of the Gonesse accident). No fire followed. (At full thrust

and with reheat an Olympus engine uses over 7 litres per second).

To prevent an incident similar to that at Washington, Concorde was fitted with stronger tyres and wheels, improved protection for the hydraulic pipes and a tyre deflation detector. The detector works by sensing the twist in the undercarriage bogie beam. Should a tyre deflate in the speed range of 10 to 135 knots, this failure is signalled to the crew and the take-off stopped. This system avoids exposing the neighbour of a deflated tyre to the major part of the take-off run.

When the Certificate of Airworthiness was suspended, Claude Freeman (BA Engineering Manager, Concorde) described his feelings in a television documentary: 'It was only a piece of paper ...but it did represent Concorde's right to fly.' Was suspension inevitable? If a similar incident occurred to the world's most common airliner, the Boeing 737, instead of to the world's least, would the B737 have been grounded?

Concorde had been flying for almost 25 years; however, the 84,000 flight cycles achieved equalled those flown by the Boeing 737 in a matter of weeks. Even if it were considered statistically impossible to repeat the crash circumstances, the authorities had little option than to call for the suspension of the Certificate of Airworthiness until appropriate modifications had been carried out.

Some argued that the lower wing skin was too thin to withstand impact and that the expense of strengthening it would be prohibitive. Now, they suggested, would be a good time to retire Concorde. Others pointed out that self-sealing tanks had been used in the Second World War. Nobody doubted that a remedy was possible, but would it be cost-effective?

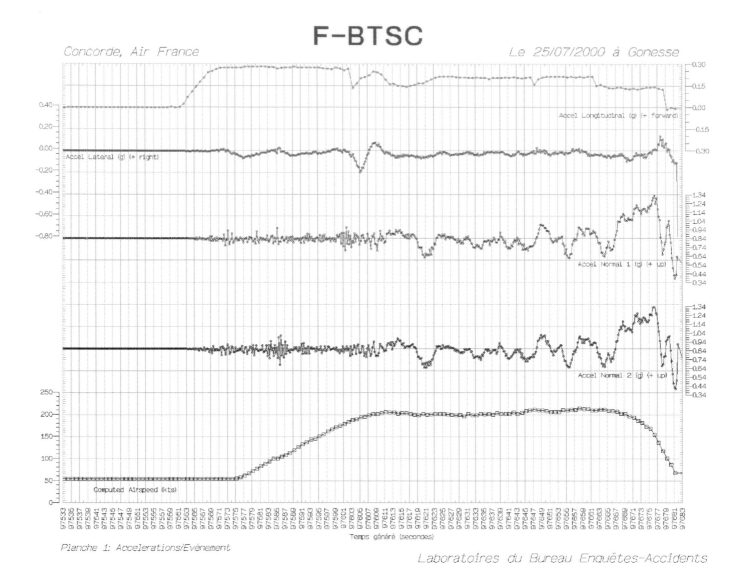

F-BTSC

Concorde, Air France

Le 25/07/2000 à Gonesse

Accel Longitudinal (g) (+ forward)

Accel Lateral (g) (+ right)

Accel Normal 1 (g) (+ up)

Accel Normal 2 (g) (+ up)

Computed Airspeed (kts)

Temps généré (secondes)

Planche 1: Accelerations/Evénement

Laboratoires du Bureau Enquêtes-Accidents

The blue line traces the acceleration along the runway. At 97602 seconds the acceleration drops due to a loss of thrust when the left engines surged. The green line shows lateral acceleration which peaks at 0.22 g to the left at 97605 seconds, caused by the loss of thrust from the left engines

At first Air France did not appear as eager as British Airways to return Concorde to service. Soon after the grounding, Jean-Claude Gayssot, the French Transport Minister, said this was not the end of supersonic flight. Even before the crash France had set up a commission to study an environmentally acceptable successor to Concorde. European or worldwide funding would be needed, he noted. Was this in preparation to announcing an end to Concorde with the connivance of Air France? The airline's attitude probably had more to do with its being in shock. Soon both sides of the Channel became equally dedicated to returning Concorde to service.

On 31 August the preliminary report was published. Its summary said:

During take-off from runway 26 right at Roissy Charles de Gaulle Airport, shortly before rotation, the front right tyre of the left landing gear was damaged and pieces of the

tyre were thrown against the aircraft structure. A major fire broke out under the left wing. Problems appeared shortly afterwards on engine No 2 and for a brief period on engine No 1. The aircraft was neither able to climb nor accelerate. The crew found that the landing gear would not retract. The aircraft maintained a speed of 200 knots and a radio altitude of 200 feet for about one minute. Engine N° 1 then stopped. The aircraft crashed on to a hotel at La Patte d'Oie in Gonesse.

The preliminary report revealed that extra baggage had been loaded but not properly accounted for; the 'ground' copy of the loadsheet could not be found. Only 800 kgs of the two tonnes of fuel loaded for the taxi had been used. The extra baggage and fuel made the aircraft at least one tonne over structural weight for take-off, although this resulted in a negligible difference to performance.

The almost intact central and right-hand flight deck panel reveals some of the last second readings. The nose and visor selector (to the right of the top row of four dials) is in the landing position

The centre of gravity on engine start was 54.2%, which after taxiing had moved forward to 54%. The report told how data from the recorders had been retrieved. Ten seconds before the start of the take-off run, the cockpit voice recorder (CVR) reveals that the tower informed the crew of a tail wind (easterly at 8 knots) and cleared AF4590 for take-off. If this were a steady wind, then due to the tyre speed limit, the aircraft's performance weight was too great by about 5 tonnes. The crew did not audibly discuss this. In reality the *average* wind was very light from the north-east. The report said:

At 14 h 44, the average wind at the threshold of runway 26 was 020°/3 kt and 300°/3kt at the threshold of runway 08. [the reciprocal runway]

All goes normally to V_1 – 33 seconds after start of take-off. Six seconds later, at 175 knots, there is a noise and a second later a change in background noise – the ignition of the fire and engine surge (akin to a backfire).

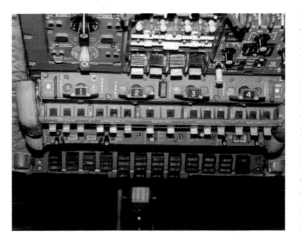

One second later, at 185 knots, the rotation is commenced.

The report shows pictures of the 43 cm x 3 cm strip of metal that cut the tyre from shoulder to shoulder, and the piece of damaged tyre itself, measuring 100 cm x 30 cm and weighing more than 4 kilograms. The profile of the cut corresponds to that of the metal strip. On visual inspection the metal appeared to be a light alloy. There is no mention of where it could have come from. The photograph of the 30 cm x 30 cm portion of fuel tank found on the runway shows that it suffered no impact damage but it was slightly bowed outwards. The mechanics of its ejection from the lower wing surface are not discussed.

There is a runway diagram showing where the debris was found, the tyre marks of the left-hand undercarriage and trail of soot from the fire. Both the strip and the tyre debris were found together on the north side of the runway. This puzzled Alan Simmons, an investigator from the AAIB. Had someone put them together?

Why the rotation was commenced some 10 knots below the calculated V_R has not been satisfactorily explained, even in the final report which was published in January 2002. Possibly to compensate, the rate of rotation was slow, about 1° per second. Immediately after rotation, there is evidence of an explosion when a piece of concrete (10 x 25 x 1 cm³) was detached from the runway probably where the two left engines surged simultaneously. The increasing angle of attack changes the airflow pattern under the wing. This caused the hot gases to be ingested into the engine via the auxiliary intake, behind the main intake in the floor

The engine shut-down handles are located on the overhead panel within reach of the Flight Engineer. A fire is indicated by a flashing red light in the respective handle and an audio warning. Pulling the handle shuts off the fuel and closes other functions associated with the engine. The two push buttons on either side of the handles are for operating the fire extinguishers

Concorde, Air France

Le 25/07/2000 à Gonesse

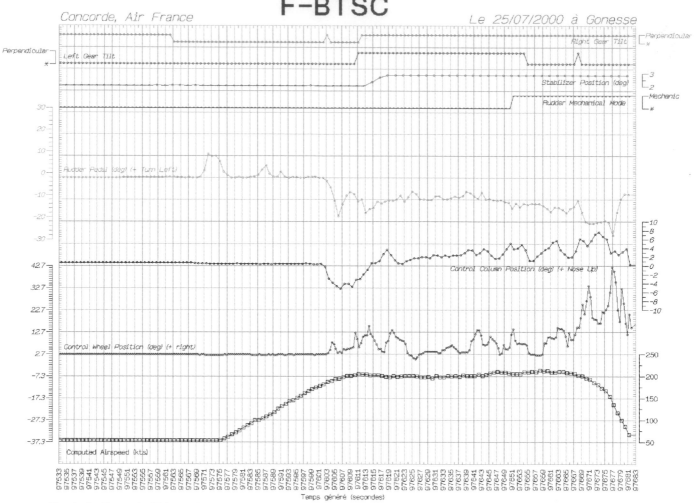

Planche 3 : Commandes/Evénement

Laboratoires du Bureau Enquêtes-Accidents

The yellow trace shows rudder position. At 97571, with the plane having wandered to the right, the pilot applies left rudder. The missing spacer from the left undercarriage therefore did not pull the plane to the left. At 97603, to counter the loss of thrust of the two left engines, right rudder is applied. Simultaneously rotation is commenced (blue trace: despite annotation positive on the chart = control column forward). The green trace shows roll input. To keep the wings level, right bank is increasingly applied

of the ducting to the engine (see appendix). The double surge gave the aircraft an impetus to the left, causing the left gear to strike a runway edge light before becoming airborne.

In conjunction with the physical evidence, the 'traces' of the flight are read and are shown in the report. Each 'trace' plots, with respect to time, a parameter: airspeed, pitch angle, engine thrust and other data. When the Black Box or Flight Data Recorder (FDR) reads 97602.5 seconds, which equates with 41 seconds from the start of take-off, there is a sudden decrease in acceleration. Fractionally later there is a strong lateral acceleration to the left (the double engine surge), which is countered with the application of right rudder. On rotation, the runway centre line becomes progressively obscured. Without visual cue the Captain maintains runway heading on his compass while the aircraft continues its drift to the left from the impetus caused by the surges. The final report says the lateral acceleration sensed

on the flight deck is less than that at the centre of gravity, which helps to explain the lack of track correction.

Within 3 seconds of the fire igniting and within 1 second of rotation, the control tower tells the crew there are flames behind them.

Two seconds later (45.5 seconds), at 195 knots, nosewheel off the ground and with less than 2,000 metres of runway remaining, from the cockpit voice recorder (CVR) the Flight Engineer possibly says 'stop' [the take-off]. Perhaps he thought there had been a double engine failure, because when he announces 'engine failure' there is a hesitation about which engine has failed. Then he announces 'shut down number 2 engine'. (The standard procedure would be for the Captain to ask the Engineer to shut down an engine once at a safe height. On this occasion, the situation probably appeared to require instant action).

One second later, the Captain asks for the Engine Fire Procedure. The fire warning for

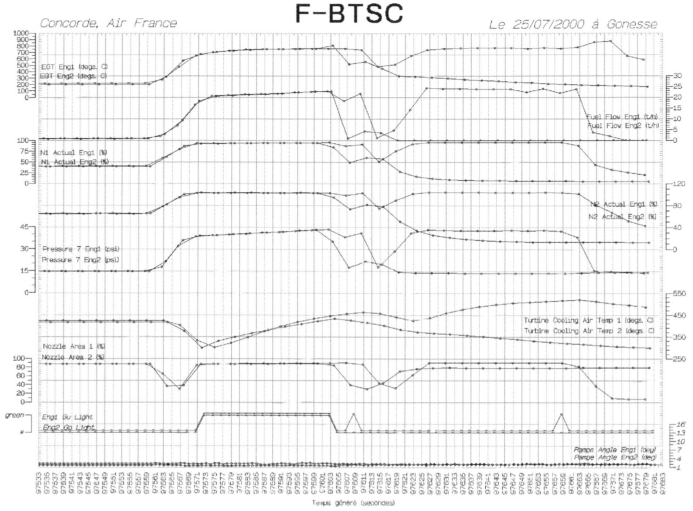

F-BTSC

EGT Eng1 (degs. C)
EGT Eng2 (degs. C)

Fuel Flow Eng1 (t/h)
Fuel Flow Eng2 (t/h)

N1 Actual Eng1 (%)
N1 Actual Eng2 (%)

N2 Actual Eng1 (%)
N2 Actual Eng2 (%)

Pressure 7 Eng1 (psi)
Pressure 7 Eng2 (psi)

Turbine Cooling Air Temp 1 (degs. C)
Turbine Cooling Air Temp 2 (degs. C)

Nozzle Area 1 (%)
Nozzle Area 2 (%)

green
x

Eng1 Go Light
Eng2 Go Light

Rampe Angle Eng1 (deg)
Rampe Angle Eng2 (deg)

Temps généré (secondes)

Planche 5 : Moteurs 1&2 / Evénement

Laboratoires du Bureau Enquêtes-Accidents

The thrust can be assessed from 'p7' readings. At 97600 (39 seconds from start of take-off) the 'p7' of engine 2 drops, indicating a loss of thrust when it surged. Two seconds later the 'p7' on engine 1 falters then recovers. Engine 2 starts to recover but is shut down. By 97662 engine 1 surges again before running down

The missing lower left wear strip from the thrust reverser of engine 3 of DC10 registered 'N 13067'. An Air France B747 took off between F-BTSC and the DC10

167

the number 2 engine sounds, supporting their diagnosis. In fact the heat of the fire outside the engine nacelle has set it off. Meanwhile, the number 1 engine recovers to give almost full thrust. The aircraft struggles up to 200ft above the ground. The speed barely reaches 210 knots, 5 knots above V_{ZRC} with three engines operating and gear down. If the number 2 engine had been operating they might have been able to accelerate despite fire damage but with no way of putting out the fire.

In the Northern Hemisphere the wind veers and increases with height. On this take-off, although the wind direction was momentarily due east, the surface wind was generally north-easterly and very light. So on climbing to the west, their airspeed was not augmented with an increasing headwind, if anything the reverse.

The selections made on the flight deck can be interpreted through analysis of the sound signature of the recorded 'clicks'. For instance, the pulling of the fire handle can be heard 58 seconds after start of take-off. This occurs just after an unknown source, presumably another aircraft, has told them the flames are large and do not seem to be coming from the engine.

The landing gear does not retract. This and the low airspeed (le badin) are of great concern to the crew. 'Le badin, le badin,'

Frank Debouk (former General Manager Concorde Air France) on the left with the late Captain Christian Marty and F-BTSC

calls the First Officer. A toilet smoke alarm sounds; smoke in the cabin? Air Traffic Control offers them 'an immediate return to the field'. This would involve a right turn for a landing to the east on the northernmost of the three runways at Charles de Gaulle (runway 09). The First Officer acknowledges. From 88 seconds after take-off the engine fire alarm sounds continuously and the terrain warning system urges them to 'pull up, pull up'. Then 100 seconds after the start of take-off, the number 1 engine, which had staged a recovery, surges and fails. The crew elects to try for Le Bourget, which by then is less than 2 kilometres ahead and slightly left.

At 205 knots with the gear down their speed is 100 knots below the two-engine V_{ZRC} for their weight. The aircraft can only decelerate. The rudder loses effectiveness, the aircraft banks to more than 90° to the left and pitches up – the loss of fuel has moved the centre of gravity aft. It turns almost through 180°. In an attempt to level the wings the crew probably throttled back the two right engines. With very little forward speed the aircraft impacts, breaks up and burns. The accident is unsurvivable.

A Japanese passenger took two photographs of the fire from a Boeing 747 waiting for F-BTSC to take off before crossing runway 26R. By coincidence President Jacques Chirac of France was on board. Could the 747 have triggered the early rotation? It was too far away to be a factor, on the last of a group of three taxiways.

Once on fire what else could the crew have done? The final report says that if the crew had tried to stop at the first indication of a problem at 183 knots or when the engineer may have said 'stop' at 196 knots, they would have overrun the runway at 75 knots or 115 knots respectively. Maximum braking on seven wheels and reverse thrust on three engines was used in the calculations. Neither course would have improved their chances of survival. The crew could do nothing more than they did; circumstances, through a set of cruel coincidences, had blocked all avenues of escape.

The report gives a résumé of the members of the crew, their qualifications and licences held. Christian Marty, at 54, had been a Concorde Captain for two years. Previously he had flown the Airbus A340 and before that a variety of mainly shorthaul airliners. He had an adventurous streak. In 1982 he had crossed the Atlantic on a windsurfer.

He had refused to sleep on his support boat, preferring to be strapped to his board; therefore he could truly say that he had spent the entire crossing on a windsurfer. On another occasion he flew over a volcano in a hang-glider.

Jean Marcot, 50, had been a First Officer on Concorde since 1989. Rather than bid for a command on another type of aircraft, he had elected to remain in the right-hand seat of Concorde. In theory his licence medical had expired eight days before. This oversight was more administrative than careless. The regulations had recently changed. Previously a medical certificate had remained valid to the last day of whichever month it was due to expire. In July 2000 it was only valid six months from the date of the last medical. In November 2000 the rules reverted. He was flight simulator instructor for the Air France Concorde fleet.

Gilles Jardinaud, 58, the Flight Engineer, had had just over three years on Concorde.

The preliminary report confirmed the decision to keep Concorde grounded, with this final paragraph:

The Certificates of Airworthiness of Concorde be suspended until appropriate measures have been taken to ensure a satisfactory level of safety as far as the tyre destruction based risk is concerned.

On 4 September 2000, the 10th bulletin announced that the metal strip that had caused the tyre burst had fallen from the thrust reverser mechanism of a Continental Airlines DC10. This flight had left for Newark in the United States some minutes before the ill-fated Concorde. The author of the bulletin was at pains to emphasise that Continental had co-operated fully with the investigators.

Several major questions remained unanswered. How was the fuel leak caused? What was the source of the ignition? Why did the landing gear not retract?

When the wheels are down, the gear doors are closed. After take-off, the gear doors are opened before retraction. Failure of the left door to open may have prevented the undercarriage retracting

Concorde's Return to Service

Concordes 'resting' at Heathrow. Without hydraulic pressure the two rudder surfaces are not aligned. Each surface is, on its own, capable of applying sufficient force in the event of an engine failure (Mark Wagner)

The pessimists declared that Concorde was a victim of its slender delta design. To meet all the aerodynamic criteria, the wheels, they said, had been placed too close to the engine intakes. Even if the tyres were stronger, they would only shed heavier pieces of rubber on bursting. To the optimist, historical precedence gave more hope. The will had been there to remedy the fault in Comet 1 for it to return as the Comet 4. A similar spirit had been shown in the case of the Space Shuttle returning to service following the Challenger disaster.

Meanwhile, British Airways was counting the cost of keeping its flagship inactive; a year's grounding would be sustainable, two probably not. The airline has always maintained that Concorde is profitable, and an indication of this came with the board's decision to take advantage of Concorde's down-time to start a £14m cabin refurbishment. But without a Certificate of Airworthiness, Concorde was going nowhere, even if Sir Terence Conran was about to refurbish the cabin.

In early November 2000 a meeting was arranged at Gatwick to discuss the options for Concorde's future. Considering the meeting too crowded for useful discussion, Jim O'Sullivan (BA Technical and Quality Director) took five key people to a quieter room. Together Captain Mike Bannister (BA Chief Concorde Pilot), John Britton (Airbus UK, Chief Concorde Engineer), Alain Marty (Airbus France Chief Concorde Engineer), Hervé Page (Air France Concorde Engineering Manager) and Roger Holliday (Chief Airworthiness Engineer Airbus UK) came up with a plan of action which O'Sullivan outlined on a flip chart.

In essence it sought to:
• reduce fire risk by looking for leak and ignition sources
• study the behaviour of engines 1 and 2 and how hot gasses cause engine surges
• validate performance
• check the hydraulics and the reason for non-retraction of the undercarriage.

In a lecture to the Royal Aeronautical Society (RAeS) at Farnborough in February 2002, John Britton spoke about the chain of events that led to the accident at Gonesse.

Starting with an incident that causes a tyre to break up, subsequent events can be traced through the chain depending on their seriousness. Thus tyre debris might cause 'structural expulsion' which would lead to either a major or minor fuel leak. If it is a major fuel leak and there is an ignition source, then this will lead to a 'catastrophe' after take-off. If there was either a minor fuel leak or no ignition source, then there would be no catastrophe. (Ideally, of course, there should be no tyre debris in the first place.)

According to the statisticians, the probability of a tyre burst causing a catastrophe was less than once in 10 million flying hours. In 25 years the Concorde fleets accrued a total of 235,000 flying hours; at this rate a hull loss, resulting from a tyre burst, would occur once in over 1,000 years. The likelihood of a repeat of the Gonesse circumstances was minuscule. Was this the one event in 1,000 years that had merely happened early? That was a risk that the authorities would not take. There had already been too many incidents with tyres. Until the problem had been solved, Concorde would be grounded. British Airways and Air France set August 2001 as a target date.

The final report into the accident was released in January 2002. It describes some of the research that led to the remedy.

When the tank burst, the fuel was forced vertically downwards, initially at 100 litres per second before it stabilised at an average of 60 litres per second. A fuel stain on the runway before the soot deposits is evidence of this.

Showing no sign of having been impacted, the portion of tank 5 found on the

Sir Terence Conran included the BA speed motif in the armrest of the new seats

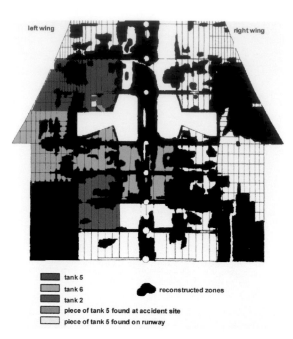

tank 5
tank 6
tank 2
piece of tank 5 found at accident site
piece of tank 5 found on runway

reconstructed zones

Computer reconstruction of lower wing surface, showing where pieces of tank 5 were found on the runway and at the crash site. The fire after impact was so intense that little remained of the structure

Painstaking work was undertaken to reconstruct the aircraft. With the nose to the right of the photograph, the upper half shows the left main gear bay, and the lower the right bay

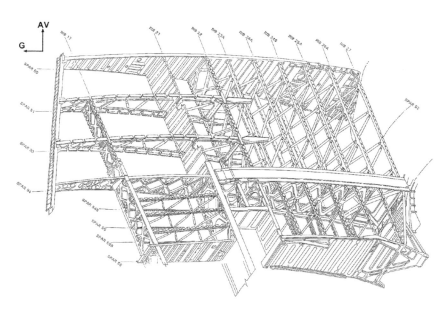

Left main landing gear strut

Piece of tank 5 found on runway

Tank 5

Piece of tank 5 found at accident site

Aircraft longitudinal axis

Right main landing gear doors

runway must have been forced *out* of the tank. If so, it showed an entirely new phenomenon. Had the 4½-kilogram tyre segment caused an hydraulic shock to over-pressurise the tank? Possibly, but the fuel tanks of military aircraft penetrated by high-speed shrapnel had burst in a similar way.

Intense research followed. A computer model was assembled to simulate the mechanics of the incident. AU2GN, Concorde's aluminium alloy, is no longer produced but when some had been tracked down, a full-scale model of tank 5 was built. Centre d'Essais Aéronautique in Toulouse (CEAT) built a gun which could fire 4½-kilogram lumps of tyre against the mock-up at 106 metres per second.

On 25 July 2000, a perfectly acceptable procedure had been followed to 'overfill' tank 5 to increase fuel quantity. As the aircraft accelerated, the fuel in tank 5 was forced to the rear, displacing any air towards the front. This effectively meant the tank was full in the vicinity of the external impact point, making it more susceptible to hydrodynamic shock. On the test rig, the impact causes the tank to be deformed inwards (direct mode), then outwards in an adjacent area in compensation (indirect mode). The rig did not burst but proved the principle.

The computer model, after being hit, shows a wave propagating along the lower tank surface. The skin then ruptures. Whatever the cause of the massive leak, a self-sealing device was required.

Kevlar is the name Dupont gave to the aramid rubber mix they had already developed. It is a light, black, flexible and very tough material suitable for bullet-proof vests. Any tank that might be exposed to

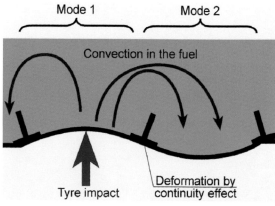

Mode 1   Mode 2

Convection in the fuel

Tyre impact

Deformation by continuity effect

Left Plan of tank 5 in the left wing. Forward is to the top of the picture

Above Plan showing the effect of a piece of rubber hitting the lower surface of a full tank

impact from an exploding tyre would be lined with Kevlar moulded to the interior contours. The Kevlar liner is suspended less than a centimetre above the tank floor, and each cell of the liner has a 4 millimetre hole in it. As the outer skin of the aircraft is warmed during cruise at Mach 2, these holes allow convection of the warmed fuel away from the tank floor.

As the liners were being fitted, it was discovered that the tanks on each Concorde were slightly different in size. The liners had

Above Jim O'Sullivan shows Captain Mike Bannister a piece of moulded Kevlar

Left Dennis Morris demonstrates a length of Concorde's Kevlar lining

Left Every Kevlar section was specifically moulded for each individual Concorde

Above *Mark Morley, BA engineer, fitting a piece of 'tailor-made' Kevlar in the cramped confines of a fuel tank*

Right *View of left undercarriage bay (gear down). The 'Gonesse' leak in tank 5 appeared just forward of the bay*

to be made to fit each individual aircraft – 'bespoke tailoring' as one engineer quipped. It was realised that there would be a weight penalty attached to the liners as well as to some 'unusable fuel'. This is the fuel that remains beyond the reach of the pumps, ie below the liner. The average rate of leak at Gonesse was 60 litres per second. The Kevlar liner would reduce such a leak to about half a litre per second. Only the most vulnerable tanks were to be lined.

The fuel leak patterns were studied when Concorde F-BVFB was flown to Istres near Marseille for ground testing. Accelerating on the runway to 175 knots, a leak (of an inert fluid) was simulated from an identical point to that in the Gonesse tragedy. Two other possible leak points were also assessed. Finding where the fuel went could reveal an ignition point and a flame stabilisation area – thought to be in the turbulent wake behind the undercarriage leg.

There were three likely sources of ignition – the reheat, an engine surge or an electric spark in the landing gear bay. The bay in question is just inboard of the engine nacelle and to the rear of the hole that had appeared in tank 5. From the distance between the fuel stain and the soot deposit on the runway, it was determined that ignition had occurred in less than a second after the tank was ruptured. All three ignition possibilities were tested at British Aerospace's Warton factory near Blackpool.

A full-size mock-up of the left under-wing section, the side of the engine nacelle, and extended gear leg were built and set up on a concrete platform. The airflow for the flame tunnel came from the exhaust of Warton's high-speed tunnel. The flow required was 106 metres per second (206 knots).

Fuel was released from the 'Gonesse hole'. Streaming over the open undercarriage bay to the rear of the wing, the fuel was lit by gas burners simulating the reheat. The fuel ignited, but the flames were unable to advance up the fuel stream traveling at 106 metres per second. The advance rate was less than 10 metres per second. This ruled out reheat as a likely source of the ignition. The French believed that the fire might have advanced in the slower moving air of the boundary layer (1 millimetre thick) or through the various engine ducts. Neither theory proved likely.

To test whether the fuel leak was ignited by an engine surge, a 70-millisecond explosion was detonated and projected forward from the intake. A surge from the auxiliary

intake of number 2 engine did ignite a fire that moved forward to the undercarriage bay. This cause was ruled out since the surge occurred after the fire had started; engines 1 and 2 then surged again, probably due to the aircraft's rotation changing the angle of attack. This change of airflow allowed hot gas to be ingested by the engine through the auxiliary intake.

A spark was generated in the undercarriage bay at the point where the brake cooling fan cable ran. On this occasion, a fire started in less than a second. It became stabilised in the eddies in the wake of the undercarriage leg and side stay. The flame pattern closely resembled the photograph of Concorde on fire, much to the distress of some observers.

Before the crash the crew had tried several times to retract the undercarriage. The final report, published in January 2002, suggests that the door of the left wheel bay had failed to open. This has to happen for the undercarriage raising sequence to begin. The door could have been damaged by the fire or debris, but unfortunately after the impact the evidence was destroyed. The hydraulic power for operating the undercarriage is from the 'green' system. Engines 1 and 2 generate this system's pressure. No evidence exists to suggest that 'green' failed, until engine 1 ran down.

Left *A full-scale mock-up of the left undercarriage bay was constructed at Warton to investigate possible ignition sources. Here the cable to the brake cooling fans is being checked as such a source*

Above *This shows how the resulting flames stabilised themselves in the turbulent wake downstream of the gear leg and side stays*

Left *Not only is the power to the cooling fans isolated during take-off, but the cable has been protected with a woven steel mesh. Seen here along the top of the bay*

Inability to open the left main gear door (closed when the wheels are down) was considered the most likely reason for the non retraction of the undercarriage. Non alignment of the bogie beam could have been another cause. Note the position of the auxiliary intakes,the dark oblongs to the rear of the main intakes, They open to augment airflow at low airspeed and high thrust (Mark Wagner)

If the undercarriage could have been retracted the fire might have put itself out. But survival would have depended on how much damage had been done to the fuselage – which may have already been breached – and whether the number 1 engine could have been kept going.

A jet engine surge is a momentary reversal of flow through the engine, not dissimilar to a backfire on a car. The phenomenon is measured in milliseconds, and sometimes a flame can be seen in the engine intake. A surge can be caused by the engine demanding a greater airflow than is being supplied, and vice versa. Internal damage and foreign object ingestion are other causes of surge. The investigators wanted to study engine surges caused by the ingestion of neat fuel or of hot gasses.

Accordingly, at Shoeburyness near the Thames estuary, an Olympus engine was mounted on a rig (which had lain idle for 25 years) fitted with a simple air intake. The tests proved that the engine performed as per the evidence from the Gonesse tragedy. Following a rupture in a lined tank, there is an emission of an initial 'slug' of fuel. This was represented by accelerating the flow to half a litre per second, at 30 litres per second per second. The engine surged but recovered and coped well with the steady leak rate.

In January 2001, the first of two interim reports said that a 'spacer' had been found to be missing from the left gear of F-BTSC. An 'AO1' check had been carried out eight days before the accident, during which the left gear leg had been replaced. The spacer from

the removed gear leg should have been fitted to the replacement unit. It keeps two bushes in place. Without their proper positioning, the whole gear 'truck' might wobble or shimmy, causing drag, thereby heating and damaging the tyres and impeding acceleration. Immediately questions were raised, particularly during a television documentary. Had the acceleration been sufficient? Had the aircraft been dragged to the left? More seriously, had the number 2 tyre already become overheated and damaged, so that on encountering the metal strip it burst even more violently than could have been predicted?

On 10 April the BEA addressed these points in its 12th bulletin:

- The brake temperatures were symmetrically warm during taxi
- F-BTSC did not require right rudder to keep on the runway centre line before the tyre burst. In fact, a little left rudder was applied (due to a north-easterly breeze)
- The left gear did not leave rubber marks on the runway before the tyre burst, but tyre marks do appear on the concrete after it happened
- The achieved acceleration of 0.268 g was normal.

From this study the BEA concluded that the lack of spacer, though a bad oversight, did not contribute to the accident.

Early in 2001, the team working on Concorde's return to service were told that Michelin was putting the finishing touches to a tyre that promised to meet the most stringent requirements. The new tyre was almost impossible to burst, but should it do so the debris would be small enough not to be a threat to the fuel tanks above. It was called the Near Zero Growth (NZG) tyre, and was a development of the company's radial ply tyre.

Michelin had been making radial ply tyres for road vehicles since 1946. In 1981 the Mirage III became the first aircraft to be fitted with radial tyres. The NZG tyre is an evolution of the radial tyre, and the tyre for Concorde is reinforced with Kevlar. Its advantage is that it does not expand significantly with inflation and centrifugal force. The outer surface of the tread is not under tension. This makes it less vulnerable to foreign object damage – it is easier to cut an elastic band when it is being stretched than when it isn't. Furthermore, the tyre is lighter than a reinforced cross-ply tyre. To prove these claims the new tyre was extensively tested.

Before trials on the actual aircraft, laboratory tests were carried out in the Michelin test centre and at the Centre d'Essais Aéronautique (CEAT) in Toulouse. Tyres were subjected to extreme conditions laid down by the aircraft manufacturer.

There was an important point to establish – could the tyre run over a similar strip of metal and continue to perform normally? Two tests were devised, one a low-speed test and the other high-speed. The NZG tyre performed better than expected throughout.

Once, when the original cross-ply tyre was tested on a dynamometer, it burst and damaged the test equipment so badly that it took a week to rebuild. In contrast, the NZG tyre survived cut but inflated. In the end, only the Michelin NZG met the requirements of the damage resistance specification.

This was almost too good to be true. In case it was, British Airways kept up the momentum on fitting the tank liners and reinforcing the electrical power cable in the undercarriage bays. The tyre, the company said, could be seen as a bonus. Once the tyre had fulfilled its promise, it became an airworthiness requirement.

In May 2001 the tyre was tested on an Air France Concorde at Istres. The regulations governing the anti-skid braking system had to be altered slightly to accommodate the characteristics of the new tyre. Luckily there was a heavy rainstorm while Concorde was at Istres, so on one of the three days of wet-surface performance tests the runway did not have to be artificially flooded.

Several modifications and stipulations were stipulated:

- Tanks 1, 4, 6 and 7 were partially lined, 5 and 8 fully.
- The cabling in the gear bay to the brake cooling fans was reinforced.
- There would be a change in crew procedures to cut the power to the brake fans during take-off and landing.
- Michelin NZG tyres would be fitted.
- The anti-skid braking protocol would be modified to give the aircraft identical performance to that with the old tyres.
- There would be a redesigned water deflector for the NZG tyre profile, without reinforcing steel wire.
- The tyre deflation detector would have to be serviceable for every take-off, ie it would no longer be acceptable to fix it later.

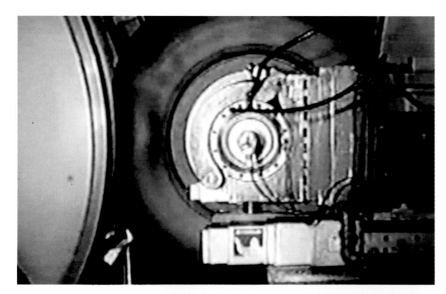

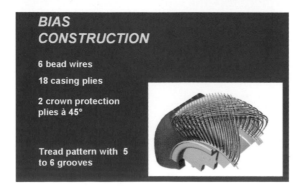

BIAS CONSTRUCTION

6 bead wires

18 casing plies

2 crown protection plies à 45°

Tread pattern with 5 to 6 grooves

NZG RADIAL CONSTRUCTION

2 bead wires

4 casing plies

7 crown plies

1 crown protection ply

Tread pattern with 4 grooves

Top *The new tyres
and water deflectors
were tested at Istres in
a similar manner to
this*

Above *Michelin
should be justifiably
proud of this superb
tyre*

Right *The Michelin
NZG Kevlar reinforced
tyre fitted to Concorde.
Since the profile of the
new tyre is different
from the 'bias' tyre, a
redesigned water
deflector had to be
fitted. This one is not
reinforced with a steel
cable*

On 17 July 2001 a BA Concorde under the command of Captain Mike Bannister, accompanied by Jock Reid, CAA Chief Test Pilot, prepared to take off at Heathrow for a test flight over the Atlantic. Members of the world's press were perched on a scaffold near the runway, reminiscent of Concorde's first commercial service 25½ years before. An ordinary subsonic aircraft took off. Then it was Concorde's turn, but there was a delay. Had some irritating gremlin lit a warning light? The reason soon became clear – the runway was being inspected for foreign objects. After the yellow inspection truck had left the runway, a distinctive roar could be heard coming from the threshold of 09R. Then that familiar shape was in the sky, reheats burning, undercarriage retracting, right turn commencing and the press applauding.

There were three main reasons for the flight. The first was to measure the unusable fuel remaining, held between the Kevlar and the lower skin. Second, it was to find out whether the liners had affected the tempera-

ture of the lower wing surface, normally kept evenly warm by fuel convection. Third, it was to monitor all the systems to see whether anything had suffered during the year's grounding. The plan was to fly on the normal Atlantic track, then at 20°W turn north towards Iceland. Here, at about 55,000 ft, they would find the relatively warm air (-50°C and warmer). The more northerly the latitude, at high altitude, the warmer is the atmosphere. At such temperatures the 'stagnation' temperature limits Concorde's maximum speed, no more than 127°C on the nose. Using the readings from thermocouples fitted in the fuel tanks, the engineers would assess whether the circulation had been jeopardised.

Concorde G-BOAF landed 3½ hours later at RAF Brize Norton in Oxfordshire. The world's press was there, and the low cloud, heavy rain and cold (for July) could not dampen the spirits. 'Concorde is back where she belongs, Mach 2 and 60,000 ft,' announced a smiling Bannister. The flight had proved everything that it had set out to. On 6 September 2001 the Certificate of Airworthiness was reinstated.

Then came the 'dress rehearsals', with Concorde G-BOAF carrying 100 BA staff on a trip out to the mid Atlantic and back, partly by way of reward for their work. The flight was an overwhelming success. In a matter of weeks, once three aircraft had been modified, services to New York would recommence. The date was 11 September, and while the BA team were disembarking, news came through about the destruction of the World Trade Center and attack on the Pentagon. Would anybody want to fly now?

On 20 September, Brian Trubshaw's memorial service was held at St Clement Dane's Church in the Strand, London. The previous March he had died peacefully at his home in Gloucestershire. Jock Lowe, former Director Flight Crew BA and retired Concorde Captain, praised Trubshaw's life in test flying, and his contribution to Concorde. Trubshaw had been in regular contact with Mike Bannister, giving enormous encouragement to the Concorde relaunch effort. Sadly he died before Concorde had once again taken to the skies.

On 7 November, Lord Marshall, the Chairman of British Airways, his Chief Executive Rod Eddington, and BA guests, boarded G-BOAF for the first trip to New York since 15 August 2000. Valerie Grove of The Times was among the guests. She reported that Tony Benn was there to see them off. Benn told how he had fought for Concorde when the Treasury wanted to cancel it. He had also been on the test flight in 1970 equipped with a parachute. Then, with customary mischievousness, he told what he had said about the final 'e' of Concorde.

'E is for entente cordiale, 'E' is for England.'

'But parts of it are made in Scotland,' had come the reply.

'Well 'E' is for Ecosse,' said Benn.

Concorde's modifications may have cost £17m, but the aircraft's return was due to the dedication and enthusiasm of the engineers,

the pilots and the management of the two airlines. Would any other fleet of 12 aircraft with 25 years of service behind them have engendered such loyalty? With the exception of the Spitfire, it is difficult to think of another aircraft that has excited the imagination so much.

Post-September 11, New Yorkers wanted to get back to normal as quickly as possible. On 7 November 2001, Mayor Rudolph Guiliani came to JFK airport to congratulate those whose hard work had restored Concorde to service. In so doing he praised the two airlines as Valerie Grove's reported in *The Times*:

Sir David Frost, Concorde's most frequent traveller, sat at the back of the aircraft, having fallen into a light, refreshing doze. He woke in time to meet the outgoing Mayor of New York, Rudolph Guiliani, who boarded Concorde to welcome us all 'to New York City, the capital of the world', adding:

'Do me a favour. Spend a lot of money.'

He was addressing the right audience, as the flight was packed with captains of industry, chaps from Schroders and Allied Domecq and RM Rothschild. Dr Neville Bain, of Hogg Robinson, chairman of Consignia, professed himself thrilled to be back on Concorde, which gets him to New York for a late breakfast meeting and back home to London the same night. 'I'm no use at video conferencing, it's not the same,' he said. 'I need to eyeball people, and touch them on the elbow.' Also, you do not get Krug and caviar in a video conference.

As he spoke, the Air France and British Airways Concordes were parked nose to nose, a re-enactment of their pose at Washington on their first arrival in the United States in May 1976.

Captain Edgar Chillaud (left) with Captain Mike Bannister, Chief Pilots of Concorde Air France and British Airways respectively, at JFK, New York, on 7 November 2001 following the return of supersonic services

When Concorde first went into service the invitation was to 'fly Concorde and arrive in better shape'. In June 1997, British Airways unveiled its new livery. Although not visible in this picture the new Concorde tail fin is consistent with this; in that it displays the familiar Union Flag elements. Unlike the other fleets however, it does not sport any of the new ethnic designs.

Outlook

Flying westward time moves backwards, by two hours from Paris, one from London. Eastward, with the spin of the Earth, the Concorde passenger loses weight, thereby justifying the superb cuisine (Mark Wagner)

The regular supersonic traveller to New York has learnt that Concorde saves the days of the week by saving the hours of the day. During Concorde's enforced sabbatical, British Airways hosted a reception in a Heathrow hangar for its supersonic clientele. Concorde, having been regarded as a luxury by some, had turned into a necessity for others. To reassure these VIPs, Mike Bannister was anxious to keep them fully informed about the ongoing safety modifications. This approach was well received and a similar exercise took place in New York. Advance bookings looked encouraging.

On 7 2001 November, with only three modified aircraft available, a daily (except Saturdays) return service to New York was established along with the weekly Barbados run over the winter. The London to New York departure was, as ever, at 10:30am, with the aircraft getting back to London at 9.10pm. The twice-daily service would be resumed when economic conditions allowed.

At the time of writing, there are many years left in Concorde. But what about a replacement? Previous chapters in this book have outlined the problems facing the designers. Boom muffling has become more of a possibility.

The sonic boom consists of three elements:

- a sudden pressure rise to above ambient. This is the shock from the nose and is heard as a boom

- a relatively slow pressure drop to below ambient, which is inaudible

- a sudden pressure increase back to ambient. This is the shock from the tail and is heard as the second part of the boom.

When plotted on a graph, the pressure trace with respect to time forms the letter N, hence it is frequently referred to as the N wave (see the chapter A Stormy Beginning). The startle factor of the boom depends more

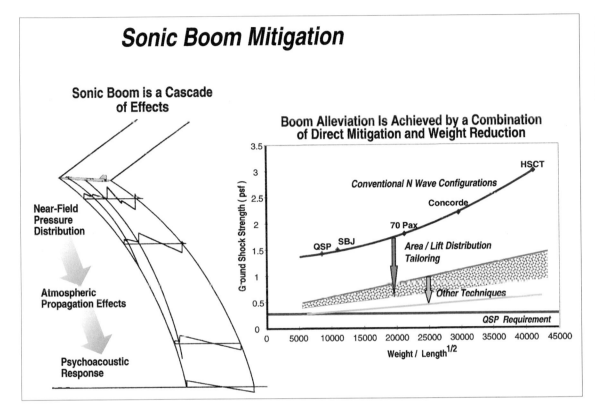

The 'N' wave is made up of the coalescence of the minor shock waves. Suppression of this effect will muffle the boom

This US Navy photo by John Gay is of a supersonic F/A-18 Hornet flown by Lt R.. Candiloro from the USS Constellation. The condensation shows the low pressure surrounding the fuselage. At the tail the pressure returns rapidly to ambient so the cloud disappears

Right Possible
configuration of an
SSBJ; note the 'area
ruling', seen here
where the fuselage
thins to compensate
for presence of the
wings. Engines placed
above the wing aid
boom suppression, but
interfere with low-
speed vortex lift

Far right SSBJ
executive layout

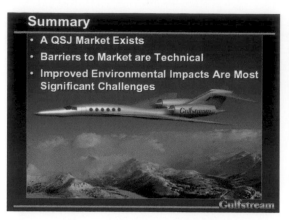

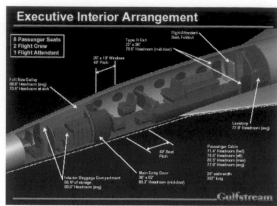

Right Chart showing
world accessibility
within 5 and 10 hours
from New York using
the SSBJ

Far right Preconditions
for an SSBJ to be
viable

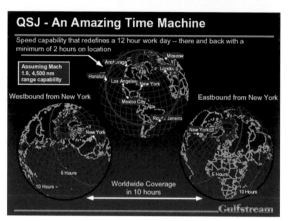

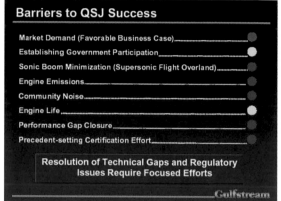

on the sharpness of the pressure rise than the quantity of the overpressure, but this has a bearing too. The overpressure measured on the surface directly beneath Concorde at Mach 2 is at least 2 lbs per sq ft, about a thousandth of sea level atmospheric pressure. The boom carpet width varies with altitude, weight and weather conditions, but can be detected by a person ten miles either side of track. The sound varies from a distant rumble of thunder to a nearby discharge of a shotgun.

During accelerating flight, the shock-waves made at a low supersonic speed arrive at the same time and place as those made at a higher one. This 'focused' boom is much louder. Further along the track two booms are heard, still further on just the one. Turning flight focuses the boom on the inside of the turn. Concorde routes are arranged accordingly. During deceleration there is no focusing.

In the United States, Gulfstream, Boeing and Lockheed Martin are researching ways of reducing the sharpness of the pressure rise, along with DARPA (Defense Advanced Research Projects Agency). A supersonic business jet (SSBJ) with overland capability should find a big market. In Europe, Dassault is interested, but is waiting for a suitable engine.

Contours and protuberances of an aircraft flying above transonic speed produce shock waves. As the waves propagate downwards, they coalesce and form an N wave. Once flying in excess of about Mach 1.2, an aircraft's shock waves are audible on the surface as the boom. Research suggests that by shaping the lower surface of an aircraft appropriately, it should be possible to prevent the intermediate shocks from coalescing. The sharpness and extent of the pressure rise will have been reduced. As the strength of the shock decreases with reducing weight, a supersonic jet of, say, 35 tonnes, would benefit more from this research than an aircraft of 300 tonnes (cf Concorde: 185 tonnes).

Gulfstream and Lockheed Martin both favour a highly swept platform. The former likes tail-mounted engines and intakes above the wing, good for boom suppression, but bad for low speed aerodynamics. The latter prefers engines mounted conventionally beneath the wing. The Boeing research features a slewed wing, at right angles to the fuselage on take-off and landing, but fully stowed along the top fuselage for supersonic flight. All the lift at supersonic speed would be generated by two unswept laminar flow wings, one fore and the other aft.

*Three Rolls-Royce
engine designs under
consideration for the
SSBJ*

Variable Cycle 'Conventional' Turbofan (VCT)

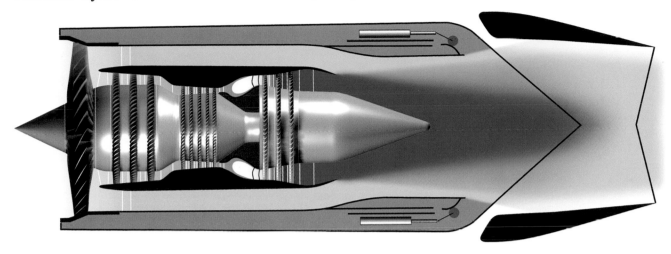

Mixed Nozzle Ejector (MNE)

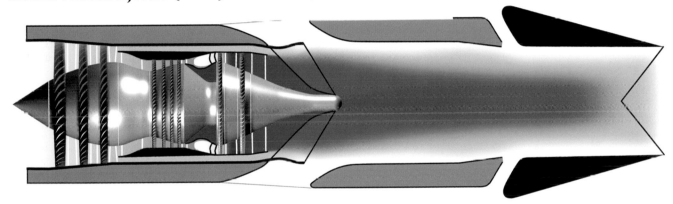

Mid-Tandem Fan (MTF)

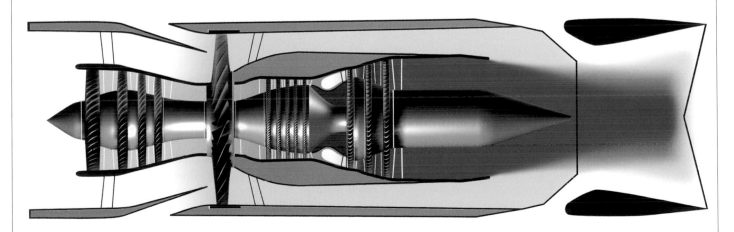

Under DARPA's Quiet Supersonic Platform (QSP) programme, Northrop Grumman planned to fly a Grumman F-5E modified with a lengthened forward fuselage. The target was to reduce the overpressure to 0.3 lbs per square foot – a seventh of Concorde's. If successful, the QSP could lead to a long-range supersonic military aircraft as well.

The amount of internal volume in an aircraft is constrained by the fineness ratio. This applies particularly to a supersonic aircraft. For minimum 'wave' drag (from shockwaves) the ratio of length to diameter should be high. The fuselage, therefore, has to be long enough to give it sufficient diameter to carry the payload and fuel, as well as to muffle the boom. If too long, then it becomes costly to build; if too short, range and comfort would be prejudiced.

Boeing and Princetown University have been studying ways to increase length 'virtually', through transmission of microwave energy ahead (50 metres) and angled below an aircraft's nose, focused to form a hot spot. The new bow shock forming at this point theoretically softens the original N wave. Power consumption would be high; pulsing the beam could offset this.

Preston Henne, Gulfstream Vice-President, has put a $70m–$100m price tag on an 8–14 seat twin-engine SSBJ. He believes a range of 4,000 to 5,000 nautical miles is possible. Provided supersonic flight overland is allowed, Henne has predicted a market for between 180 and 350 SSBJs.

The power plant for such aircraft presents a challenge. In October 2001 *Flight International* quoted John Whurr (Rolls-Royce Advanced Programmes Executive): 'The SSBJ market is insufficient to justify the development of a completely new propulsion system.' The engine would have to meet noise and emissions criteria. Should an engine fail when crossing oceans, good subsonic single-engine performance would be required (to comply with similar rules governing twin-engine subsonic airliners). If Concorde has to fly subsonic, for instance having shut down an engine, its range is reduced by 25%. Options for this contingency are considered before flight, and monitored during.

According to Rolls-Royce, there are three choices of engine cycle suitable for the SSBJ ('cycle' refers to the way the air is distributed within the engine and ejected from it – see previous page).

1. Conventional Turbo Fan (CTF);

2. Mixed Nozzle Ejector (MNE);

3. Mid Tandem Fan (MTF).

The simplest solution, according to Rolls-Royce, is to develop a conventional turbofan with a bypass ratio of three. It would be a low-risk venture using conventional turbo machinery. Its noise characteristics would be good through all stages of flight, with good specific fuel consumption (SFC refers to the ratio of the rate of fuel use to the thrust given) in all flight conditions, particularly when supersonic, but only up to Mach 2. Its weaknesses are that it would need a large intake, engine nacelle and nozzle. As a

result, it would suffer from high installed drag and weight, and from spillage drag when transonic. In order to accelerate the exhaust flow of the CTF for supersonic propulsion, attention would have to be paid to the design of the nozzle.

The MNE is the easiest of the three to build. It consists of a low bypass engine directly behind which air is entrained through an auxiliary intake. The final nozzle, as on Concorde, is arranged to entrain yet more ambient air for noise suppression. For high speed, the auxiliary intake is closed and the nozzle opens to form a divergent duct. It has the lightest turbo machinery, smallest intake and nozzle, and good installed performance with low drag. It would allow a cruise speed up to Mach 2.4.

The weight of the MNE would be critical.

A desirable thrust to weight ratio might be hard to meet on account of the performance at low speed. Its design is critically dependent on the ejector and the efficient mixing of the entrained ambient air with the exhaust flow. Furthermore, complying with future noise rules might be difficult. A similar problem had to be faced when Concorde went into service five years later than planned.

The variable cycle of the MTF would give it good performance with low noise in all flight conditions up to Mach 2. However, the turbo machinery associated with varying the cycle could be complicated and heavy.

In 2000 Airbus was not showing any interest in building either an SSBJ or a successor to Concorde. Instead there was talk of an aircraft big enough to contain shopping malls and saunas. In December 2000 came the announcement that the A3XX proposal had become the A380 project, with first flight scheduled in 2004 and entry into commercial service in 2006. The first version of the A380 is designed to carry 555 passengers over a range of 8,000 nautical miles.

Boeing had decided that there was no economic justification for one let alone two large aircraft projects, so had quietly folded up its B747X plans. Instead, on 29 March 2001, it unveiled 'Sonic Cruiser', a programme to build an airliner capable of flight at speeds just below Mach 1. Boeing denied its announcement had been intended to steal Airbus' thunder. Some commentators had their doubts. Adam Brown (Vice-President Market Forecasts, Airbus Industrie) pointed out that although Sonic Cruiser had been heralded as a new idea, in fact the proposal had been published in the 1970s and in much the same words. The Europeans complained that the fuel consumption on Sonic Cruiser was environmentally unacceptable. In the early 1970s the pro-subsonic lobby had accused Concorde of the same thing.

Sonic Cruiser is still at the conceptual stage. Both a 200 and a 250-seat version with ranges of 6,000 nm or perhaps even 9,000 nm have been mentioned. Boeing hopes to make some of the structure out of composite materials, replacing the denser aluminium.

Sonic Cruiser would not quite take a pair of big engines off the shelf – some development is required. However, each air intake, requiring an 'S' bend, would not be as complicated as Concorde's. Artist impressions show Sonic Cruiser with a double delta, canard and a nose blunter than Concorde's. Boeing anticipates that it will cruise at Mach 0.98. To satisfy airworthiness requirements, it will have to be capable of exceeding Mach 1.0. Boeing plays down rumours that it could also cruise at Mach 1.02, where there is supposed to be an efficient point. The drag rise experienced at Mach 1 means that overall efficiency is not, in theory, restored until Mach 1.5.

Flying at upto Mach 1.154, in a Standard Atmosphere, the path of the shock wave is refracted away from the surface, so no boom is audible on the surface (C606 Operations Support 1976). This is known as the cut-off Mach number. It increases in climbing flight, and when the atmosphere is cold with respect to the surface (eg, over the Equator). It also increases when the aircraft encounters a head wind stronger than the wind on the surface.

The speed of sound varies with air temperature. Assuming temperatures found in the International Standard Atmosphere (see Appendix), at 40,000 ft, Mach 0.98 is approximately 565 knots. On the Earth's surface, Mach 0.98 would be 645 knots. Most subsonic, long-range aircraft fly at a maximum of Mach 0.85. In average temperatures of -55°C, this would give Sonic Cruiser an advantage of only 70 knots and not 80 knots as has been suggested.

On a 6,000 nautical mile sector, 1 hour 45 minutes would be saved. Boeing says that could save even more time, avoiding airport and airspace rush hours. Furthermore, with high rates of climb, Sonic Cruiser would quickly reach its cruising level of over 40,000 ft where there is less congestion. The first commercial flight is expected in 2008.

Historically civil aviation has grown at 5% per year. Crises like the 1990 Gulf War put a temporary stop to the trend. Six months on from September 11 passengers started to return. On 18 March 2002, British Airways announced the restoration of all but two of its subsonic transatlantic services and a return to Concorde's Saturday New York flight.

The American high-speed research programme has been shelved. Only the Japanese continue active research into a Concorde

The 550-seat Airbus A380 is being built at Toulouse at the time of writing. Airbus Industrie has chosen a conventional planform; for an economical cruise, Mach 0.86 would probably be the limit. Note the full-length double deck

successor. In 1997 Japan's National Aerospace Laboratory (NAL) launched the Next Generation SST program (Nexst). There was no point, they thought, in competing in the subsonic field against Boeing and Airbus. Britain and France had been similarly driven in the early 1960s. Even so, there is liaison between Boeing, Japan Aircraft Industries and the Japan Aircraft Development Corp 'to conduct research and development work on technologies including composites for the Sonic Cruiser and other potential new airplanes'.

Engineering opinion in Japan favours the devclopment of an SSBJ first. Once the problems of noise, sonic boom and pollution have been overcome, then a larger version would be attempted. Using computational fluid dynamic (CFD) techniques, NAL has developed an 'inverse design method'. This means that engineers tell the super-computer what performance they want, and the computer designs an aerodynamic shape to fit their requirements. The use of lighter composite materials for the structure in place of aluminium alloy will be essential.

For success the aircraft must achieve a lift to drag ratio of 9 at Mach 2, (cf Concorde's 7.5); but the target is 10 in the Breguet Range Equation (see appendix). Laminar flow control will be essential. The computer does not handle boundary layer behaviour well, so a

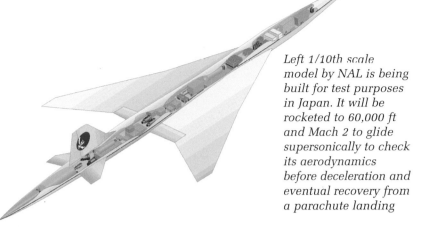

Left 1/10th scale model by NAL is being built for test purposes in Japan. It will be rocketed to 60,000 ft and Mach 2 to glide supersonically to check its aerodynamics before deceleration and eventual recovery from a parachute landing

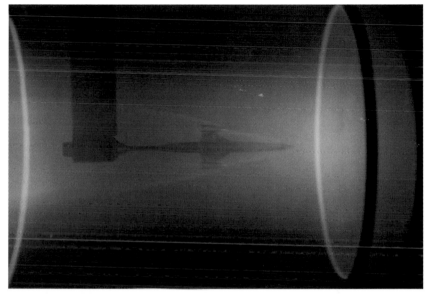

Above *Alan Bond's team (Reaction Engines Ltd) continue with their investigation into Skylon, a 'single stage to orbit, craft. Thanks to QinteQ at Farnborough a model has been tested in a low density tunnel at Mach 9.5 in a steady stae with nitrogen excitation*

Left *President Georges Pompidou of France (left) with Henri Ziegler, President-Directeur Général de l'Aerospatiele on board Concorde 001 in May 1972, surrounded by state-of-the-art computers. Whether public money will be used to fund a successor is open to question*

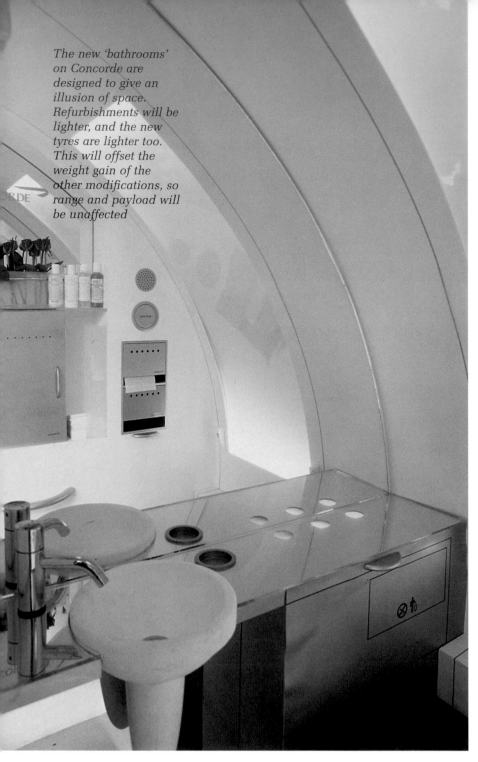

Above right The 1972 World Tour arriving at Heathrow. With the Queen are Brian Trubshaw and Michael Heseltine. George Edwards (head of BAC) is on the left. The Queen was not to fly Concorde until 1977, her Jubilee year

one-tenth scale, rocket-propelled model is being prepared. From 60,000 ft at Mach 2, it will descend at supersonic speed, finally deploying a parachute before recovery. Later in the programme a twin-engine powered model will be launched from a Tristar. Other questions concerning nitrous oxide emissions and sonic boom suppression will be addressed.

Since the chapter Sub-Orbital Travel was written, rocket engine inventor Alan Bond has received a small amount of funding. Reaction Engines Limited has established itself at Culham near Oxford. The goal is still to develop an engine capable of burning fuel with atmospheric oxygen, then with oxygen carried on board. In 2002 the problem of icing on the heat exchanger had been addressed. Ways of using helium instead of hydrogen as the cooling medium were being studied. Bond's basic idea is evolving. If the UK wants to move into this arena efforts such as Bond's will need more support.

The problem with Concorde is that once it became a reality, it was never allowed to evolve. The Concorde that went into service is the 'A' winged version. The 'B' version would have had leading edge slats, greater fuel capacity, an extra engine compressor stage and no reheat. Quieter and with a longer range, (25%) it would have been a more attractive proposition to many European airlines. No wonder the 'A' version was difficult to sell.

However, the triumph of Concorde is its combination of far sighted functionality and supreme beauty. With these it generates great pride and loyalty. Not only has it survived financial and technical crises, but it has done so profitably. I for one hope that the sun will not set on Concorde until there is a satisfactory successor.

'I, for one, hope that the sun will not set on Concorde until there is a satisfactory successor.'

Appendices

Max take-off weight	185,070 kg (408,000 lb)
Max landing weight	111,130 kg (245,000 lb)
Max weight without fuel	92,080 kg (203,000 lb)
Max payload (approx)	13,150 kg (29,000 lb)
Max number of passengers	128 (but BA Concordes are fitted with 100 passenger seats)
Max fuel at specific gravity 0,800 limited by volume:	95,680 kg (26,400 gallons)

The dimensions of Concorde. The measurement marked with the asterisk is for the 'Aerodynamic Root Reference Chord'. It is used when referring to the position of the centre of gravity moved by the transference of fuel (see accompanying diagram). Thus the centre of gravity on most take-offs (53.5%) is 48 ft 6 in behind the forward point, and 53 ft 6 in at its most rearward (59%) during the supersonic cruise.

Concorde – Leading dimensions

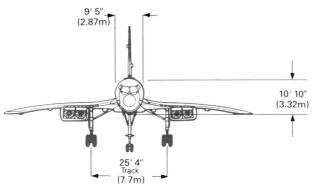

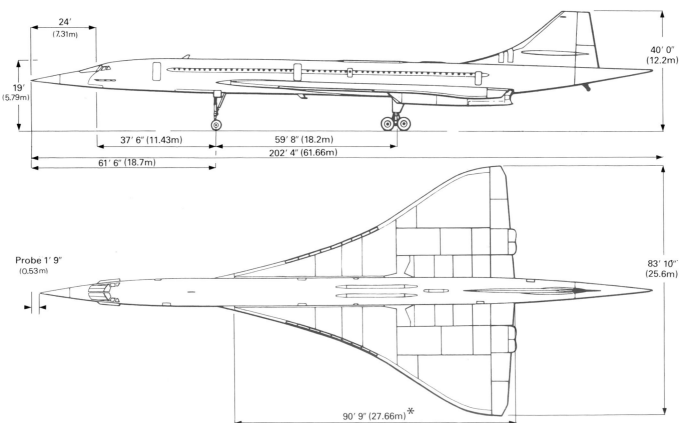

Breguet Range Equation

The maximum range is constrained by several factors including payload, reserve fuel required on arrival, weather conditions and the amount of the route that can be flown supersonically. A typical maximum range on Concorde with 100 passengers plus baggage (10,000 kg total payload) and normal fuel reserves, is 3,500 nm (4,030 sm). The route between Bahrain and Singapore was flown in the colder air found over the tropics; this improved the efficiency of the engines allowing a range of 3,720 nm to be flown regularly. Although the payload limit on this sector was 7,500 kg (75 passengers) it could usually be increased to close on 100 passengers when conditions were favourable. The maximum recorded range on Concorde under very favourable conditions, and therefore difficult to plan in advance, was between Washington and Nice, a distance of 3,965 nm (4,565 sm) flown on 11 September 1984 with 54 passengers in G-BOAB taking 4 hours and 7 minutes.

The range (R) in nautical miles (no wind) of an aircraft can be expressed as:

$$R = \frac{V \times L/D}{SFC} \times \log_e (w_1/w_2)$$

Where V is the cruising speed in knots; L/D the lift to drag ratio; SFC is the specific fuel consumption of the engine – pounds of fuel per hour per pound of engine thrust; (w_1/w_2) is the ratio of weights at the start and end of the sample of range to be investigated. The natural logarithm of the final term is a measure of the structural efficiency of the aircraft – the amount of fuel available for aircraft weight (including payload). For Concorde travelling at Mach 2, V is circa 1120 kts; L/D is 7.5; SFC 1.18 (each engine consuming fuel at just over 11,000 lbs per hour will give, during the cruise, about 9300 lbs of thrust). If the two weights were 165 (w_1) and 110 (w_2) tonnes (t) respectively, Concorde could travel just under 2900 nautical miles on 55 tonnes of fuel. Should the weights have been 155 t and 100 t respectively, then the range improves to 3120 nms. In practice over 90 tonnes of fuel is loaded including approximately 15 tonnes of 'spare' fuel for diversion etc, and much of the fuel is burnt during the 'off design' period of the flight. However, the equation can be applied to each segment of the flight.

Powerplant

Four Rolls-Royce/SNECMA Olympus 593 Mark 610 turbo jet engines. Maximum thrust at take-off with afterburner (reheat) contributing about 20% to the total – 38,050 lb.

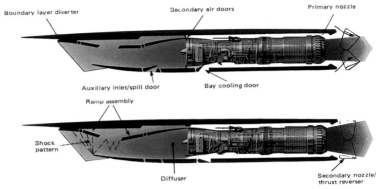

At take-off 95% of the thrust is delivered by the engine and 5% by the nozzle and intake assemblies.

During supersonic cruise only 50% of the thrust is delivered by the engine; the remainder is delivered, equally shared, by the variable ramp assembly and the convergent/divergent nozzle system. The purpose of the diffuser is to slow, and therefore compress, the air, which is now subsonic, still further before it enters the engine face.

Note *A convergent passage slows and compresses a supersonic airflow, while a divergent passage slows and compresses a subsonic airflow.*

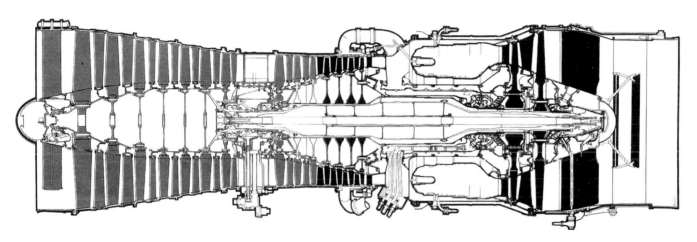

Above *The Olympus engine is a two-spool engine. The inner, or low pressure (1p) shaft revolves within the outer, or high pressure (hp) shaft. There are fourteen compressor stages, seven on each shaft, driven by their respective turbines. As the air approaches the combustion chambers, during the supersonic cruise, it becomes very hot due to its compression (over 80:1 total), hence the need to construct the final four compression stages from a nickel-based alloy – usually reserved for the turbine area. (The darker shades, green in the cutaway engine below, show the more heat resistant alloys.) To the rear of the turbines is the reheat assembly. The amount of fuel burnt in the combustion chamber controls the rpm of the hp shaft, whilst varying the area of the primary nozzle (see top) controls, at a given rpm of the hp shaft, the rpm of the low pressure shaft.*

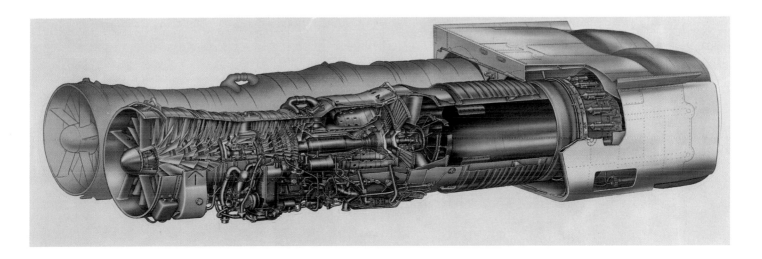

The anatomy of Concorde

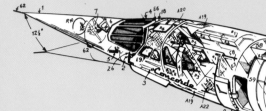

Emergency equipment
E1 Oxygen-bottle stowage
E2 Drop-down masks
E3 First-aid oxygen in galley top
E4 Four 36-man life rafts
E5 Chute stowage
E6 Windscreen (electrically heated), hydraulic wipers and fluid rain clearance
E7 Emergency radio
E8 Fire-suppression bottles
E9 Direct-vision panel and exit
E10 Spraymat de-icing

General structure
1 Variable-geometry drooping nose
2 Droop guide-rails
3 Droop hinge-joint
4 Retracting visor
5 Visor guide-rails
6 Visor refracting link
7 Visor jack
8 Outward-opening, plug-type passenger door (66 in × 30 in, sill 16 ft 5 in above ground)
9 Service door (48 in × 24 in)
10 Underfloor baggage hold (pressurised), 26 ft × 38 in × 55 in (308 cu ft)
11 Rear baggage compartment (pressurised), door to stbd (429 cu ft)
12 Middle passenger doors (port and stbd) 73 in × 34 in
13 Metal-faced floor panels
14 Rear emergency door (port and stbd) 68 in × 34 in
15 Light alloy/balsa sandwich floor panels
16 Machined window panel
17 Triple-gap window, removable as a unit
18 Multi-layer windscreen, removable as a unit
19 Forged wing/fuselage main frames
20 Stringer carry-through
21 T-section spot-welded stringers (front fuselage)
22 Z-section spot-welded stringers (rear fuselage)
23 Single-flange frames (front fuselage)
24 Double-flange frames (rear fuselage)
25 Rolled-aluminium RR58 skin
26 Front pressure bulkhead
27 Rear pressure bulkhead and tank wall
28 Spar-box, machined girder side pieces
29 Spar-box, machined cap strip/boom
30 Pre-stretched, integrally machined wing-skin panels
31 Lattice-tube pin-jointed ribs
32 Machined ribs
33 Corrugated, machined tank wall and spars permitting thermal expansion
34 Single-web spars
35 Forged wing (forward tanks) adjustable mountings
36 Pressure-floor curved membranes (to relieve thermal stress)
37 Pressure/passenger floor-support beams
38 Machined pressure-floor support beams over wheel bay
39 Machined, pressurised keel box carrying services
40 Stressed (15 g upward impact) tank roof
41 Vapour seal over tank roof
42 Unpressurised aft systems bay
43 Pressurised forward systems bay
44 Fin support structure (tube and extruded members)
45 Machined fin spars (rivetted to fuselage frames)
46 Removable leading-edge sections
47 Machined ribs
48 Chemically milled skin

49 Expansion joints between sections
50 Removable outer wing (tank 5A, port, and 7A, stbd)
51 Wing fixing by 340 bigh-tensile steel bolts
52 Quick-look removable inspection panels
53 Inspection panels, screw-fixed
54 Honeycomb structure (control surfaces, engine nacelles and intakes)
55 Seat rails
56 Floor supports, permit longitudinal expansion
57 Toilet
58 Galley unit
59 Coat stowage
60 Overhead baggage racks with doors
61 Passenger-service units on underside of baggage racks
62 Pilot heads

Air conditioning
A1 Intake-air tapping to heat exchangers
A2 Primary heat exchanger (one per engine)
A3 Secondary heat exchanger (one per engine)
A4 Heat-exchanger exhaust air
A5 Delivery to cold-air unit
A6 Fuel-cooled heat exchanger (one per engine, both systems)
A7 Cold-air unit (one per engine both systems)
A8 Delivery to cabin air-distribution system
A9 Distribution duct
A10 Riser to distribution duct
A11 Duct to forward risers
A12 Window ventilating air (all windows)
A13 Air-recirculating duct
A14 Individual punkahs on service panels, adjustable to seating arrangement
A15 Cabin-air exhaust through roof filter via trim to under-floor
A16 Heat and sound insulation (glass fibre and polyester sheet)
A17 Baggage-compartment cooling air
A18 Cabin-floor-level exhaust duct to ventilate equipment bays
A19 Flight-deck air duct
A20 Window demisting
A21 Equipment venting air
A22 Equipment-air extraction duct

A23 Automatic discharge/relief valve (normal diff. 10.7 lb/sq in)
A24 Manual discharge valve
A25 Thrust-recovery nozzle
A26 Low-pressure venting air between vapour seal and tank roof
A27 Ground-conditioning connection
A28 Undercarriage-bay cooling air

Controls
C1 Control cable runs under floor
C2 Rod linkage to surface power control units (stand-by linkage, electrics primary)
C3 Power control unit mounting
C4 Electrically signalled, manual stand-by power control unit
C5 Twin output from power control unit
C6 Control-unit fairing
C7 Elevon
C8 Flexible joint
C9 Elevon outer hinges, permit spanwise expansion
C10 Ram-air turbine
C11 Retracting jack

Flight deck
D1 Captain's seat
D2 Second pilot's seat
D3 Third crew member's station
D4 Roof panel
D5 Third crew member's panel

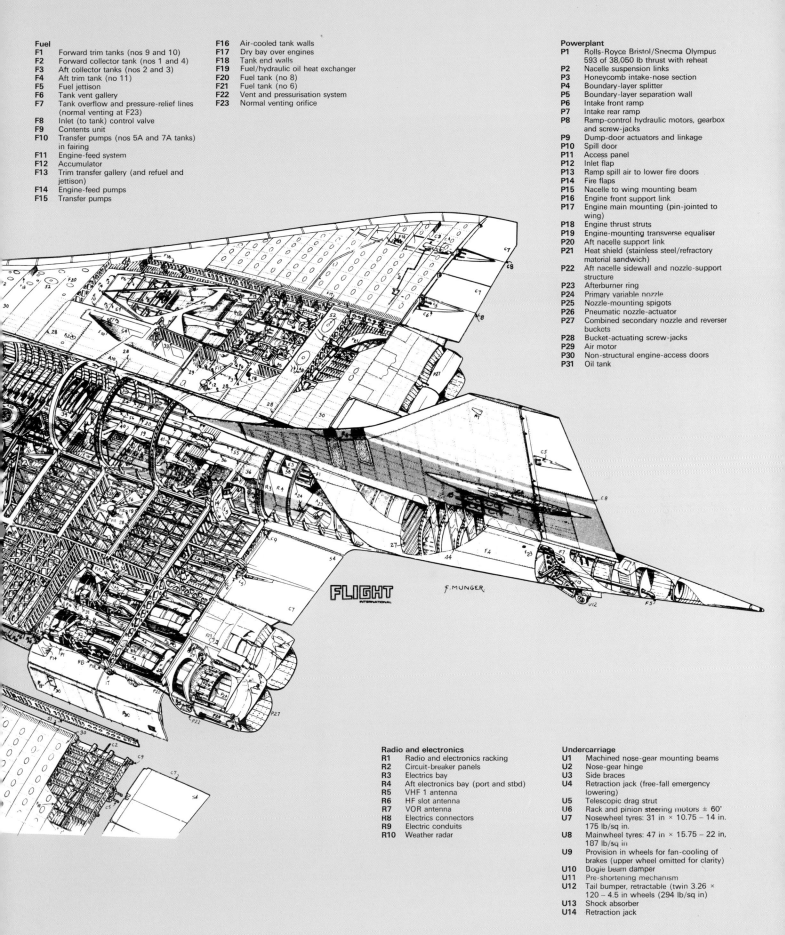

Fuel

F1	Forward trim tanks (nos 9 and 10)
F2	Forward collector tank (nos 1 and 4)
F3	Aft collector tanks (nos 2 and 3)
F4	Aft trim tank (no 11)
F5	Fuel jettison
F6	Tank vent gallery
F7	Tank overflow and pressure-relief lines (normal venting at F23)
F8	Inlet (to tank) control valve
F9	Contents unit
F10	Transfer pumps (nos 5A and 7A tanks) in fairing
F11	Engine-feed system
F12	Accumulator
F13	Trim transfer gallery (and refuel and jettison)
F14	Engine-feed pumps
F15	Transfer pumps
F16	Air-cooled tank walls
F17	Dry bay over engines
F18	Tank end walls
F19	Fuel/hydraulic oil heat exchanger
F20	Fuel tank (no 8)
F21	Fuel tank (no 6)
F22	Vent and pressurisation system
F23	Normal venting orifice

Powerplant

P1	Rolls-Royce Bristol/Snecma Olympus 593 of 38,050 lb thrust with reheat
P2	Nacelle suspension links
P3	Honeycomb intake-nose section
P4	Boundary-layer splitter
P5	Boundary-layer separation wall
P6	Intake front ramp
P7	Intake rear ramp
P8	Ramp-control hydraulic motors, gearbox and screw-jacks
P9	Dump-door actuators and linkage
P10	Spill door
P11	Access panel
P12	Inlet flap
P13	Ramp spill air to lower fire doors
P14	Fire flaps
P15	Nacelle to wing mounting beam
P16	Engine front support link
P17	Engine main mounting (pin-jointed to wing)
P18	Engine thrust struts
P19	Engine-mounting transverse equaliser
P20	Aft nacelle support link
P21	Heat shield (stainless steel/refractory material sandwich)
P22	Aft nacelle sidewall and nozzle-support structure
P23	Afterburner ring
P24	Primary variable nozzle
P25	Nozzle-mounting spigots
P26	Pneumatic nozzle-actuator
P27	Combined secondary nozzle and reverser buckets
P28	Bucket-actuating screw-jacks
P29	Air motor
P30	Non-structural engine-access doors
P31	Oil tank

FLIGHT INTERNATIONAL

F. MUNGER

Radio and electronics

R1	Radio and electronics racking
R2	Circuit-breaker panels
R3	Electrics bay
R4	Aft electronics bay (port and stbd)
R5	VHF 1 antenna
R6	HF slot antenna
R7	VOR antenna
R8	Electrics connectors
R9	Electric conduits
R10	Weather radar

Undercarriage

U1	Machined nose-gear mounting beams
U2	Nose-gear hinge
U3	Side braces
U4	Retraction jack (free-fall emergency lowering)
U5	Telescopic drag strut
U6	Rack and pinion steering motors ± 60°
U7	Nosewheel tyres: 31 in × 10.75 – 14 in. 175 lb/sq in.
U8	Mainwheel tyres: 47 in × 15.75 – 22 in, 187 lb/sq in
U9	Provision in wheels for fan-cooling of brakes (upper wheel omitted for clarity)
U10	Bogie beam damper
U11	Pre-shortening mechanism
U12	Tail bumper, retractable (twin 3.26 × 120 – 4.5 in wheels (294 lb/sq in)
U13	Shock absorber
U14	Retraction jack

The Flight Envelope

How the fuel is used to move the centre of gravity on Concorde. The position of the centre of gravity is measured as a percentage of the 'Aerodynamic Root Reference Chord' (see dimension chart). The position of the centre of gravity restricts the aircraft to a speed range shown by the 'limit bugs' on the Machmeter; or alternatively, at a given speed, the centre of gravity must be within limits shown by 'bugs' on the centre of gravity indicator (see photographs on pages 89, 92 and 100)

Concorde must be flown within the slightly shaded area shown on the graph. The maximum operating indicated airspeed limit (V_{MO}) varies not only with altitude, but also, to a small extent, with Concorde's weight. Above 51,000 ft the maximum operating Mach limit (M_{MO}) over-rules V_{MO}; by 60,000 ft M_{MO} (Mach 2.04) corresponds to 440 knots indicated airspeed. The lowest authorised speed limit below 15,000 ft is not shown on this graph since it is related either to weight on take-off from a particular runway, or to landing weight.

Although M_{MO} is Mach 2.04, Concorde generally cruises at Mach 2. There are, however, further constraints to the speed. One is derived from the position of the centre of gravity; at the furthest forward position of the centre of gravity, the top Mach number limit is Mach 0.8; during the acceleration the centre of gravity is moved progressively rearward and at its most rearward point the Mach number range is from Mach 1.55 to over Mach 2.04; however, the top speed is then limited by M_{MO}, V_{MO} or T_{MO}. T_{MO} is the maximum operating temperature limit, representing another constraint to the speed; the maximum temperature at the nose must not exceed 127°C.

In practice this does not become a limiting factor to Concorde until the outside air temperature is warmer than −50°C, at altitudes above 48,000 ft.

Next to the altitude, in thousands of feet, is shown the outside air temperature corresponding to the International Standard Atmosphere (ISA). Next to this is shown the speed of sound for that given temperature. The true outside air temperature is usually at variance from the 'standard' by a few degrees either way over the North Atlantic, so the figure for the speed of sound must be regarded as approximate. Over the equator, where the tropopause is higher, temperatures between 50,000 and 60,000 ft are of the order of ISA −20°C (i.e. −77°C). At this temperature the speed of sound is 545 knots (627 mph).

The formula for the speed of sound (a) is

$$a = constant \times \sqrt{absolute\ temperature}$$
assuming temperature in °K and speed in knots, the constant = 38.89

For an outside air temperature of −57°C (216°K)

$$a = 38.89 \times \sqrt{216}$$
$$= 571\ knots$$

The formula for giving the approximate rise in temperature (ΔT)°C for a given speed is

$$\Delta T = \left(\frac{speed\ in\ mph}{100} \right)^2$$

Thus at Mach 2 when the outside air temperature is −57°C the temperature rise is

$$\left(\frac{2 \times 657.5}{100} \right)^2$$
$$\simeq 173°C$$

Under these conditions the total temperature is 173° − 57° = 116°C.

Note At the speeds associated with a Space Shuttle (or HOTOL) re-entering the earth's atmosphere this formula is not applicable.

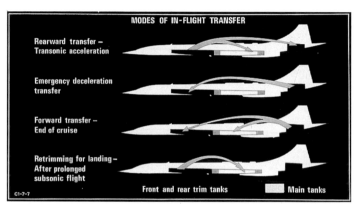

MODES OF IN-FLIGHT TRANSFER

Rearward transfer – Transonic acceleration

Emergency deceleration transfer

Forward transfer – End of cruise

Retrimming for landing – After prolonged subsonic flight

C1-7-7

Front and rear trim tanks   Main tanks

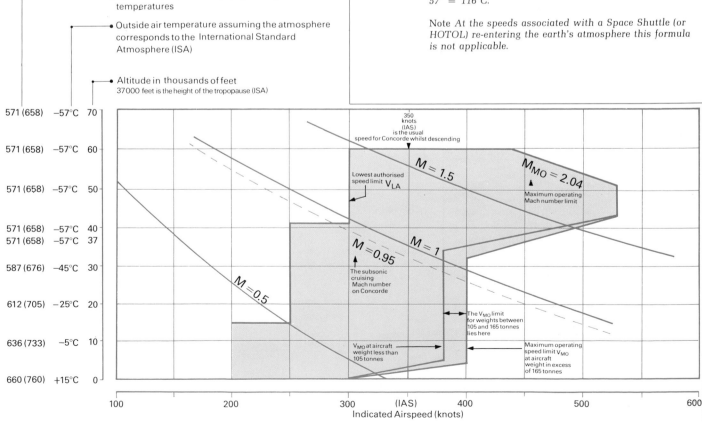

● Speed of sound in knots (mph) at the given temperatures

● Outside air temperature assuming the atmosphere corresponds to the International Standard Atmosphere (ISA)

● Altitude in thousands of feet
37000 feet is the height of the tropopause (ISA)

350 knots (IAS) is the usual speed for Concorde whilst descending

Lowest authorised speed limit V_{LA}

M = 1.5

M_{MO} = 2.04

Maximum operating Mach number limit

M = 0.95

M = 1

M = 0.5

The subsonic cruising Mach number on Concorde

The V_{MO} limit for weights between 105 and 165 tonnes lies here

V_{MO} at aircraft weight less than 105 tonnes

Maximum operating speed limit V_{MO} at aircraft weight in excess of 165 tonnes

571 (658)	−57°C	70
571 (658)	−57°C	60
571 (658)	−57°C	50
571 (658)	−57°C	40
571 (658)	−57°C	37
587 (676)	−45°C	30
612 (705)	−25°C	20
636 (733)	−5°C	10
660 (760)	+15°C	0

Indicated Airspeed (knots)
100   200   300   (IAS)   400   500   600

Concorde Utilisation Details for British Airways and Air France

BA figures, 31 July 2000 (effectively November 2001)

Aircraft registration	Aircraft number	Hours flown	Supersonic cycles	Landings
GBOAA	206	22,769	6,842	8,064
GBOAB	208	22,297	6,688	7,810
GBOAC	204	21,531	6,543	7,511
GBOAD	210	22,300	6,690	8,083
GBOAE	212	22,383	6,708	8,087
GBOAF	216	17,297	5,359	5,765
GBOAG	214	15,091	4,730	5,294
BA total		**143,668**	**43,560**	**50,614**

Air France figures, 31 July 2000 (effectively November 2001)

Aircraft registration	Aircraft number	Hours flown	Supersonic cycles	Landings
FBVFA	205	17,347	5,315	6,780
FBVFB	207	13,874	4,791	5,021
FBVFC	209	12,249	4,129	4,601
FBVFD*	211	5,814	1,807	1,929
FBVFF	215	12,421	3,734	4,259
FBTSC*	203	11,989	3,655	4,481
FBTSD	213	12,162	3,672	4,672
Air France total		**85,226**	**27,103**	**31,743**
Grand total		**228,894**	**70,663**	**82,357**

* 'FD' was taken out of service in 1982 and dismantled in 1994. 'SC' was destroyed 25 July 2000.

The rig at Farnborough achieved 20,000 equivalent supersonic cycles. Originally measured in 'Supersonic Flight Cycles', the new yardstick is 'Reference Flights' which includes a compensation for light take-off weights (see Chapter: 21 Years in Service). However there is no finite limit to the life of the airframe.

The Aircraft

Type	Registration	Number	First flight	Retired at	Notes
Prototype	F-WTSS	001	March 69	Le Bourget	
Prototype	G-BSST	002	April 69	Yeovilton	
Pre-prod.	G-AXDN	01	Dec 71	Duxford	
Pre-prod.	F-WTSA	02	Jan 73	Orly	
Production	F-WTSB	201	DEC 73	Toulouse	
Production	G-BBDG	202	Feb 74	Filton	
Production	F-BTSC (1)	203	Jan 75	Lost 25 Jul 2000	
Production	G-BOAC	204	Feb 75		
Production	F-BVFA	205	Oct 75		
Production	G-BOAC	206	Nov 75		(1) Formerly F-WTSC
Production	F-BVFB	207	March 76		(2) Formerly F-WJAM
Production	G-BOAB	208	May 76		(3) Formerly G-BFKW
Production	F-BVFC	209	July 76		(4) Formerly F-WJAN
Production	G-BOAD	210	August 76		(5) Formerly G-BFKX
Production	F-BVFD	211	Feb 77	Dismantled 1994	
Production	G-BOAE	212	March 77		
Production	F-BTSD (2)	213	June 78		
Production	G-BOAG (3)	214	April 78		
Production	F-BVFF (4)	215	Dec 78		
Production	G-BOAF (5)	216	April 79		

British Airways Concorde Crews 1976-2002

Captains

RPW Allen
R Anderson
A Baillie*
M Bannister*
S Bates*
KP Barton
RJL Boas
JAD Bradshaw
DA Brister
NA Britton
LD Brodie
AL Budd
JD Butterley
JW Burton
BJ Calvert
JL Chorley
JD Cook
RV Dixon
PM Douglas
PRW Duffey
JD Eames
DA Edmondson*
DH Ellis
M Emmett
V Gunton
JA Harkness
T Henderson
JW Hirst
PW Horton
JC Hutchinson
KD Leney
HJ Linfield
WD Lowe
P Mallinson*
AJ Massie
CB McMahon
HC McMullen
IC McNeilly

AR Meadows
A Mills*
RA Mills
CJC Morley
CC Morris
GF Mussett
K Myers
C E Norris*
M O'Connor
T Orchard*
R Owen*
DJM Rendall
E Reynolds
MA Riley
S Robertson
M Robinson
DG Ross
DC Rowland
L Scott*
RS Smith
D Studd*
A Thompson*
BGT Titchener
NV Todd
J Smith
BO Walpole
SD Wand
R Weidner*
R Westray*
JR White*
D Woodley*

First Officers

AB Atkinson
RP Babbé
P Bandall
A Barnwell*
J Bedforth*
P Benn*

P Benson
AJ Bird
S Bohill-Smith
ME Boyle
RJS Burchell
MW Burke
C Burrough
D Byass*
AD Cobley
AR Darke
J Downey
L Evans*
J Graham
CD Green
P Griffin*
B Harmer
AI Heald
BR Holland
J Hornby
JG Huson
B Irven
M Jealous*
DA MacDonald-Lawson
A Macfarlane
DG Mitchell
G Mitchell
EER Murton
J Napier*
BR Oliver
CJD Orlebar
D Payne
JH Phillingham
J Phillips
R Pike
WJ Piper
AF Quartly
NS Rendall
JM Reynolds
R Reynolds

CA Robey
ML Robson
J Rooney
RA Routledge
PT Sinclair
WI Smith
K Snell
K Strocchi
RJ Taylor
J Tye
M Walden*
MHJ Watson
MH Watson
D Whitton
K Williams
MR Withey
MR Young
AJ Yule

Engineer Officers

K Appleton
SL Bolton
GS Bowden
RC Bricknell
K Brotherhood*
AA Brown
WJ Brown
PC Carrigan*
A Chalmers*
TF Caster
C Coltman*
L Cooper
M Cooper
TB Dewis
W Dobbs
FW Duffy
R Eades
PE Egginton
T Evans*

A Everett*
IR Fellowes-Freeman
P Finlay*
SG Floyd
F Ford*
J Goatham
M Harrison
M Hollyer*
WG Hornby
D Hoyle*
S Hull*
D Jackman
WD Johnston
WA Johnstone
RA Jones
IV Kirby
JE Lidiard
PA Ling
DA Macdonald
R Maher*
PJ Newman
T Norcott*
PJ Phillips
A Price*
TJ Quarrey
I Radford
JA Rodger
IF Smith
J Stanbridge
D Tracey*
G Tullier
A Walker*
RN Webb
NC West
AF Winstanley
J Wood*
R Woodcock*

This is a list of all the BA crew members that have ever been qualified to operate Concorde. In 1980 there was a maximum of 28 qualified crews, since then the average has been around 20, dropping to 14 in the mid 1990s and around 8 in November 2001. Those qualified to operate or return to Concorde as of April 2002 are marked with an asterisk. A 'crew' consists of Captain, First Officer and Engineer Officer.

Air France Concorde Crews 1976-2002

Captains

Andreani F.
Arondel G.
Biras B.
Boye J.
Brulant M.
Butel M.
Caillat G.
Campion G.
Catania C.
Chanoine Martiel P.
Chatelain J-L
Chauve J.
Chauvin J.
Chemel E.
Chillaud E.
Conte P.
Contresty R.
Debets P.
Delorme C.
Demeester R.
Doguet R.
Doublait J.
Duchange A.
Dudal P.
Duguet G.
Dupont M.
Dupont W.
Ferry M.
Fournier HG.
Gely A.
Gilles P.
Girard P.
Gourguechon P.
Grandjean H.
Hertert F.
Hetru C.
Jacob G.
Lacoux P.
Lalanne J.
Le Gales G.
Le Guillou M.
Le Moel J-P.
Leclerc C.
Lesieur J-C.
Lortsch M.
Machavoine R.
Malbrand D.
Manchon D.
Marty C.
Massoc A.
Michel J-F
Mims J.
Moron J.
Pecresse Y.
Plisson P.
Pouligny M.
Prunin J.
Quilichini
Rio M.
Robin J.
Rossignol J.
Rude F.
Sagory R.
Schwartz J.
Tardieu G.
Terry R.
Verhulst A.
Vicens F.
Voog C.

First Officers

Adibi F.
Bachelet B.
Barras G.
Bataillou A.
Bernigaud A.
Bonnot P.
Celerier E.
Chambrier D.
Colloc A.
Compagnon D.
Croise A.
D'Haussy P.
Decamps PA.
Delangle P.
Delorme JC.
Depouez B.
Doumax M.
Dubreucque A.
Durieux C.
Duval G.
Fady D.
Fourtier G.
Geoffry A.
Gibouin JF.
Giron P.
Grange P.
Guegan J.
Holbecq AJ.
Jaillet J.
Lapersonne P.
Le Breton J.
Le Chaton D.
Macot J.
Marchand B.
Martin M.
Mauroy G.
Metais G.
Morisset S.
Neutre P.
Ortiz R.
Othnin Girard R.
Peloffy JM.
Pradon F.
Proust JM.
Puyperoux R.
Ravera L.
Ringenbach G.
Rogon G.
Tonnot E.
Vacchiani R.
Vialle B.

Engineer Officers

Aubry JP.
Babot A.
Barbaroux G.
Baty P.
Benard H.
Beral R.
Billerey C.
Blanc A.
Bonzi R.
Brugeroux G.
Buisson R.
Cappoen V.
Cazin
Cesari D.
Clement G.
Collette B.
Crouzet JP.
Cucchiaro G.
Czmal A.
Desserprit J-P
Detienne M.
Diou M.
Drouard M.
Dubourg P.
Duguet R.
Escuyer R.
Faviez L.
Frot L.
Jardinaud G.
Jarrousse J.
Lafaye
Lajarge J-J
Lavillaureix A.
Le Berre P.
Lebrun C.
Ledoux J.
Lombart J.
Marquis F.
Masselin JL.
Menoret B.
Michaut H.
Moustier G.
Pellerin G.
Piccinini A.
Pluchon Y.
Poulain C.
Ranty H.
Roger A.
Schwaller L.
Suaud M.
Thomas J.
Vallet S.
Vasseur D.

Concorde Chronology

1956
November 5: Supersonic Transport Aircraft Committee (STAC) established.

1959
March 9: STAC recommends design studies of two supersonic airliners (Mach 1.2 and Mach 2).

1959-61
French & British SST feasibility and design studies initiated.

1961
First Anglo-French discussions on possible SST collaboration. *June-July:* First BAC/Sud discussions in Paris and Weybridge.

1962
October: Anglo-French Mach 2.2 transport specification published *November 29:* Anglo-French agreement for joint design development and manufacture of a supersonic airliner.

1963
Preliminary design presented to airlines. *January 13:* President de Gaulle uses name 'Concorde'. *June 3:* Concorde sales option signed by Pan American Airlines. *June:* BOAC and Air France sign Concorde sales options. *June 5:* US supersonic transport programme announced.

1964
Projected medium-range version abandoned: design of long-range version enlarged. *May:* Enlarged Concorde design announced. *July:* Olympus 593D first run, Bristol.

1965
April: Metal cut for Concorde prototypes. *May:* Pre-production Concorde design announced.

1966
Manufacturer and airline engineering liaison established. *April:* Final assembly of prototype 001 begins, Toulouse. *June:* Concorde flight simulator commissioned. *August:* Assembly of prototype 002 begins at Filton. *September:* First flight of Avro Vulcan test bed with Olympus 593 engine. *October:* Olympus 593 achieves 35,190lb thrust on test at Bristol. *December:* Fuselage section delivered to RAE, Farnborough for fatigue testing.

1967
Design for pre-production aircraft revised to reduce drag; rear fuselage extended, new nose/visor. *February:* Concorde interior mock-up presented to airlines at Filton. *April:* Complete Olympus 593 engine first test-run in high altitude chamber, Saclay. *December 11:* 001 rolled out at Toulouse. British partner adopted 'Concorde' spelling.

1968
February: UK Government announces £125m loan for Concorde production. *August:* 001 taxi trials, Toulouse. *September:* rolled out at Toulouse. British aircraft design redefined. *December:* Olympus 593 ground-testing reaches 5,000 hours. *December 31:* First flight of Tupolev Tu-144 prototype.

1969
March 2: First flight of 001, Toulouse. *March:* Government authority given for construction of nine airframes (two ground test airframes, two prototypes, two pre-production aircraft and three production aircraft). *April 9:* First flight of 002, Filton (to Fairford). *June:* First public appearance of both prototypes, Paris Air Show. *October 1:* 001 achieves Mach 1. *November 8:* Airline pilots fly 001. *December:* Authority given for construction of three more production aircraft.

1970
March 25: 002 achieves Mach 1. *September 1:* 002 appears at SBAC show, Farnborough; lands at Heathrow. *November 4:* 001 achieves Mach 2. *November 12:* 002 achieves Mach 2.

1971
January: 100th supersonic flight. *March 24:* Congress stops US supersonic transport programme. *April:* Authority given for four more production aircraft. *May 25:* 001 appears at Paris Air Show; flies to Dakar. *June:* Total Concorde flight test time reaches 500 hours. *August:* 100th Mach 2 flight. *September 20:* First pre-production Concorde, 01 rolled out at Filton. *December 17:* First flight of 01, Filton.

1972
February 12: exceeds Mach 1. *April 13:* Production aircraft 11-16 authorised. *April 22-23:* 002 appears at Hanover Air Show. *May 25:* BOAC announces intention to order five Concordes. *June:* 002 sales demonstration tour of Middle East and Australia. *July 24:* China signs preliminary purchase agreement for two Concordes. *July 28:* BOAC orders five Concordes, Air France orders four. *August 28:* China signs preliminary purchase agreement for a third Concorde. *September 28:* Concorde 02 rolled out at Toulouse. *October 5:* Iran Air signs preliminary purchase agreement for two Concordes plus option on a third.

1973
January 10: First flight of 02, Toulouse. *January 22-February 24:* 002 completes 'hot and high' trials at Johannesburg. *January 31:* Pan American and TWA decide not to take up their Concorde options. *June 3:* Production Tupolev Tu 144 crashes during Paris Air Show. *June 30:* 001 flight to Fort Lamy (Chad) gives 80-minute scientific observation of solar eclipse. *September 18:* 02 leaves Paris for first US visit for opening of Dallas/Fort Worth Airport. *September 26:* Breaks Washington-Paris record (3hr, 33 mins) on return flight. *October 19:* 001 retired to French Air Museum at Le Bourget. *December 6:* First flight of 201, first production Concorde.

1974
February 17-19: 02 completes low-temperature trials at Fairbanks, Alaska. *February 13:* First flight of 202, second production Concorde (G-BBDG). *June 25:* Concorde static test specimen at CEAT tested to destruction. *July 19:* Initial production programme of 16 aircraft agreed. *August:* Middle East demonstration flights by 202. *September 12:* Flight testing total reaches 3,000 hours. *October 20-28:* American Pacific coast demonstration tour. *October 21:* Supersonic flight total reaches 1,000 hours.

1975
January 31: First flight of 203.

February 11: Completion of passenger emergency evacuation certification trials. *February:* Tropical icing trials. *February 27:* First flight of 204. *February:* Certification trials at Madrid. *May 28:* Special category C of A for 203 awarded; registration changed to F-BTSC, start of 'endurance' flying by this aircraft (completed August 2nd). *May:* Static display and flying programme at Paris Air Show. *June 30:* CAA special category C of A for 204 awarded. *October 9:* Concorde receives French C of A. *October 14:* British Airways and Air France open reservations for Concorde scheduled services. *October 25:* First flight by 205. *November 5:* First flight by 206. *November 13:* final Environmental Impact Statement published by FAA. *December 5:* Concorde receives British C of A. *December 19:* Air France receives its first Concorde (205).

1976
January 5: Concorde public hearing held by US Secretary of Transportation. *January 6:* Air France receives 203. *January 15:* British Airways receives its first Concorde (206). *January 21:* Airline service begins; London-Bahrain (British Airways, 206) and Paris-Rio via Dakar (Air France, 205). *February 4:* Concorde services to New York and Washington for 16 months trial period approved by US Secretary of Transportation. *February 13:* British Airways receives its second Concorde (204). *March 4:* 002 retired to Science Museum (based at RN Air Station, Yeovilton). *March 6:* First flight of 207. *April 8:* Air France receives 207. *April 9:* Air France service extended to Caracas via Santa Maria, Azores. *May 18:* First flight of 208. *May 20:* 02 retired to Orly Airport, Paris. *May 24:* Transatlantic services begin, from Paris and London to Washington. *July 9:* First flight of 209. *August 13:* Air France receives 209. *August 25:* First flight of 210. *September 30:* British Airways receives its third Concorde (208). *November 30:* Fairford flight test base closed. *December 6:* British Airways receives 210. *December 8:* Concorde 203 returned by Air France to Aérospatiale.

1977
February 10: First flight of 211. *March 17:* First flight of 212. *March 26:* Air France receives 211. *July 20:* British Airways receives 212. *August 20:* 01 retired to Duxford, under care of Imperial War Museum. *October 19:* Proving flights to New York begin. *October 26:* Singapore Airlines/BA agreement on London-Singapore flights via Bahrain announced. *November 2:* HM The Queen and HRH Prince Philip return from Barbados on Concorde. *November 22:* Services to New York begin, from Paris and London. *December 9:* Service from London to Singapore via Bahrain begins.

1978
Prolonged talks on Malaysian Concorde ban. *April 21:* First flight of 214. *June 26:* First flight of 213. *August 10:* BA carries its 100, 000th Concorde passenger. *September 18:* Air France receives 213. *September 20:* Air France opens service Paris to Mexico City via Washington. *December 26:* First flight of 215.

1979
January 9: US type certificate awarded. *January 12:* Braniff subsonic service between Washington and Dallas/Fort Worth inaugurated. *January 24:* BA/Singapore Airlines extension Bahrain-Singapore resumed. *February 22:* British Government announces BA to write off Concorde purchase cost; Government to receive 80 per cent of operating surplus. *April 20:* First flight of last production Concorde (216), Filton. *September 21:* British and French Governments announce unsold aircraft and support engines to be placed with British Airways and Air France. *December 16:* BA Concorde flies London-New York in 2hrs 59mins 36 secs.

1980
February 6: British Airways receives 214. *June 1:* Braniff ceases Dallas/Fort Worth service. *June 13:* British Airways receives 216. *October 23:* Air France receives 215. *November 1:* Singapore service discontinued.

1981
January 21: Five years in airline service, 50,000 hours, 15,800 flights, 700,00 passengers. *January-February:* Evidence on Concorde presented to Commons Industry and Trade Committee. *April 14:* Report on Concorde published by Commons Industry and Trade Committee expresses dissatisfaction with cost figures and urges efforts to ensure costs are shared equally with France. Government reply in July describes committee's criticisms of forecasts as 'unwarranted'. *September 11:* Anglo-French 'summit' meeting: British and French Governments commission joint studies on future of Concorde. *October 29:* British and French ministers meet in London to discuss Concorde. Three options proposed (1) cancellation. (2) a phased rundown, (3) indefinite continuation. *December 2:* British Government review of relative costs presented to Parliament by Department of Industry. *December 9:* Department of Industry ministers and officials give evidence to Commons Industry and Trade Committee.

1982
March 31: Air France services to Caracas and Rio discontinued. *February:* British Industry and Trade Committee reaffirm dissatisfaction with cost aspects. *May 1:* Formation of Concorde Division within British Airways, responsible for profitability of Concorde operations. *May 6:* British and French ministers meet in Paris to discuss Concorde (cost reductions, officials's report, cost-sharing). *Aug:* Ian Sproat (Government Minister responsible) writes to Chairman of BA Sir John King stating that the Government will cease to fund Concorde's British manufacturers (Rolls-Royce and British Aerospace). *October:* Sir John King replies to the Sproat letter saying that BA will examine the possibility of Concorde funding the support costs out of revenue. *Nov:* Group set-up within BA to examine support costs.

1983
Jan 1: fastest transatlantic crossing west to east: New York to London in 2 hours 56 minutes. *April 13:* SFO Christopher Orlebar is technical consultant to BBC TV programme on Concorde in QED series, broadcast today

1984
March 27: Concorde inaugural flight to Miami via Washington. Henceforward a thrice weekly service to Miami. *March 31:* After eighteen months of negotiations British Government involvement in the Concorde project becomes minimal with BA becoming responsible for funding Concorde's British manufacturers. *Sept 11*: Distance record Washington-Nice by G-BOAB 3,965nm (4,565 statue miles). *Nov 16:* Concorde (G-BOAB) inaugural charter to Seattle from London via New York.

1985
Feb 13: First commercial service London-Sydney by Concorde under charter establishing a record time of 17h 3m. *March 28:* Concorde under a commercial charter establishes the record between London and Cape Town of 8h 8m. *April 25:* New livery unveiled by Concorde G-BOAG (214) returning into service. This aircraft had been out of service for a long period with much of its equipment having been removed for use in the other Concordes. *May 11:* Concorde special charter inaugural to Pittsburgh. *Dec 19:* Highest recorded ground speed, to date, achieved by Concorde G-BOAC in commercial service 1,292kt (1,488mph). Throughout 1985 Concorde inaugurates several routes within Europe for publicity reasons and to destinations within the Americas in conjunction with the Cunard Shipping Line.

1986
Jan 21: Concorde celebrates 10 years of commercial operations. *April 5:* First Concorde charter to New Zealand, viewing Halley's Comet over the Indian Ocean. *July 11:* Prime Minster Margaret Thatcher makes her first supersonic flight on Concorde from London to Vancouver to visit EXPO 86. She is presented with a copy of *The Concorde Story*. *Nov 8-23:* Concorde's first round-the-world charter, special edition of *The Concorde Story* commissioned by John Player to mark the event.

1987
Jan: Concorde spearheads advertising for the privatisation of British Airways. *March 7:* Second round-the-world trip by Concorde, organised by Goodwood Travel. *Sept 6:* Captain Brian Walpole sets new transatlantic record - just 95 minutes between Hopedale, Newfoundland and the northwest Irish Coast. *Oct 5:* BA Concorde carries one millionth transatlantic scheduled passenger - Patrick Mannix of Reuters. *Nov 22:* Concorde celebrates tenth anniversary of operations into John F. Kennedy International, New York, Richard Noble, landspeed record holder, sets new record by crossing the Atlantic three times in one day - on Concorde. *Dec 12*: Concorde commences new scheduled service, once weekly to Barbados for the winter season.

1988
Feb 7: Concorde G-BOAA makes record New York to Heathrow flight - 2h 55m 15s. *April:* G-BOAA, first Concorde to undergo 12,000 flying hours check. Structure pronounced sound for service well into 21st century. *June 15:* Inaugural Concorde twice weekly to Dallas, Texas, for summer period till August. *June:* Captain Walpole awarded OBE in Queen's Birthday honours. *Dec:* Concorde resumes Barbados service for winter season. Captain Walpole retires from BA.

1989
Feb 7: Noel Edmunds features Captain John Hutchinson on BBC programme about Concorde, aviation and travel, *March 2:* Aerospatiale host party to celebrate 20th anniversary of Concorde' first flight at Toulouse in 1969. *March:* HM Queen flies to Barbados on Concorde. *April 1:* Concorde leaves Heathrow on supersonic circumnavigation charter - to cover 38,343 miles. *April:* Concorde loses part of rudder between Auckland and Sydney, circumnavigation continues safely after repair. *Nov 19:* Channel 4 TV '*Faster Than A Speeding Bullet*' by Captain Christopher Orlebar features Concord in the history and future of supersonic flight.

1990
Jan 21: Concorde's 14th anniversary of commercial service. *Jan:* Goodwood Travel notch up 37,153 charter passengers on Concorde. *April 6:* Prince Michael of Kent presents awards to Concorde engineers. *April 14:* Capt. Norman Britton takes New York to London record: 2hr 54min 30sec. *May 5:* BAe & Aerospatiale unveil plans for Concorde successor; BA will take 'more than usual interest'. *June 1:* Concorde Honolulu to Hong Kong in 6hr 30min (subsonic time 13hr 10min) *June 6:* Celebration of 50th anniversary of Battle of Britain, Capt. Jock Lowe flies Concorde in formation with Spitfire over the White Cliffs of Dover. *Aug 10:* Concorde assists at Gatwick Airport's diamond jubilee. *Sept 7:* Concorde model installed at Heathrow's main entrance roundabout. *Sept 14:* Concorde appears at Farnborough airshow. *Nov 30:* Concorde twice weekly winter services to Barbados recommence.

1991
Jan 11: Announcement that Concorde Washington to Miami services will cease as from March 31. *Jan:* Second Concorde suffers rudder delamination. *April 4:* Capt Hutchinson celebrates 15th anniversary of Washington's supersonic service. *May 5:* Capt. WD (Jock) Lowe becomes Director of Flight Crew BA. *May 14:* HM Queen & HRH Prince Philip fly in Concorde to Washington to start official tour of USA, Capt. Lowe i/c. *June 7:* New computerised Concorde flight planning system introduced. *July 12:* Concorde 101 at Duxford repainted. *July 19:* Gen. Sir Peter de la Billiere awards tickets to Gulf War veterans. *July 26:* Concorde celebrates opening of Birmingham's new Airport Terminal. *Oct 18:* IMF bankers to Bangkok on Concorde. *Nov 1:* Capt. Lowe hosts Jackie Mann - former Beirut hostage. *Dec 12:* Capts Hutchinson and Mussett each break a record: Acapulco to Honolulu via Las Vegas, and Bali to Colombo via Mombasa; Lord King awards FAI certificates.

1992
Jan 22: Mary Goldring, former fierce critic, looks forward to a Concorde successor in her TV programme 'Goldring's Audit'. *Feb 21:* Capt Hutchinson, nearing retirement, broadcasts on BBC World Service: 'A personal view'. *March:* Concorde to visit Nigeria & South Africa. *March 27:* Neil Kinnock electioneering for Labour party visits BA Concorde. *April:* Tories win general election. *July 17:* Capts Horton, Hutchinson & Musset - Concorde speed record holders - to Buckingham Palace garden party. *July:* Former BOAC chairman Sir Basil Smallpeice dies. *Oct:* 'Concorde Spirit Tours' charters Air France Concorde for record earth's circumnavigation 33h 1m. *Nov 11:* Concorde pulled 440yds by RAF team for Children in Need Charity. *Dec:* Capt. David Rowland becomes Concorde Flight Technical Manager (FTM). *Dec 18:* Concorde to Barbados again for winter with one extension to Mexico at end of March '93.

1993
Jan 29: Lord King, pictured with Concorde model tucked under arm is honoured for Outstanding Contribution to International Aviation during Chairmanship of BA; he is to become President of BA for life. *March 26:* Senior First Officer Barbara Harmer of BA becomes first lady pilot of Concorde. *May 21:* Concorde G-BOAF to become first of seven to have £1m internal and external refurbishment. *July 2:* Capt. Rowland (FTM) to be Concorde Business Manager as well. *Aug 27:* Concorde human tow to raise money for BA's Charity 'Dreamflight'. *Sept 12:* Capt. Orlebar, former Concorde First Officer, consultant for 'Your Flight', Channel 4 documentary on Air Traffic Control. *Oct 10:* Special flight Concorde to Jeddah. *Nov 12:* Concorde with Capt. Morris at Athens celebrating 60th anniversary of Greek association. *Nov 19:* G-BOAA receives new £1m upper rudder, solution to previous rudder problem. *Dec 3:* Fastest show on earth - Bee Gees charity (Children in Need) flight around Bay of Biscay organised by Concorde SEO Bill Brown.

1994
Jan 7: Concorde BA001 LHR to JFK first with the new Cabin Crew uniform. *Feb 4:* Student from Southampton awarded Sword of Honour on Concorde's flight deck. *March 2:* 25th anniversary of Concorde 001's first flight from Toulouse is celebrated. *March:* Concorde dinner at which Sir George Edwards and Brian Trubshaw are guest speakers; *Jun:* Capt. Rowland resigns from being combined FTM & Business Manager. *Aug:* Cracks in Concorde wing in a rear spar web structure, non-primary and easily repaired. *Aug:* Three outer window panes cracked at Mach 2 and 57,000, no loss of pressurisation - inner ply taking it all. Replacement outer windows now double ply as well. *Oct:* Richard Branson announces possibility of his airline - Virgin - leasing Air France Concorde plus crews, *Oct:* Concorde exhaust analysed in flight near New Zealand. *Nov:* Concorde takes BA delegates on Official Visit to India. *Nov:* Concorde ceases services to Washington. This will save 300 sectors per year.

1995
Jan: Capt. Mike Bannister to become Flight Technical Manager (FTM) Concorde. *March:* Concorde dinner at RAF Club, *April 2:* John Major (PM) flies to Washington on Concorde 'to trump US President Clinton'. *May:* Disagreement between Aerospatiale and partners over future SST (a Mach 2, 350 seater); Germany and Britain favour development of subsonic 600+ seater; Terrazoni (GM of Aerospatiale) doubts if the $20b required could be found but sees a market for reducing the 14h subsonic flights especially over the Pacific. *May 29:* Sir Archibald Russell CBE FRS, British designer of Concorde, dies aged 90. *Aug:* Capt. Mike Bannister takes over Concorde training responsibilities as Flight Manager Concorde. *Aug 15:* Air France Concorde leaves New York for world record circumnavigation, *Sep:* NASA tests a hypersonic wing configuration in Langley (Virginia USA) windtunnel. *Sep 25:* Victorious European Ryder Cup team returns via Dublin with Trophy onboard Concorde, *Sep:* NASA prepares to make supersonic choices as the HSR (High-Speed Research) programme. *Sep:* Olympus 593 engines clock up half a million hours of supersonic flight time; meanwhile R-R and SNECMA continue work on the Mid Tandem Fan non reheat engine. *Sep 21:* RAeS lecture by Iain Gray of BAe: 'Is the Concorde successor getting closer?' - yes! *Oct:* UK and French airworthiness authorities will decide in 1996 on necessary modifications to extend Concorde life up to 8,500 Reference Flights. *Oct:* NASA commences flight tests on Supersonic Laminar Flow Control. *Nov:* Sir Colin Marshall to become non-executive Chairman in January 1996 and Mr. Robert Ayling to become Chief Executive. *Dec:* Capt. WD (Jock) Lowe to stand down as Director of Flight Crew

1996
Jan: Collision avoidance radar, essential for flight over USA, fitted successfully to Concorde, overcoming problems associated with overheating of aerial caused at supersonic speeds. *Feb:* UK & French airworthiness authorities rule that only six changes to maintenance schedules (so no modifications) will be required for Life Extension Programme - due to excellent state of airframe. *Feb 7:* Capt. Leslie Scott breaks New York - London record to 2h 52m 59s. *Mar:* NASA completes synthetic vision landing system tests using video and infra red sensors, thus future SST would not need droop nose. *Mar 17:* A modified TU144L is rolled out for six months of joint Russian-US (NASA) research. *Mar:* Proposals for the X-33 reusable single stage to orbit will be submitted to NASA by May. *April 2:* Air France Concorde painted blue to advertise Pepsi-Cola's new can. *April 15:* NASA unveils supersonic concept aircraft, Mach 2.4, range 9,200kms (5,200nms), 310 seats, noise: stage 3 rules less 3 dB. *May 20:* BA announces record profits for year 1995/96 - £580m. *May 27:* Concorde G-BOAG in for 'major' & refurbishment *Jun 2:* Concorde and the RAF's Red Arrows in formation fly-past for 50th anniversary of Heathrow Airport. *Aug 8:* Sir Frank Whittle, inventor of the jet engine, dies aged 89. *Aug 22:* Channel 4 TV doc suggests that 1973 Paris airshow crash of TU-144 was caused by Soviet pilot's violent manoeuvre to avoid collision with 'spying' French Mirage - story denied due to Soviet/French collusion. *Sep 3:* Julian Amery (Lord Amery of Lustleigh), former Minister of Aviation and signatory of 1962 'Concorde' Treaty with France, dies. *Sep 7:* Concorde appears at Farnborough Airshow *Oct 10:* G-BOAG (216), 'Major' check completed - last BA Concorde 'major' till the millennium. *Oct 1:* Boeing predicts that future Supersonic Transport would create turmoil by 'siphoning' off First,

Business and Full Fare Economy equating to two thirds of the revenue on a conventional service. *Nov29:* TU-144LL flew again from Zhukovsksy for a series of 32 joint Russian-US research flights. *Dec:* TBB - former Concorde hangars at Heathrow dismantled; purpose built facility with 'tail end docking' introduced.

1997
*Jan 21:*Concorde celebrates 21 years in service with BA and Air France. *Feb 11:*Rush for £10 New York return Concorde tickets (normal price over £5,000) issued to celebrate 10th Anniversary of BA privatisation. *Jan 21:* Concorde celebrates 21 years in Service. *Feb 12:* 30 million telephone calls (worldwide) made for Concorde return to New York £10 tickets. *April:* Air France reactivates Concorde F-BVFB from storage, cost put at $5.2m, as others in the fleet approach their 12,000 hour 'major' checks. *May 15:* BA announces that Concorde services to Barbados will run in the summer too - from June to August. *May 18:* 'Gas shroud' proposal from California University could cut noise from turbojet engines on take-off. *May 28:* BA Concorde fares up 15% to £5,596 LHR-JFK return, passenger numbers unaffected thanks to soaring UK economy. Air France Concorde fares up only 8%. *June 20:* Concorde Alpha Foxtrot displaying the new BA 'Union Flag World Image' livery conveys Prime Minister Blair to the Denver Summit. *July:* Aleksandr Pukhov - Tupolev Chief Designer announces that fewer than 32 missions will complete flight testing of the Tu-144LL (joint Russian/US project) - 5 flights versus 15 sufficed for subsonic testing. The remaining 10 flights will start in September. Maximum speed achieved to date is Mach 2, - $30,000 of fuel is consumed on each flight. *July:* 'Life extension' now confirmed up to 8,500 reference cycles with capability to exceed this after review in 2004/5 - no modifications required, merely changes to routine inspections. *Aug:* MDC flies 6% scale model of the inherently unstable 'Blended-Wing-Body' design for very efficient subsonic flight - 800 seats over 7,000nm. A Concorde successor might benefit from such technology. If the BWB is successful the economic criteria for the Concorde successor might be more difficult to meet. *Aug:* David Gower, former cricketer, to present Concorde on forthcoming BBC documentary *The Air Show Aug 27:* Japan announces intention to build Concorde successor, 300 seats with Mach 2.4 (1600 mph) cruise. *Sep:* Brad Faxon, of the US Ryder Cup team, achieves an 8 mile putt on Concorde at 1330mph (lasting 23 seconds) during a record breaking, 3h25m flight from New York to Malaga Captained by Jock Lowe. *Sep 23:* Brian Trubshaw, Jock Lowe, Jim O'Sullivan (Chief BA Concorde Engineer) & Bob McKinlay present 21 Years of Concorde with BA at the Royal Aeronautical Society London. *Nov:* United Space Alliance, responsible for Space Shuttle servicing, visit BA to learn techniques of Concorde servicing which address similar problems to those encountered by the Shuttle. *Nov 20:* 'Lottery Live' shows winner Mark Gardiner arriving in Barbados on Concorde with some lucky friends.

1998
Jan 21: Concorde celebrates 22 years of service with BA and Air France. *Feb 4:* With Capt. Jock Lowe i/c, Prime Minister Tony Blair flies Concorde to Washington summit with US President Clinton, discussions centre around Iraq arms inspection crisis. *April:* Tu-144LL experimental flight test programme ends, having achieved 39h over 19 flights. *April:* General Electric starts feasibility study into non-variable cycle engine for Dassault's proposed Supersonic Business twinjet 'Falcon SST' - 67kN dry and 98kN with reheat, M1.8 cruise. *May 20:* 75th Anniversary of Farnborough celebrated with Concorde visit - Capt. Lowe i/c. *May 25:* Part of left middle elevon breaks off one hour into flight to JFK, safe return to London, no long term problem envisaged. *July 1:* England World cup team, defeated by Argentina, returns in Concorde. *July 7:* Sir Robert Lickley, chief Designer Fairey Delta 2 (FD2) dies aged 86. *Sept 12:* Concorde takes part in 50th Anniversary of the Farnborough Airshow. *Oct:* TU-144 to take part in a further eight test flights with NASA; L/D ratio, ground effect and kinetic heating to be analysed. *Nov 21:* Capt. Dave Studd and crew celebrate 21st anniversary of Concorde operations into New York. *Dec 1:* BA announces supersonic service between New York and Barbados for 6, 13 & 20 Feb 1999. *Dec 23:* Article in 'Flight' discusses solutions to noise and sonic 'boom' for HSCT (High Speed Civil Transport); a fifth engine of high bypass used in conjunction on take-off could reduce noise and a microwave 'spike' might form a plasma ahead increasing the speed of sound thus reducing the 'boom'. Reducing financial support is threatening these studies.

1999
Jan 17: Sunday Times article predicts Dassault Falcon Supersonic 8 seater business jet will fly by 2006. However there will be competition from Gulfstream and Lockheed Martin combining with their 'SSBJ'. *Jan 18:* Dr Cunningham MP, Labours 'enforcer' critisized by Tories for using Concorde to Washington. *Feb:* NASA abandons HSR programme after Boeing decides there is no near term market for Concorde successor. *Feb:* Franco-Russian programme to study 'Scramjet' engine for Mach 2.5-12 speed range. *Mar 2:* 30th anniversary of Concorde 001's first flight from Toulouse celebrated. *Mar 4:* Trade war with USA threatens Concorde's landing rights in New York. *Mar 17:* Dassault shelves SSBJ due power plant problems - noise and economic reliability. Gulfstream to continue studies. *Mar 23:* Air France seeking to phase out Concorde due high maintenance costs; BA looking forward to 'many more years' of Concorde operation. *April 9:* Capt. Jock Lowe celebrates 30th anniversary of Concorde 002's maiden flight with Goodwood Special Flight to Filton. *May:* US ban on Concorde landing rights lifted as EU climbs down in trade war over hushkitted older jets. *May 24:* FA cup victors Manchester United fly by Concorde to Barcelona for European Cup Final vs. Bayern Munich. *May 26:* Man United win 2-1 (at the very last minute). *June 5:* BA announces replacement of 'ethnic' tailfin logos on subsonic aircraft with design similar to Concorde's fin. *Jun:* NASA rolls out X-34 low cost orbital technology demonstrator, to be launched from a Tristar, suborbital flights could take place by end of 1999. *June 10:* A very apologetic Harvey Weinstein, producer of *Shakespeare in Love* & *The English Patient*, fined £200 for smoking in a Concorde lavatory. *June 30:* Executive Jet (pioneer of 'Fractional Ownership') joins Lockheed Martin and Gulfstream in pressing NASA to fund Business Jet X-plane in wake of cancelled High Speed Research programme. Stealth technology could help in designing wing shape which avoids coalescing shock waves; a suppressed sonic boom might legalise supersonic flight over land. *July 1:* Concorde GBOAE, in formation with Red Arrows, flies over Princes Street Edinburgh to celebrate the opening of the Scottish Parliament by the Queen. *Aug 8:* BA to announce Concorde £14m cabin refurbishment plan with designer Sir Terence Conran acting as consultant. The weight saving new carbon fibre seats will reduce fuel usage, saving £1m pa. *Aug 11:* Concorde special flight tracks final solar eclipse of the millennium. *Sep 10:* Retired Concorde Captain David Ross dies. *Sep 18:* James Doyle 76, alias Jimmy Cameron, admits to being 'Ace' - the BAC electrical engineer recruited by the KGB who divulged Concorde secrets which assisted Tupolev in the design of the TU-144. *Dec31:* Concorde, heard but not seen (low cloud), overflies 'The London Eye (BA's Ferris Wheel) as part of the Millennium Celebrations.

2000
Jan: Lockheed Martin and Gulfstream reveal possible design for a minimised boom business jet under their QSAT (Quiet Supersonic Aircraft Technology) programme, with a 4000nm range at Mach 1.8. A 'Demonstrator' could be flying in five years, with development in ten. *Jan:* £14m to be spent on cabin refurbishment. *April 12:* Lionel Haworth, Aero-engine who developed R-R Olympus engine for Concorde dies aged 87. *May:* Infrared technology - to detect atmospheric turbulence ahead of 2-D inlet for QSAT - to be tested on a Lockheed SR-71. *Jul:* Cracks reported in some Concorde wings, spar 72. *Jul 25:* Air France Concorde 203 crashes near Paris CDG. No.2 engine fire causing No.1 failure as well thought to be cause. 109 souls on board killed, 4 in hotel at Gonesse die too. Capt. Christian Marty was in command of this German charter Flight to New York. BA and AF suspend Concorde flights. *Jul 26:* BA resume Concorde flights; AF states: no resumption until cause has been established. *Jul 29:* Fuel leak caused by tyre burst and subsequent fire ignited by reheat, now thought to be the cause. *Jul 30:* Due to possible fuel smell on a BA flight to New York, Concorde diverts to Gander. *Aug 7:* 40cm piece of metal found on runway, after V1 point, could have contributed to Concorde crash; main gear water deflector also implicated; parallels to Air France Concorde incident at Washington Dulles 14 Jun 1979 noted. *Aug 15:* BA grounds its Concorde fleet due to imminent withdrawal of C of A. Capt. Les Brodie fears he might be the last BA Concorde pilot to fly from JFK. *Aug 16:* DGAC and CAA withdraw Concorde's C of A. *Aug 31:* Preliminary report published. *Nov 7:* Judicial report states that the piece of metal on the r/w came from the Continental Airways DC10 and that traces of rubber from a Concorde tyre had been found on it. *Sep:* Edgar Chillaud returns 'stranded' AF Concorde from JFK to CDG. *Sep 15:* Leslie Appleton, designer of Fairey Delta 2 (FD2) dies aged 86. *Nov 17:* Remains of Concorde F-BTSC in process of reconstruction at Hangar 12 Dugny – near Le Bourget. French Magistrate Xavier Salot states 'we know it was not a bomb'. The two engines that failed are under examination at the Centre for Propulsion Studies, Sanglay (a suburb of Paris) *Dec:* Approval for modifications given. *Dec:* First Michelin NZG tyre to Dunlop for fitting too Concorde main wheel. CEAT Toulouse perform dynamometer tests on new combination.

2001
Jan: Damage tests carried out on Michelin NZG tyre Almeria Spain. *Jan 5:* Interim Report on Concorde crash published by BEA. *Jan 14:* Air France Concorde flies CDG to Istres, near to Marseille, to investigate behaviour of fuel leaks in airflow under the wing. Cause of fire still not understood. *Jan 16:* £17m to be spent on structural modifications at same time as cabin refurbishments. *Feb:* AF Pres J-C Spinetta announces that AF is as keen as BA to return Concorde to service. *Mar 24:* Brian Trubshaw, British Concorde test pilot dies aged 77. *May:* AF Concorde F-BTSD returns from Istres after tyre and brake tests. *May 12:* Alexei Tupolev designer of Tu144 ('Concordski'),dies aged 76.*Jul 5:* Richard Wiggs, founder of Anti-Concorde dies, aged 72. *Jul 17:* G-BOAF test flight LHR to Brize Norton via Atlantic for supersonic cruise to check modifications, 'a very successful flight', says Capt. Bannister. *Aug:* BA pilot retraining, Concorde at Shannon, Ireland. *Sept 5:* Concorde's C of A restored. *Sep 11:* Following a 'dress rehearsal' flight, the Concorde return to service team hears of the attacks on the Pentagon and World Trade Center *Sep 20:* Brian Trubshaw memorial service St Clement Dane's Church, The Strand, London. *Oct 22:* G-BOAF returns to JFK for an 'operational assessment flight', Capt. Les Brodie i/c - 'last out first in' (see Aug 00). *Nov 7:* BA and AF resume services to New York. Mayor Rudi Guiliani greets Concorde's clientele. BA Capt. Mike Bannister, AF Capt. Edgar Chillaud. *Nov 7:* PM Tony Blair takes Concorde (i/c Capt. Les Brodie) [dubbed 'Blair Force One'] to Washington, for talks with President GW Bush concerning Afgan war and Middle East. *Dec 1:* Concorde resumes weekly Barbados services. *Dec:* Mayor Guiliani arrives by Concorde to receive honorary Knighthood from Queen Elizabeth. *Dec 16:* Promotional tickets for New Year period at one third normal price sell out in 3 minutes.

2002
Jan 21: 26th anniversary of Concorde service. *Jan 27:* Fourth modified Concorde in each airline ready for testing. *Mar 24:* Jeremy Clarkson in the Sunday Times, writes amusing and supportive article about 'the big white dart'. *Apr 16:* Barbados winter flights season comes to a successful end. *Apr 16:* Eastbound service rescheduled dep JFK 08:30 arr LHR 17:25. *Apr 18:* Gordon Brown, British Chancellor, flies Concorde to US for

BA Concorde destinations from London Heathrow as of 2002

April 2002 scheduled services

Barbados (non-stop) *once weekly (or more) during winter season and August.*
To New York *daily 10:30 - 09:25;* from New York *daily 08:30 - 17:25; six weekly in August.*

Past scheduled services:
Bahrain *thrice weekly*
Dallas Fort Worth *(via Washington with BA, then Braniff) thrice week/v*
Miami (via Washington) *thrice weekly*
Singapore (via Bahrain) *thrice weekly*
Toronto *various schedules over summer months*
Washington Dulles *thrice weekly*

Diversions:
Atlantic City
Bangor
Boston
Gander
Gatwick
Halifax
Lajes
Montreal
Newark
Shannon
Windsor Locks

Charter Destinations of both Air France & BA
(AF) = exclusive to Air France (up to 1998).

Africa:
Abidjan
Agadir (AF)
Antanarivo (AF)
Aswan
Bamako (AF)
Bujumbura (AF)
Cairo
Capetown
Cartagene (AF)
Casablanca
Conakry (AF)
Dakar
Djerba (AF)
Douala (AF)
Djibouti (AF)

Harare
Johannesburg
Kigali (AF)
Kinshasa (AF)
Kilimanjaro
Lagos (AF)
Lome (AF)
Libreville (AF)
Lusaka (AF)
Luxor
Marrakesh
Mauritius (AF)
Moroni (AF)
Mombasa
Nairobi
Ouagadougou (AF)
Reunion (AF)
Robertsville (Monrovia) (AF)
Seychelles (AF)
Tangier (AF)
Tozeur (AF)
Tunis (AF)
Yamoussoukro (AF)

The Americas:
Abbotsford
Acapulco
Albany
Andrews AFB (AF)
Anchorage (AF)
Antigua
Aruba
Asheville
Atlanta
Atlantic City
Austin (Texas)
Baltimore
Bangor
Barbados
Barreirinhas (AF)
Battle Creek
Bermuda
Boston
Brasilia (AF)
Bogota (AF)
Buenos Aires (AF)
Buffalo
Calgary
Caracas
Cayenne (AF)
Charleston
Chicago (AF)
Cincinnati
Cleveland
Colorado Springs
Columbus
Dayton
Denver
Detroit
Edmonton
Fort-de-France (AF)

Fort Lauderdale
Fort Myers
Goose Bay
Grand Cayman
Hampton (AF)
Harrisburg
Hartford/Springfield
Havana (AF)
Honolulu
Houston Ellington
Houston Intnl
Iguassu (AF)
Indianapolis
Jackson
Jacksonville
Kailua-Kona
Kansas City
Kingston
Las Vegas
Lexington
Lima
Little Rock
Llanbedr
Lubbock
Mexico City
Miami
Midland-Odessa
Moncton (AF)
Montego Bay
Montevideo (AF)
Montreal
Nashville
Nassau
Newburg Stewart
New Orleans
Newport
New York
Oakland
Oklahoma City
Omaha
Ontario (USA)
Orlando
Oshkosh
Ottawa
Papeete (AF)
Philadelphia
Phoenix
Pittsburgh
Pointe-a-Pitre (AF)
Port-au-Prince (AF)
Portland
Port of Spain
Providence
Puerto Rico
Quebec (AF)
Raleigh
Recife (AF)
Regina (AF)
Reno (AF)
Richmond
Rio de Janeiro

Rochester
Rockford
Sacramento (AF)
St Louis
St Lucia
Saint Martin (AF)
Salt Lake City
San Antonio
San Diego (AF)
San Francisco (AF)
San Juan (AF)
Santa Maria
Santiago
Santo Domingo (AF)
Sao Paulo (AF)
Schenectady
Seattle Boeing Field
Seattle Tacoma
Springfield
Syracuse
Tahiti
Tampa
Tampa Macdill
Toronto
Trinidad
Tucson
Val d'Or (AF)
Vancouver
Waco
Washington Dulles
Washington Andrews
Wichita
Wilmington
Windsor Locks
Windsor Ontario

Australasia:
Auckland
Brisbane
Christchurch
Darwin (AF)
Easter Island (AF)
Fiji
Hao (AF)
Jakarta (AF)
Learmonth
Mururoa (AF)
Noumea (AF)
Perth
Sydney

Europe and Middle East:
Aarhus (AF)
Aalborg (AF)
Abu Dhabi (AF)
Albacete (AF)
Amman
Amsterdam
Ancona
Ankara (AF)
Aqaba

Athens
Badajoz (AF)
Baikonour (AF)
Bahrain
Barcelona
Basel
Bastia (AF)
Beauvais (AF)
Beirut (AF)
Bergen
Berlin
Biarritz (AF)
Billund
Bologna
Bordeaux
Bratislava
Brest (AF)
Brussels
Budapest
Cambrai (AF)
Charleroi (AF)
Chateauroux
Clermont-Ferrand (AF)
Cologne
Copenhagen
Dijon (AF)
Dhahran
Dubai (AF)
Dublin
Epinal (AF)
Faro
Frankfurt (AF)
Geneva
Graz
Grenada
Grenoble (AF)
Gothenburg (AF)
Hamburg (AF)
Hanover
Haifa (AF)
Helsinki
Ibiza (AF)
Istanbul
Ivalo (AF)
Jeddah
Kangerlussuaq (Sondrestrom)
Keflavik
Klagenfurt (AF)
Kish (AF)
Kuwait
Lajes (AF)
Lanzarote (AF)
Larnaca
Las Palmas (AF)
Leipzig
Liege (AF)
Lille (AF)
Linz
Lisbon
Luxembourg

Lyon (AF)
Madrid
Malaga
Malta (AF)
Marseille (AF)
Metz (AF)
Milan Linate
Milan Malpensa
Montpellier (AF)
Moscow
Mulhouse (AF)
Munich
Munster
Muscat (AF)
Nantes (AF)
Nice
Novossibirsk (AF)
Nuremberg (AF)
Oporto
Oslo
Ostend (AF)
Patina
Paris CDG
Paris Orly
Paris Le Bourget
Pescara
Pisa
Poitiers
Prague
Reins (AF)
Riyadh
Rome Fiumicino
Rovaniemi
Sana'a (AF)
S-J de Compostella (AF)
St Petersburg
Salzburg
Seville
Stavanger
Stockholm
Strasbourg
Tarbes (AF)
Tenerife
Tel Aviv
Toulouse
Tours
Turin
Turku (AF)
Vasteras
Valladolid (AF)
Venice
Vichy (AF)
Vienna
Warsaw

Far East:
Bali
Bangkok
Bangui (AF)
Beijing
Bombay

Calcutta
Chiang Mai (AF)
Colombo
Dacca (AF)
Delhi
Denpasar (AF)
Djakarta
Guam
Hong Kong
Islamabad (AF)
Kathmandu (AF)
Kuala Lumpur
Madras
Nagasaki (AF)
Osaka/Kansai (AF)
Singapore
Tashkent
Tehran (AF)
Tianjin (AF)
Tokyo (AF)

United Kingdom:
Aberdeen
Belfast
Birmingham
Boscombe Down
Bournemouth
Brize Norton
Cardiff
Coltishall
Derby (AF)
East Midlands
Edinburgh
Exeter
Fairford
Farnborough
Filton
Finningley
Gatwick
Glasgow
Hatfield
Humberside
Kinloss
Leeds
Leuchars
Liverpool
Luton
Macrihanish
Manchester
Manston
Mildenhall
Newcastle
Prestwick
St Mawgan
Stansted
Teesside
Yeovilton

Air France Concorde destinations from Charles de Gaulle Airport (Paris)

April 2002, scheduled services: Paris - New York, *five days per week 10:30 - 08:25* New York - Paris, *five days per week 08:00 - 17:45*
Past scheduled services: Caracas (via Santa Maria) Mexico (via Washington) Rio de Janeiro (via Dakar) Washington Dulles

---

Bibliography

An Introduction to the Slender, Delta Transport, BAC/ Aerospatiale, 1975

British Airways and Concorde Finances, Report of the Review Group, Department of Trade and Industry, February 1984.

David Beaty, *The Water Jump,* Secker & Warburg, 1976.

Charles Burnet, *Three Centuries to Concorde,* MEP, 1979.

Dr. P. H. Calder and P. C. Gupta, *Future SST Engines,* SAE, 1975.

Brian Calvert, Flying Concorde, Airlife, 1981.

Concorde, Second Report from the Industry and Trade Committee, Session 1980-81.

Flight International – various articles.

P.C. Gupta, Rolls-Royce Ltd., Aero Div., Bristol, *Advanced Olympus for Next Generation Supersonic Transport Aircraft,* SAE, 1981.

History of Aviation, New English Library, 1972.

Sir Stanley Hooker, *Not Much of an Engineer,* Airlife, 1984.

Jane's All the World's aircraft – various editions.

Geoffrey Knight, *Concorde, The Inside Story,* Weidenfeld & Nicholson, 1976.

Sir Frank Whittle, *Jet, the Story of a Pioneer,* (Frederick Muller, 1953).

C. S. Leyman BAe, Bristol, *After Concorde What Next?,* (Presentation at A.I.A.A. annual meeting, Washington, 1985).

J. E. Morpurgo, *Barnes Wallace,* Longman, 1972.

Kenneth Owen, Concorde, *New Shape in the Sky,* Jane's, 1982).

Richard H. Peterson and Cornelius Driver, *Advanced Supersonic Transport Status,* (Presentation at A.I.A.A. annual meeting, Washington April, 1985).

Arthur Reed, *Britain's Aircraft Industry, What went Right? What went Wrong?,* Dent 1973.

Darrol Sinton, *The Anatomy of the Aeroplane,* Granada, 1966 (reprinted 1980).

Sir Basil Smallpeice, *Of Comets and Queens, Airlife,* 1981.

Index

References to illustrations are shown in **bold**.

Illustration Acknowledgements Photographs and diagrams were kindly supplied by the following: *Aeroplane*; Aerospace Publishing Ltd., Peter A. Bisset; The Boeing Company, Alan Bond; Braniff International; British Aerospace; British Airways; British Tourist Authority; The Brooklands Museum; Avions Marcel Dassault, John M. Dibbs; Frank Debouck; Evening Echo - Bournemouth; *Flight International* (Quadrant), Image Industry; International Air Radio Ltd; Jack Leffler/Sky Eye Aerial Photographers; Adrian Meredith Photography; Metro Dade Country; M. L. Nathan; National Aeronautics and Space Administration; Christopher Orlebar; Nigel Paige; Christine Quick Photography Ltd; RAF Museum; Rolls Royce; Jeppesen Sanderson Inc; Alan Simmons; Southampton University; Tony Stone Associates; Syndication International; Michael Taylor; Mark Wagner.

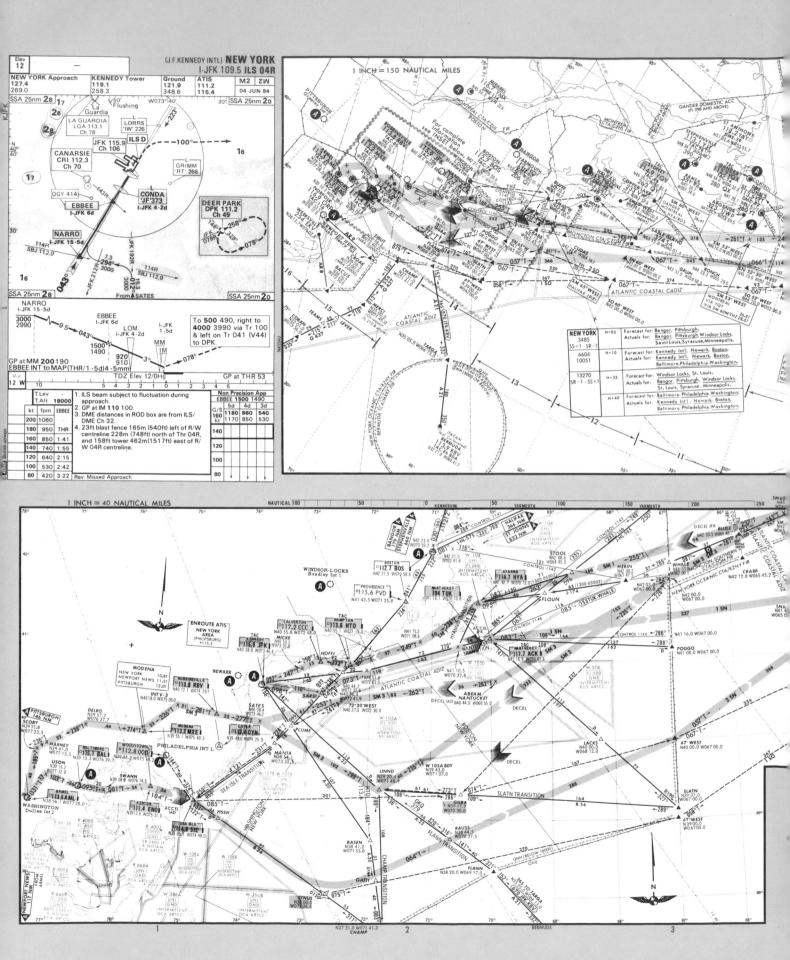